429288

POWELL, Michael
The last voyage of the
Graf Spee.

THE LAST VOYAGE OF THE GRAF SPEE

For
Kevin and Columba
and
their Mother

The last voyage of the Graf Spee

Michael Powell

WHITE LION PUBLISHERS LIMITED
London, Sydney and Toronto

First published in Great Britain
by Hodder & Stoughton 1956

Copyright © Michael Powell 1956

White Lion Edition 1976

ISBN 7274 0256 0

Made and printed in Great Britain
for White Lion Publishers Limited,
138 Park Lane, London W1Y 3DD
by Hendington Limited,
Lion House, North Town, Aldershot, Hampshire

AUTHOR'S PREFACE

THERE can be small excuse for writing a book today unless one has a unique story to tell. I claim that privilege. The genesis of this book was a suggestion by Emeric Pressburger, in the Spring of 1954, that we should write and produce a film about the Battle of the River Plate. For the next year we prepared it and during the following year we made it. We met and talked with all the principal living persons of the episode; we went twice to Montevideo; and with the co-operation of the Admiralty and of the United States Secretary of the Navy we executed all the movements of ships at sea. As the director of the film I began to realise that I was enjoying a unique opportunity: one which had never occurred before and would seldom occur again: I knew all the principal actors of the drama personally, except Admiral Harwood and Captain Langsdorff, who were both dead: I knew what had happened and why it had happened: in the course of my reconstruction of the Battle I had, as it were, stood upon the Bridge of Harwood's Flagship; and upon the Bridge of the *Exeter* and of *Achilles*; and in the *Graf Spee* herself. I had tried to imagine myself in Captain Langsdorff's place; and in Captain Dove's. I knew the thoughts of the Ministers on the spot; and I knew the spot.

I began to wish that this varied and unique experience could be preserved in some more permanent shape than a film. I have two sons. I wanted them to read this story and possess it. I wanted unborn boys and girls to pick it up one day and read it and absorb it into their experience. A film can entertain millions, but it can seldom be possessed by them. A book can; and that is why I have written this book.

My thanks are due to many people, and particularly to those who contributed personal narratives which have been drawn upon freely: Captain P. P. G. Dove, of the *Africa Shell*; Admiral Sir W. Edward Parry, K.C.B., of the *Achilles*; Admiral Sir Charles Woodhouse, K.C.B., of the *Ajax*; Captain F. S. Bell, C.B., R.N. (retd.) of the *Exeter*; and especially to Captain R. E. Washbourn, D.S.O., O.B.E., R.N., who was the Gunnery Officer of the *Achilles*. I would like to thank the Kemsley Press for permission to use certain copyright material contained in 'I was a prisoner of the *Graf Spee*' by Captain Dove. I am deeply indebted to the Admiralty for advice and assistance on every phase of the story; and to Captain A. W. Clarke, C.B.E., D.S.O., R.N., for many valuable suggestions. I owe a debt to both Lady Harwood and Frau Ruth Langsdorff for their advice and encouragement; to Admiral Sir Henry W. U. McCall, K.C.V.O., K.B.E., C.B., D.S.O., Commodore R. C. Medley, D.S.O., O.B.E., Sir Eugen Millington-Drake, K.C.M.G., Dr Alberto Guani, General Alfredo Campos, Admiral Rodriguez Varela, Miss Esther Shaw and many others; and to the J. Arthur Rank Organisation who own the copyright of the original screenplay by Emeric Pressburger and myself.

I have tried to portray the principal characters as I believe they talked and thought, but I have felt free to reject, adapt and invent as it suited me. My facts, times and dates are as correct as I can make them but this is not an historical document, it is an adventure-story.

CONTENTS

CHAPTER I

THE *AFRICA SHELL*

AT HALF-PAST ten in the morning off the coast of Portuguese
East Africa, Captain Patrick Dove, Master of the Tanker *Africa
Shell*, 706 tons, received a violent shock. The steamy East African
atmosphere, the rain, the squally, and the choppy sea which was
running in the Mozambique Channel, made for bad visibility,
but still, standing on his bridge and looking out to sea, he could
see, clearly defined against a dull background of rain-clouds, a
big battleship, coming directly for the *Africa Shell* at full speed,
throwing up a great bow-wave of white foam.

First Officer Mansfield stood beside Dove on the bridge, his
thumb pressed on the button of the alarm gong which was ringing all over the ship. A native boy stood at the wheel. He held
the course steady although his eyes rolled anxiously to port. The
Africa Shell was brand-new for use on the coastal trade. Although the world was at war, she had never expected to get into
action so soon. She hadn't even a gun. The crew could be heard
jumping to emergency stations, whilst the officers came running
aft along the cat-walks. They reached the bridge more or less
together and out of breath.

Dove lowered his glasses and said, in a conversational tone:
'One of those German Pocket battleships is coming straight at
us.' The others grinned, and Chief Engineer Low said, 'Got a
mosquito in your glasses, Skipper?' 'Some mosquito,' replied
Dove, 'and some sting! Take a look.' He handed his glasses to
the Chief. Second Officer Jeffcote grabbed the spare pair from
the bridge; First Officer Mansfield had his own. All three pairs
of glasses were pointed towards the east. By now the huge battle-
cruiser was much closer. Her square control-tower was unmis-
takable and her compact shape and high speed gave her an air
of extraordinary menace as she came rushing towards them. In
spite of the need for urgent action, hardly any of the men could
take their eyes from their glasses.

The Chief was the first to speak. 'By gum, Skipper, you're
right.'

'It's a battleship right enough,' said Mansfield. 'Might be one
of ours,' he added hopefully.

'It might be a Frenchman,' said Jeffcoat. 'She's coming from Madagascar.'

Dove ignored this chat and bellowed, 'Sam!' His coloured Boy answered from below. 'Sam! bring that photo from my cabin, the one from the Naval Review – quick!' Then turning to Mansfield, he asked, 'What's our position?' He dropped his glasses on his broad chest, gripped the rail, and watched the approaching stranger with a frown.

'Thirty miles north of Mozambique,' replied Mansfield.

'She's hoisting a flag. Take a look, Skipper,' said the Chief, always an optimist. 'Isn't that the French flag she's got up?'

Dove grunted sceptically, but took another look and said, 'How far off would you say she was?'

'Seven or eight miles,' estimated Jeffcoat.

Sam came panting on to the bridge with the photograph and handed it to his Captain. Dove looked alternately at the photograph and then, through his glasses, at the approaching ship, comparing the two and mumbling, 'Same ruddy big control-tower . . . Hm!' He turned and looked at the long, low coastline, which lay about six miles away, and said, 'Once we get inside the three mile limit, I don't mind if the whole German Navy comes after us.' Suddenly he leapt into action. 'Turn for the shore, Mr Jeffcoat! . . . Whack her up, Chief! if you ever want to see the Tyne again. Get the boats slung out, Mr Mansfield! Put a man for'ard to watch out for shoals. I am going in close.'

The Chief hurried below, the others jumped into action. Orders were given. The ship swung west and headed straight for the shore. The telegraph was rung for Full Speed Ahead.

Very soon the little ship was going at a speed never intended by her makers. She was running into a wide, shallow bay. The water was brown and sandy and choppy and the *Africa Shell* bumped along over the waves like a runaway tractor over a frozen ploughed field. She was heading straight for the shore. Dove stood with his back to it, facing his pursuer. Like all his officers he wore a tropical kit and his brief white shorts and his shirt with the short sleeves made his square figure look squarer than ever.

'What are we doing?' he yelled.

Mansfield answered proudly: 'Twelve knots – maybe a little more.'

The ship was shaking with the vibrations of her unaccustomed speed, as much as from the bumpy water.

Dove groaned, 'They're doing twice that. Check our position, Mr Jeffcoat, and keep checking it.' The Second Officer dashed

10

into the wheel-house and bent over the chart table.

Dove shouted to him, 'Take a bearing on the two light-houses, Cape Zavora and Quessico Point.' Then he turned and said down the voice-pipe, 'Chief, you're doing fine. Whack her up a point or two more if you can.' He looked through his glasses at the approaching ship. 'She's signalling!' Mr Mansfield joined his Captain and both of them looked through their glasses, spelling out together 'International Code! "Heave – to – I – am – going – to – board – you"!'

They exchanged a look and Dove growled, 'Ruddy pirate! What's our position now?'

Jeffcoat answered from the wheelhouse, 'Another half mile will do us.'

Dove said to Mansfield, 'Hoist the Acknowledge. Tell the boy to take his time. You go with him and fumble the hoist.'

Jeffcoat yelled, 'They're signalling again, sir.'

The two officers raised their glasses and again read out, 'Forbid – use – of – radio.'

Meanwhile Mr Mansfield and one of the native crew were creating an artistic delay with the flag-hoist. They got the acknowledging flag half way up, managed to foul it, and hauled it down again. By now nobody needed any glasses to see that their pursuer was a Pocket battleship. She was only a mile away and coming up fast. Suddenly there was an orange flash and a puff of smoke. One of her forward guns had fired! Captain Dove dropped his glasses and the strap jerked at his thick neck. A few seconds later a five-inch shell passed over his head. It brought back unpleasant memories of the First World War. A fountain of sand and water went up in the air ahead of the ship. The steersman rolled his eyes at Dove, but held his course. The others looked open-mouthed at Dove for orders.

He roared, 'Hoist – hoist! What are you waiting for? Do you want your blooming heads shot off? What's our position now, Mister?'

'Just checking, sir,' came the reply from the chart-house, whilst Mansfield shouted, 'She's signalling again, sir.'

Dove raised his glasses and grunted, ' "Heave to or I sink you"! I know that one all right. Well, Mr Jeffcoat?'

'We've done it,' yelled Jeffcoat, bursting out of the charthouse, 'we're inside the three mile limit, we're only two and a half miles off the beach!'

Dove leapt to the Engine Room telegraph, and rung to Slow. The Chief acknowledged almost before he rang. It was obvious he had been watching his engines leap in their beds and had one hand on the throttle. The noise and vibration stopped. Dove looked again at their pursuer.

'You can come aboard now, my lad!' he said. Then down the voice-pipe he reported, 'We made it, Chief. Come up on deck.' Then he shouted again, 'Boy!' His Boy shot up the ladder.

'She may still be a Frenchman,' said Mansfield, 'just wants to check on us.'

'That shell didn't hum the Marseillaise for me,' said Dove, then: 'Get out the gin, Boy. Maybe Mr Mansfield's right. Let's welcome our gallant Allies. So get the French vermouth as well.'

He looked again through his glasses and said, with scorn, 'French, my rear end! That's the Nazi flag!'

He could see the flag clearly, flying at the gaff. Half of it had been frayed by the wind, and the other half had been discoloured by smoke and exposure.

'It's the skull and cross-bones all right,' said Dove. 'Mister! Stand by to receive visitors. Keep edging in towards the beach. You take charge, I've got to get the ship's papers from my cabin.

He half-jumped, half fell, down the steep ladder, burst into his sea-cabin, opened the safe and took out a bag which was already weighted. He hurried out on deck, dropped it overboard and watched it sink. He went in to his cabin again and grabbed from a drawer a Colt .45 and a box of ammunition. He came out with them in his hands and looked around him. By now half the crew were watching, and his personal Boy, highly delighted, shouted to a friend below, 'Tom! Tom! Come over diss side. Dere's going to be big battle.'

A second later he was disappointed to see his Skipper drop both gun and ammunition into the sea after the bag, just as Tom stuck his head out of the galley and called, 'Where? Where de battle?'

'Him finished already,' was the sad reply.

By now the *Africa Shell*, with her engines almost stopped, was rolling heavily in the swell. First Officer Mansfield was down in the waist, ready to welcome the visitors. The others stood on the bridge watching the war ship. Captain Dove rejoined them. The Pocket battleship, thirty times their size, was now only half a mile away. Already they had swung out an electric crane aft and lowered a launch into the water. It was a powerful affair, loaded with men, and was heading swiftly towards them. The battleship, moving slowly, was swinging around to get between them and the shore. As the launch came nearer, the officers transferred their interest in the battle-ship to the occupants of the launch. It was a boarding-party.

Quite suddenly, the cold reality of his situation struck Patrick Dove. Simultaneously he and Mr Jeffcoat lowered their glasses and looked at each other. 'It looks like a free trip to Germany for yours truly,' said Dove.

Jeffcoat nodded, 'Maybe for all us Officers.'

In a low, serious tone, Dove said, 'Mr Jeffcoat! and you Sam! Get together any valuables you may want to take. Get mine, too. Tell the men to do the same. Hurry! These boys mean business.'

Suddenly his Boy was at his elbow with a tray of glasses. Dove scowled, 'What's this, Boy? Lime juice?'

'Eight bells, sir,' answered the Boy in a sepulchral tone. 'Cook say you must have your tray of lime juice at eight bells, Hitler or no Hitler.'

'Give me the tray, Boy,' said Dove impatiently. 'Go to my cabin – you know where I keep my gold cuff-links, don't you?'

The Boy's eyes gleamed, 'Oh, yes, sir.'

'Well, get 'em,' said Dove. He grinned in a half shame-faced way at Jeffcoat. 'They were a wedding present from my old woman.'

A yell came from the waist. 'Here they come, sir!'

Both officers looked over the rail.

'They don't look as if they came from Sunday School,' said Dove.

Jeffcoat nodded. 'Tough looking lot!'

The big launch had come alongside. On deck was swarming Jeffcoat's 'tough looking lot': two officers and twelve seamen, dressed in every conceivable rig. Some in boiler suits, others dressed in dirty white trousers and black naval jumpers, some in caps (no name on the caps of course), some in jersey hats, some without any hat at all. One, a special one, wore clean white trousers and a leather jacket. He was the first to come aboard. All had guns in their hands and knives in their belts, and carried the Swastika displayed somewhere on their person. It was a real pirate crew. They came on board like pirates. A special party carried explosives and detonators. Mr Mansfield watched them grimly. Leather-jacket, fumbling with his gun, addressed him in good English. 'Where is your Captain?'

Mansfield jerked a thumb. 'On the bridge.'

'Show me the radio-cabin!'

'There isn't one.'

Leather-jacket waved his gun. 'Take me there at once! You

13

are forbidden to send out signals. You are forbidden to communicate with any shore station. I hold you personally responsible to see that no signals are sent about the boarding of your ship.'

Mansfield stepped up close to him, 'See here, Mister. Are you an Officer of that ship over there?'

'Gestapo,' was the reply.

'I thought so,' said Mansfield. 'Fresh-water sailor.'

During this encounter, the rest of the boarding-party had gone about their business. They knew exactly what to do. They had obviously done it many times before. Some dived into the engine-room, some ran for'ard, some aft – they were all over the ship like ferrets, while the tanker's crew gaped or scowled. Under Mr Mansfield's orders the men had swung out the boats and thrown in their kit, and were standing by ready to abandon ship. Voices shouting in German, some giving orders and some obviously cheerfully looting, could be heard all over the ship.

The Naval Lieutenant had gone straight to the bridge. As his head appeared at the top of the companion-ladder, Dove said, 'Hallo, Hertzberg! Got a new job?'

For a moment, Lieutenant Hertzberg was taken aback, then he grinned and stepped forward. He was a smart, amiable officer. 'Dove! Bully Dove! Fancy meeting you.' He spoke perfect English.

'I don't fancy meeting you,' replied Dove grimly. 'Still now you're here, won't you join me?' He indicated the tray. 'Lime juice – I wish it was arsenic.'

'Thanks,' said Hertzberg, taking a glass. He raised it in a toast. 'Well, what shall we say? . . . Fortune of War?'

'Here's mud in you eye,' retorted Dove, raising his glass.

'And in yours, too, Captain,' relied Hertzberg smartly.

They drank. He put back his glass on the tray on the chart-table, and looked sideways at Dove. 'Bit of a change, this from the Hamburg-Amerika Line, eh? No more flirtations with pretty lady-passengers. No more beers with Bully Dove.' Then he became official, 'I'm very sorry, Captain. We are going to sink your ship.'

'I'm blowed if you are,' said Dove violently, 'look here, Hertzberg, take a look at this chart. Take a bearing of those light-houses. We're in Portuguese waters, well inside the three mile limit.'

His violence was parried with a smile. 'I don't admit that.'

'The Hell you don't!'

Hertzberg winked. 'Your chart is inaccurate. You have ten minutes to get your crew away.' His tone changed to a more friendly one for a moment, 'And for Auld Lang Syne, Dove, you and your officers can go too.' He pointed over to the shore. 'You won't have far to pull.'

'Rather less than three miles,' said Dove, looking him squarely in the eye.

'I make it rather more,' replied Hertzberg coolly. 'Please take me to your cabin. I must have the Log.'

As Dove and Hertzberg went down to the cabin, the Chief passed them carrying a suitcase and the ship's cat. 'Hurry up, Skipper!' he panted, 'they've opened the sea-cocks and set time-bombs alongside the fuel-tanks.'

Some of the boats were already being lowered away. The boarding-party, their work of destruction finished, were hurrying to and from their launch, their arms full of loot: typewriters, cigarettes, bottles, radio-sets, instruments and cans of food.

'Pirates! That's what you are. Bloody pirates!' growled Dove, and led the way into his cabin.

Mansfield's voice could be heard calling to him. Dove shouted in reply, 'Coming.' Then as Mansfield appeared in the doorway, he said, with a jerk of his head towards Hertzberg, 'This Gentleman wants to pinch our Log. But he's going to give me a receipt for it!' Hertzberg smiled, 'Certainly.' He seemed to enjoy Dove's insults.

A black face appeared behind Mansfield. 'Boy,' said Dove, 'run down quick to my cabin, and get my golf clubs and my shore-clothes.'

'Out of the way, black monkey!' said Leather-jacket's voice, as he forced his way into the cabin. Hertzberg frowned. Like most of the German Navy, he had no use for the Gestapo. Leather-jacket addressed Dove: 'where do you keep your code?'

'International Code?' said Dove, wilfully misunderstanding, 'on the bridge of course.'

'Your secret code,' said the Gestapo man angrily.

Dove jerked his thumb over the side. 'In Davy Jones's Locker.'

Hertzberg had meanwhile been scribbling a receipt. He straightened up formally. 'Here is your receipt, Captain Dove. Please hand over the Log.'

On the Pocket battleship a signal-lamp was winking from the flag-deck. A German sailor came running to Hertzberg and reported in German. By now all the boats were lowered. The boarding-party was back in the launch. Dove, Hertzberg and the

Gestapo-man were the last to leave the tanker.

On receiving the sailor's report, Hertzberg abruptly left the cabin followed by Dove. As they went down the ladders, he said, 'Sorry, Dove, change of plan. You will have to come with us.' He called out to the boats, which were rising and falling on the swell, 'Pull away there! We are going to sink this ship immediately.' Mansfield called out to Dove from the stern of his boat, but Hertzberg answered him, 'Your Captain is going with us!' He said something in German to the Gestapo man. Dove protested, 'What about Auld Lang Syne, Hertzberg?' But the Officer, without a smile, replied, 'My Captain has recalled us. We have sighted another ship, which requires our attention. Come!'

'I protest,' said Dove sturdily, but obeying the order.

'You can protest to Captain Langsdorff,' was the only answer he got.

The launch bore away at high speed towards the warship. A wail came over the water – it was Dove's Boy. 'Oh, Captain, sir!' The sea boats rocked in the wash of the launch. Dove waved and shouted at the full pitch of his lungs, 'Good luck all of you,' and voices answered across the water. Dove inflated his lungs to their fullest extent, and bellowed, 'MISTER MANSFIELD! REPORT TO THE NEAREST BRITISH CONSUL!' The Gestapo-man made half a move to stop him, but at a sign from Hertzberg, he shrugged his shoulders and sat down again on the thwarts.

High up on the swell, appeared for one last moment, the figure of Dove's Boy pathetically holding up the golf clubs and Dove's shore-clothes, while a thin voice torn by the wind and the sea, wailed, 'Captain, sir. Your things! . . .'

CHAPTER II

THE TIGER OF THE SEA

BY NOW the launch was approaching her stern and the colossal steel side of the Raider rose thirty feet above them. The big crane was swung out and the hook was already coming down to meet them, as the coxswain brought the launch alongside. The tackles were ready in the boat, and were hooked on smartly. No orders were given. Everything was done to the bosun's pipe where, high above their heads, Dove could see faces looking down at him. They were mostly young faces, some of them absurdly young, mere boys of sixteen or seventeen years of age, looking down with eager interest to see what the looting party had brought back and what fish they had caught this time in their net.

Dove was expecting to have to climb a rope-ladder, but to his surprise the whistle was heard again and the whole launch, with all the men in it, was lifted cleanly and smoothly out of the water and up into the air. They rose up swiftly and soon were on the level of the deck. A few seconds later, they were far above it, and Dove could see the gun-crews at their stations and the guns slowly turning as they scanned the horizon. Now he could see the whole quarter-deck of the battleship and the super-structure towering above him. His quick eye took in the forward turrets and the rest of the armament, but the launch was already swinging amidships, and was being lowered smoothly into an open hangar. A square-built bosun came in view, a typical North German, burly and fresh faced, with his whistle at his lips. He grinned at Dove as the launch sank below his feet into the dark hold, and several other sailors waved in a friendly manner. 'Like a blooming sardine,' grumbled Dove to Hertzberg, as they were lowered between the steel walls.

Already the engines were turning at half-speed and suddenly a loudspeaker started blaring orders in German. Dove heard booted feet running on the deck above. The launch settled in the chocks on the floor of the hangar with a clunk! an eerie rumbling noise started above their heads and Dove, looking up, was startled to see a huge steel roof rolling over, to close the whole hangar. Already the gap was closing, and he could see the

17

faces of the sailors looking down at him being gradually cut off by the edge of the roof. Then the last bit of blue sky vanished and the roof closed with a grating sound. For a few seconds they were in complete darkness, then harsh lights came on and the crew started to scramble out of the boat followed by Dove and Hertzberg. He was a prisoner on board the Raider.

As Dove was marched for'ard by Hertzberg, the battleship was already moving at full speed. The roar of the forced draught was deafening as they passed near the engine room. They went through several flats and corridors. Dove kept his eyes open, and his ears cocked to all the hundred sounds to be heard on a great battleship. They arrived at the door of a cabin near the control-tower. Hertzberg knocked and went straight in, followed by Dove. A man in Captain's uniform was sitting at a desk, covered with papers. Hertzberg advanced and gave him a short report in German. Among the words, Dove caught, 'Kapitan Dove von Tanker *Africa Shell.*'

His eye was caught by a large framed photograph of a battle cruiser on the bulkhead. He stepped up and had a close look at it. It was inscribed in French, 'To the *Graf Spee* from the French cruiser *Jeanne d'Arc.*'

There was a muffled explosion not far away. Dove turned quickly round from the photograph. The two officers exchanged a look. The Captain said politely, 'I am afraid, Captain, that that was your ship.'

Dove grunted, and mumbled something about adjectival pirates, then pointing to the photograph, he said, 'So, you are the Pocket battleship *Admiral Graf Spee.*' Both the Germans smiled without replying. Kay dismissed Hertzberg with a nod, and Dove's old shipmate had the bad taste to wink as he passed and said, 'Cheerio!' before he closed the door.

The Captain pointed to a chair and said, 'Please sit down.'

Dove ignored the invitation and said, 'Captain Langsdorff! I wish to make a protest!'

He was interrupted. 'My name is Kay. I hold the rank of Captain, but I am not the Captain of this ship.'

Dove remained where he was and said bluntly, 'I want to see Captain Langsdorff.'

'Your request will be forwarded to him,' replied Kay blandly. 'Captain Langsdorff seldom leaves the bridge. Are those the only clothes you have? You are going to be cold.'

Dove looked up keenly, 'Why? Are we heading south?'

He got no answer. He went on, 'Young Hertzberg gave me no

time. I've got just what I stand up in.'

Kay was evidently determined to be pleasant. He said, 'We will see what we can find for you. Please sit down, Captain.'

Dove allowed himself to be persuaded. Kay pushed a box towards him, 'Cigarette?'

Dove took one and looked at it closely. Kay smiled, 'Yes, it's Virginian. From an English ship, the *Newton Beach*.'

Dove lit his cigarette and said, 'So it was you who sunk the *Newton Beach*.'

Kay poured some whisky and said, 'Scotch. From the steamship *Clement*.'

'Oh,' said his guest. 'And who supplies you with tea?'

Kay looked surprised in his turn. 'Tea?' Then he laughed, 'Oh, you mean that chest over there of Orange Pekoe. Ah! That is from the *Huntsman*.'

'The Captain of the *Huntsman* was a pal of mine,' said Dove rather grimly.

Kay looked shocked. 'In all the merchant ships that he has sunk, Captain Langsdorff has never lost one life. He is a fanatic on the subject. You will be seeing your friend again . . . one day.'

'Is he on board?' asked Dove eagerly.

Kay answered evasively, 'Not exactly'; and he asked Dove if he took water or soda. 'I'll take it neat,' said his guest, and knocked it back.

'You'll be glad to hear we have plenty of whisky on board. We're short of tea.'

Dove glanced at the chest of tea in the corner of the cabin. Kay followed his gaze. 'That's a Christmas present for my wife. In Hamburg, they are shorter of tea than we are.'

Dove's only comment was, 'So, we're all going home for Christmas? That's jolly!'

The alarm buzzer started to ring. All over the ship the loud-speaker system came alive. Orders and numbers were shouted. Heavy boots hurried along steel decks and up steel ladders. Dove wondered aloud what was up. Kay pressed a button on his desk without answering. It rang a buzzer on the flat outside. The door opened and a Master-at-Arms stepped in. He gave the Nazi salute.

Dove had already noticed that very few people in the ship gave anything but the regular Naval salute. As a matter of fact, it was not only uncommon, but highly unpopular, in the Germany Navy to give the Nazi salute at all, until it was made compulsory

19

after the attempt on Hitler's life in 1944.

Kay rose and said in German to the Master-at-Arms, 'Escort the English Captain to his cabin.' He took his cap from the desk and was already putting it on. The interview was over. Dove rose, paused a moment, shrugged his shoulders and walked out. The Master-at-Arms followed and closed the door. The loud-speakers continued to blare orders. The Master-at-Arms dived down a ladder into a steel corridor; the place was alive with hurrying sailors. Gas masks dangling on their chests and they were adjusting steel helmets. They all seemed very cheerful. Most of them were young boys of seventeen or eighteen. Dove and his escort went down another steel ladder and across a big flat, then down a ladder along a corridor and down yet another ladder. Everywhere men were hurrying up and down like ants disturbed in a nest. The sound of the engines got louder and louder. It felt as if the whole ship were throbbing with energy and power.

Dove asked, 'Is there going to be a fight?'

Without pausing the Master-at-Arms said, 'Pardon?' He obviously hadn't understood the English question, so Dove added pantomine and shouted, 'Fight! Battle! Boom! Pssh!'

The Master-at-Arms gave a taut laugh, 'Nein, nein. No battle. Like *Clement*, like *Huntsman*, like *Africa Shell*, eh, Kapitan?'

Dove understood, 'Another merchant ship, eh?'

'Ja, ja! Merchant Schiff,' echoed the Master-at-Arms happily. 'No battle!'

Dove said conversationally, 'Maybe it don't depend on you alone! I'd like to see that grin wiped off your face.'

'Pardon?' said the Master-at-Arms.

'Granted,' said Dove.

They were now below the water-line. There was no porthole, of course. A blue light was burning. The cabin was very small and plain – and noisy. An air conditioning fan whirred in a corner of the room. It obviously belonged to someone, for there were clothes hanging up and scattered about, books, some photos. The Master-at-Arms announced, 'You stay. I go now.' He went.

Dove grunted, 'You stay! . . . as if I could ruddy well do any-thing else.' He glanced around the cabin, looked a bit closer at a photo on the bulkhead, 'Nice looking girl. Oh, well.' He sat on the bunk, put his feet up and stretched out, his hands behind his head. 'Cheer up! We'll soon be dead.' Very soon he was sleeping peacefully.

An hour passed, then the lock clicked and the door opened.

The Master-at-Arms and a very young officer came in. They were amused to find Dove snoring, and made one or two jokes about him in German. The young officer started to collect his things, whistling a popular Berlin song. Dove woke up as calmly as he went to sleep and said, 'Hello.'

The young officer clicked his heels and bowed. He was a nice boy, blond and pugnacious-looking. He introduced himself, 'Leutnant Friedrich! Flugabwehr!' Then in good English, he went on, 'Ack-ack officer. Sorry to disturb you. I'm just collecting my things.'

Dove sat up on the bunk and said, 'Oh, it's your cabin?'

Friedrich smiled and said, 'It's yours now.'

'Sorry to turn you out,' said Dove.

Friedrich laughed, 'You're welcome. This cabin is right over the propeller shaft. I'm going higher.' He opened some drawers and started whistling again. Dove looked at the Master-at-Arms sardonically, 'Any more prisoners? Or did that ship get away?' He spoke slowly, with gestures, and this time he was understood.

The fellow answered in a superior manner, 'No get away. No Schiff get away from us. We very much speed. Japaner.'

Friedrich translated helpfully, 'She was a Japanese ship.'

'Japanese, was she?' said Dove, highly indignant. 'Then why not put me aboard her? She's a neutral!'

Friedrich said something to the Master-at-Arms, who shrugged and said slowly to Dove, 'You know much. You know this schiff Graf Spee. You know schiffs we have zoonk . . . zink. . . . ' He gave up the struggle, and said, 'Kapitan, you now have exercise on deck.'

Dove said stubbornly, 'I want to see Captain Langsdorff.'

Once more his request was blocked by the answer, 'Maybe he see you. Maybe not.'

When Dove came on deck, there was no sign of any other ship in sight. It was a fair day. Their course, as far as he could judge it, was now sou'-sou'-west, whereas before they had been travelling south-east. Dove concluded that after sinking the Africa Shell, Captain Langsdorff had gone directly away from the African coast until he was well out of distance of scouting aircraft. He had then altered course and they were going, as Captain Kay had predicted, southward and into colder latitudes. Having worked this out to his own satisfaction, Dove started to walk around the ship taking his own time, and looking with great interest at everything there was to be seen. There were young

21

German sailors everywhere, busy at various jobs. They looked at Dove as he passed with equal interest. One or two gave him a flippant little Nazi salute, half in friendliness. Dove accepted this in the spirit in which it was offered, and acknowledged it with a massive nod, and occasionally a gruff, 'How d'ye do?'

There seemed to be no restrictions on what he could see, or not see. The Master-at-Arms didn't hurry along when he stopped to admire the great eleven-inch guns in their heavy armour-plated turrets; when he stopped again to look at the batteries of quick-firing ack-ack guns; and when he counted the turrets of five-nines and all the other secondary armament with which the battleship was bristling. He stopped again to look up at the massive control-tower, quite unlike anything else he had ever seen on any other ship. A thing that puzzled him greatly, high up above the control-tower, was a strange looking piece of apparatus on the main mast, which ceaselessly turned round and round, as if searching the seas. Dove had never seen such a thing – nor had many other men at that time, Ahead in this, as in many other things, the Pocket battleship was equipped with a rudimentary form of radar.

There were a hundred things to see.

Dove was very impressed by the way the ship was kept. 'You could eat off the decks anywhere,' he observed to the Master-at-Arms.

'Ja, ja. Soon you shall eat,' said the German soothingly.

Dove decided to give him up.

A messenger came up and spoke to the Master-at-Arms, who said to Dove, 'Our Kapitan wishes to see you,' and turned to lead the way. Dove refused to budge and called out to their retreating backs. 'Here – hold on!' They stopped and turned to stare at the square, obstinate figure. Dove didn't budge, 'Is it the real one this time?' he asked, and when they continued to stare he added, 'Am I going to see Captain Langsdorff?' Both men nodded together and replied, 'Ja, Kapitan Langsdorff,' like Siamese twins.

The Captain's cabin was on the deck level, and was very large and modern. Dove's immediate impression was of dazzling cleanliness and efficiency. The furniture was of steel and modern in design, but he took this in later. His first look was for the redoubtable man, who had asked to see him.

Captain Langsdorff was a tall slender man of about forty. That was all Dove could see at first glance, for he was turned away from his visitor, and bent over a very large chart of the

South Atlantic Ocean. He had obviously just come from the bridge. He wore his binoculars slung around his neck.

The chart was large and an interesting one. It was divided into dozens of squares, about thirty miles each way. All of them were within a certain latitude and longitude. Each square had a date on it. The course of the *Graf Spee* was boldly drawn upon the chart from the moment of sailing from Hamburg to their present position. It crossed and re-crossed itself several times off the west coast of Africa. It was in this area that the *Graf Spee* had been lying in wait before she started to sink British ships. Each action had been marked on the chart and neat little counters, with the name of the sunken ship printed on them, showed the extent of Captain Langsdorff's bag to date. The *African Shell* was already spotted in the Mozambique Channel.

The Master-at-Arms had opened the door without a knock, and come in followed by Dove. The messenger stayed outside within call. After announcing 'Der Englische Kapitan Dove, Herr Kapitan,' the Petty Officer had stepped outside and shut the door, leaving Dove alone with his captor.

After a moment, Captain Langsdorff straightened up and turned around. He had a sensitive, strong face with eyes full of intelligence and imagination. He wore an elegant little piratical beard on the point of his chin. He carried himself lightly and well. He looked supremely confident.

Now that he had got to the man at the top, all Patrick Dove's indignation and sense of grievance returned. He glowered. He made no effort to hide his feelings. A dancing light appeared in the eyes of Captain Langsdorff, He was the first to speak, 'Well, Captain Dove,' he said.

'Well, Captain Langsdorff,' growled Captain Dove, giving not an inch.

There was a second's pause as each man sized up the other. Then Langsdorff broke into a charming smile, and advancing quickly, held out his hand. Dove had to shake it. Langsdorff continued to speak, in an English which was almost without accent, better even than Hertzberg's, 'How do you do, Captain? My boarding officer has reported your protest, over the seizure of your ship. You say that you were in territorial waters. If you were, that's going to be very difficult for me.'

Dove was sensible to his opponent's charm but stuck to his point, 'Not half so difficult, sir, as it has been for me already. I've lost my ship and everything in it. To my mind, there wasn't the slightest doubt that I was well inside the three mile limit,

23

and if I had my chart with me I could –'

'Here is your chart, Captain,' said Langsdorff, picking it off his desk and unfolding it, 'Show me!'

Dove was a bit taken aback, but smoothed the chart out with a horny hand, and said, 'I will. Look here! See that line? That's my course, it couldn't be clearer.' Langsdorff looked solemnly and politely at Dove's chart and appeared to give due consideration to Dove's complaint, but his eyes were twinkling, and Dove soon caught the twinkle. Langsdorff smiled and said, 'Captain, we are not likely to agree. You want the figures to prove you right and me wrong, while I – ' he left the sentence unfinished and smiled. Dove looked at him straightly. Langsdorff continued, 'Shall we compromise? You make your protest in writing, and I myself will sign it. Is that fair?'

Dove saw that that was all that he would get, and thinking of compensation after the war, he took it and said, 'Fair enough, sir.'

Langsdorff said gaily, 'Then we'll drink to that. Have some Scotch?' He crossed to the other side of the cabin, and Dove followed him saying, with a grin, 'From the *Clement*?'

Langsdorff gave him a sharp look as he poured the drink, and said, 'Yes, from the Steamship *Clement*.' Then continuing the thought behind Dove's remark he added, as he handed him his drink, 'Believe me, Captain, I don't like sending ships to the bottom. No sailor does. Nor do I like making war on civilians. Up to now it is the civilians who have suffered in this war. The soldiers are sitting in concrete and armour broadcasting to each other. The airmen are flying reconnaissance flights. As for the sailors, they're well, look at me! I have command of a fine ship, a new ship, one of the finest battleships afloat. We're fast . . . '

'Twenty-five knots,' guessed Dove aloud.

Langsdorff waved his cigar, 'More. We have immense firepower. . . . '

'Six eleven-inch guns,' interposed his attentive listener, 'and eight – or ten – five-nines?'

Langsdorff gave him another look, 'You use your eyes. Yes, we are very strong, and my orders are to sink merchant ships and to avoid a battle.'

'You never know your luck, sir,' said Dove comfortingly, 'it might happen that without you expecting it, you'll run up against one of ours.'

Langsdorff picked another cigar out of the box and lit it from the glowing butt in his mouth. He was the only man that Dove had ever seen who chain-smoked cigars. He commented on Dove's last remark by saying: 'You have only three ships who can match my guns – you're *Repulse, Renown* and *Hood.*'

Dove said quietly, 'On paper.'

Langsdorff gave him another quick look and added, 'And those big battleships are not fast enough to catch me.'

'Plenty of our cruisers are faster than you,' said his remorseless guest.

Langsdorff seemed to be enjoying the match of wits. 'Your fast cruisers are no match for my eleven-inch guns,' he said, and Dove again said, 'On paper.'

This time the remark drew rather a stern look, followed by a sudden smile and a burst of frankness, 'I have one more advantage, Captain,' he said. 'It's very difficult to find me.'

'I appreciate that, sir,' said Dove, 'I don't understand how your supply ship can even hope to find you.'

'She can't' said this modern pirate, and he looked as pleased as a boy as he added, 'I find her.'

Dove said shrewdly, 'Isn't that just as difficult?' He got what he wanted. Langsdorff led the way over to the big chart-table, which Dove had been looking at out of the corner of his eye ever since he came into the room. They both leant over it. Langsdorff swept away some cigar ash and said, 'It's the simplest thing in the world. The details are secret but the system is old. The ocean is divided into squares, and I know exactly in which square I can find my supply ship on given dates.'

Dove bent over the chart and committed as much as he could to memory, commenting that it was all very interesting. He looked up to see Langsdorff eyeing him with amusement. 'I know exactly what you are thinking, Captain,' he said, 'but this chart it safe . . . and so are you! for the duration. . . . '

He straightened up and looked down at the chart, criss-crossed with the line of his course, dotted with the various rendezvous with his supply ship, and covered with the names of the ships which he had sunk. He surveyed it as an eagle looks down upon its hunting ground and said, 'So you see, I have the Seven Seas to hunt in, from the North Pole right down to the South!'

Dove said drily, 'I hope you won't go as far as that, sir. I'm not dressed for it.'

This strange man suddenly reached out and clapped him on the shoulder, and said with great friendliness, almost affectionately, 'Our tailor will fix you up with something. I will order it myself.' Then he turned just as quickly and went to the door, opened it and called 'Lempke!' The voice of the Master-at-Arms answered at once. Captain Langsdorff said, in English for Dove's benefit, 'Escort Captain Dove to his cabin.' The interview was at an end.

But the curious thing was that both men, although officially enemies, felt that they had made a friend.

CHAPTER III

THE TIGER AND THE JACKAL

'WUNDERBAR!' said the little fat tailor.

Dove examined himself in the long glass. His new suit of thick blue serge was really an excellent fit. He had insisted on its being plain blue without any uniform stripes, but he had also insisted on having his medal ribbons from World War I sewn on to the breast. He patted the medal ribbons reflectively. The tailor, chattering away to himself in German, readjusted the set of the coat as tailors do. He was a uniformed man, of course, but obviously not a seaman. He came up to about the middle button of Dove's waistcoat and took a personal pride in his large customer. 'Wunderbar!' he repeated.

'Is it the cut that you mean, or do you allude to my figure?' asked Dove.

The tailor beamed up at him and said, as usual, 'Bitte?'

Dove suddenly cocked his head, 'Hello. We're slowing down. What's up?'

A Chinaman popped his head in at the door. Dove knew that he was one of the Chinese laundrymen on board. The yellow man's face was one large smile. 'Hell Winkle!' (The tailor's name was Herr Winkler.) 'Sie ist da!' He pointed up on deck, then checked himself suddenly, seeing the English Captain.

'Well, John,' said Dove cheerfully, 'who ist da?'

Somebody slapped the Chinaman on the back very forcibly, and the Master-at-Arms came in. He, too, looked cheerful and was also dressed in blues. Dove and he were old shipmates by now, and had considerable respect for each other.

'Kapitan Langsdorff is asking for you, Captain Dove,' he said, 'I have orders to bring you up to the forward gun deck, below the bridge.' He looked admiringly at Dove's new suit. 'That is good.'

Dove revolved solemnly before him. The little tailor stood beaming with his tape measure hanging round his neck. The Master-at-Arms addressed him, 'Fertig?' The tailor answered, 'Jawohl,' and gave a final tug to the back of the coat. Leading the way, the Master-at-Arms said to Dove, 'You will need a warm suit on deck.'

The first thing that Dove saw, when he came into the open air, was a big black tanker flying the Norwegian flag, only a few cables length away. He estimated her to be about twelve thousand tons. She was equipped for refuelling at sea, and half a dozen big pipes were swung high up on derricks like fat languid snakes; her decks were swarming with men, and Dove's keen eyes could pick out parties opening crates and bringing up stores from the holds, while others were mustering for'ard and aft rigging hoists for trans-shipping between ship and ship. This was evidently the supply-ship. As Dove watched, the two ships came closer and closer. Both of them were doing about fifteen knots and, as the passage between them narrowed, the sea foamed between like a huge mill race. His eye was caught by the Norwegian flag being struck. Another flag was run up and broken out.' It was the Nazi flag, and was greeted with cheers and yells of welcome from the crew of the battleship.

Her decks were also swarming with men; working parties were rigging hoists and preparing the oil intakes. There were other parties standing by in steel helmets, ready to receive the lines as they came aboard. But besides that, every man who could be on deck was there, and discipline seemed relaxed by common consent as shouts and chaff flew to and fro between the two ships. Their boisterous cheerfulness, at sight of their supply-ship betrayed the strain under which all these men had been living, for months at sea, under strict discipline, with every man's hand against them.

They were very far south. How far Dove never quite discovered. The sky was grey and the sea was green and icy. They might have been off Kerguelen, or Prince Edward Island. He would not have been surprised to see ice floes from the invisible ice-pack only a few hundred miles to the south. The steel work of the ship was wet and cold to the touch, and everybody was in cold-weather rig.

By now the two big ships were only about a hundred feet apart and Dove admired the seamanship of both Captains. The sea roared between them. Suddenly there was a bang as a brass gun on the tanker fired a slug, attached to a line, over to the battleship. There was a chorus of yells as the young sailors dashed from cover to be the first to grab the line and run away with it. For'ard and after other lines were coming over, and in a very short time the hoists were rigged. Officers went flying to and fro across the narrow gap; stores were being ferried over; and the great fuel pipes came weaving and bobbing down towards the battleship

28

until their open mouths brushed the deck and their masters seized on them, forcing them to disgorge their tons of oil into the empty tanks.

It was all far too efficient and well organised for Dove. 'Nice goings-on,' he said aloud to the Master-at-Arms, 'you'd think the South Atlantic belonged to you fellows!'

A voice high above him, on the topmost bridge, called: 'Good morning!' Captain Langsdorff had spotted him and was leaning over. He, too, looked relaxed and cheerful. He had been in the habit of sending for Dove every two or three days during the fortnight of captivity. They had got to know each other well, and their appreciation of each other had increased. Dove had the impression that Langsdorff sent for him because it did the Captain good to talk to somebody with whom he could relax the authority and responsibility of his position. Probably Dove, more than anybody, had seen the crushing weight of this burden upon the young Captain. Langsdorff was a passionate patriot and he felt that the prestige and naval glory of Germany depended upon him carrying out his mission successfully and bringing his ship in triumph back to port, against the might of the combined Navies who were looking for him. This determination, coupled with his other determination not to lose one civilian life if he could help it, and with his keen sense of sole responsibility for the lives of his own crew, made a heavy burden for a sensitive, imaginative man of high principles, unsupported, and belonging to a Navy which had so short a tradition of sea-service behind it.

But now he looked cheerful and confident as he shouted, in answer to Dove's thanks for letting him come on deck, 'I thought you might be interested!'

Dove looked around at the tanker, the oil pipes, the crates of stores, and said, with a meaning emphasis which was not lost on Langsdorff, 'You're right! I am!' He was standing near one of the hoists and as a big sack came zooming across the gap it burst and dried fruit showered all over the gun deck. It was treated as a great joke. The Petty Officer looked on smiling as the young sailors scrambled for the raisins and prunes. One of the boys offered a handful to Dove. He hesitated and looked up to the bridge where he had last seen Langsdorff. But a voice said at his elbow, 'Go on, take it!' Langsdorff had come down from the bridge, the inevitable cigar between his teeth, and standing there in his blue uniform, his cigar and his cap cocked at a rakish angle, his little black beard trim in the pale light, he looked more like a romantic pirate than ever.

Dove took the advice (and a handful of raisins) saying, as he munched them, 'It looks as if Father Christmas has arrived.'

'He has,' said Langsdorff gaily, 'with fresh meat, green vegetables, fruit and fuel-oil. Want to meet the Old Man?' He slung the loop of his glasses over his head and handed the binoculars to Dove.

Dove took them with eagerness. He had been intrigued by the fact that the tanker had no visible name, but now as he scanned her side through the powerful glasses, he realised that she had a name amidships which had been painted out. But to a keen eye the letters were just visible. Dove adjusted the glasses and looked again and read aloud: *ALTMARK* –

This was long before the name of the ill-famed prison ship became known, but there was something ominous to Dove, even then, in the name lurking under its coat of black paint.

When he heard Dove speak, Langsdorff gave a quick look and took the binoculars back. He looked at the *Altmark*'s name himself and frowned, then shrugged his shoulders and said carelessly, 'Not very well camouflaged, is it? Now we do things much better.' He pointed down on to the deck where some men were painting a long strip of sheet metal, about fifteen feet long and one foot wide. The name they were painting in was *Deutschland*. At a shout from the Captain the officer in charge of the party gave an order, and the sheet was turned over to show *Admiral Scheer* painted on the other side. Langsdorff explained, 'Those are two of our aliases. We rig them up for neutrals, sometimes one side, sometimes the other. Sometimes we even use our own name. Neutrals always report what they see and so – I keep your Navy guessing. . . .'

He gave a mischievous look at Dove's solemn face and said, 'I am like a pretty girl. I change my hat – I change my frock – Presto! – I am a different girl!'

There was a nervous quality in his gaiety and in his stream of talk. Dove felt the temporary relief from constant strain. Langsdorff continued to chat in the same manner as they strolled about the deck. 'That working party are putting up an new funnel . . . a dummy funnel – made of canvas . . . those fellows are rigging and extra turret – made of wood. I am changing my silhouette. We are very good at that.'

A master painter was supervising other painters mixing various colours. Langsdorff said gaily, 'The make-up department. . . . Max Factor! We are just like a Holywood studio. This is our make-up expert.' He called out, 'Leutnant Hirth!' A young officer answered the call. He was a serious type and carried a large book. Langsdorff continued, 'Leutnant Hirth is our camouflage expert. He is a real artist.' To Hirth he said in German, 'Geben Sei mir das Buch.' It was a familar book to Dove, who said, 'Oh-ho, Jane!'

Langsdorff smiled, 'Yes – *Jane's Fighting Ships,* an excellent publication – made in England!' He pointed to the book, 'This is our latest silhouette.'

Dove said, 'Well, well! An American heavy-cruiser. So that's why you've got a number painted on your bows. I suppose that means we're going West?' Langdorff and his camouflage officer exchanged a conspiratorial glance. Dove said bluntly, 'D'you think you'll get away with it?'

'Long enough to delay recognition,' answered Langsdorff, handing back the book with a word of thanks. He resumed his stroll and Dove walked beside him as he went on, 'Five minutes at thirty knots can make the difference to being in range or out of range. Two things matter in modern naval battles, Captain. Good intelligence ashore, so that you know what to expect when you see it; good spotting on your own ship, so that you know what you see when you expect it. And talking of new silhouettes, I must congratulate you,' he added, looking Dove up and down.

'Thanks,' said Dove, 'he's done a good bit of camouflage too – around the waistline!'

Langsdorff laughed, 'I want you to look your best, Captain. You have company tonight. I am transferring to this ship all the officer prisoners who are in the *Altmark.*'

This was big news, and logically Dove should have been pleased to know that he was going to have the company of his own kind. He was a gregarious man by nature. But man is such an adaptable animal that he found, to his surprise, that he suffered a slight twinge of disappointment at realising his lonely voyage on the *Graf Spee* was nearly over. Yet had it been lonely? During the whole of his life he was never to forget those two weeks. Probably at no time in his vigorous, but, of necessity, routine career at sea had he ever had so many interesting experiences, so much time for reflection, and such opportunity for close observation of a man whom he was beginning to admire greatly. He suddenly realised that this was probably the last time he would have an intimate talk with Langsdorff. (He was mistaken about this, as we shall see later.) Perhaps Langsdorff guessed what was passing in his mind, for he was watching him closely. Dove said, 'I gather it's been your practice, sir, to trans-

31

fer to the *Altmark*, as a prison ship, all the officers and crews which you have captured?'

Langsdorff nodded and Dove went on, 'May I ask why you are changing this practice?' Langsdorff answered briskly, 'Certainly, Captain. I have no secrets from you.' His friendly smile belied the irony in his words. 'The *Graf Spee* is going to be relieved by – another vessel. We have done our spell of duty.' Suddenly he showed the deep emotion which lay beneath his gay manner, and it was with deep feeling that he went on, 'Three months at sea! We are due for leave at home. And when I return, I must bring back my officer prisoners. Good for civilian morale. The *Altmark* will return at her leisure with the ships' crews under hatches. So tonight you are no more alone. Now if you will excuse me, I will tell the Master-at-Arms to show you to your new quarters. Lempke!' He gave an order and saluting Dove, vanished up a ladder to the bridge.

The steel door of Dove's new quarters had a metal plate screwed into it, labelled 'See Kadetten'. The Master-at-Arms told the ship's carpenter, who accompanied them, to unscrew the plate. Dove supposed that it would be bad form to keep the sign up now that it was going to be a prison. (There were no midshipmen on the *Graf Spee*.)

It was a large room, immediately under the main deck. The portholes were boarded up and barred. There were plenty of steel chairs and several tables bolted to the floor. A pantry and a lavatory opened off the main room. One of the corners was already marked off with white chalk. Blue electric lights were burning. The place was clean, though bare, and Dove nodded approvingly before he said, 'Very nice! Very nice and spacious.'

The Master-at-Arms agreed, 'You will be twenty-nine officers here.' Dove's smile vanished. 'Twenty-nine!' His guide grinned, 'Ja, ja. And later on, many more!' He led the way to the chalked out corner. 'You here, Captain! Orders of Kaptain Langsdorff. Reserved for you.'

Young sailors burst in, chattering and laughing and carrying a lot of baggage which they dumped in the middle of the room by the steel pillars. There was quite a procession of them. In no time, a great pile of kitbags, suitcases, brown paper parcels, even one or two cabin trunks were dumped on the floor. Dove got more and more excited as he read the labels and saw the familiar names of home ports. He was just saying, 'All I can say is they had more time to pack than I had,' when there was the sound of running feet and excited voices along the deck outside, and the first batch of prisoners burst into the flat, heralded by a broad Yorkshire voice, 'Newton Beach first! Come on, lads!'

His companion shouted, 'Quick! Get one of the corners!'

A small Welsh engineer chimed in, 'Aye! Indeed! Corners are cosy!'

Ignoring Dove's outstretched hand, they charged across the flat and took possession of the corner reserved for Dove, chucking his blankets and few personal effects into the middle of the room. The Captain who had first come in, announced to all and sundry, with an air of defiance, 'This is the Newton Beach corner!'

They were only just ahead of the others. Nobody had any time for Dove. It was quite obvious that life in the Altmark, while not improving anybody's manners, had sharpened up their sense of self-preservation to a remarkable degree. While Dove turned this way and that, trying to introduce himself, men were arriving, scrambling for the best places, in the corners, on the tables, under the tables. As each grabbed his position, he announced his ship and hailed his own people to come over and join him. Others were claiming their baggage from the mound in the centre of the room. There was a pandemonium of voices, a scraping and banging of cases, calls of 'Huntsman, Huntsman . . . ' 'Ashlea over here! . . . ' 'Newton Beach! . . . ' 'Trevanion, this is Trevanion table!'

Finally Dove, exasperated, grabbed the arm of a tall man who was pushing by him, and twisted him round, saying with emphasis, 'Good evening, Captain!'

'Why! You're one of us,' said the invader, peering at his face and his medal ribbons. The others gathered round him, exclaiming, 'I thought he was a Jerry! . . . Glory be! A new face! . . . Who are you, anyway?'

'Dove, Africa Shell,' he answered, feeling like a new boy at school.

'When was your ship sunk, Dove?' said the Captain of the Ashlea.

'November 15th, Indian Ocean.'

'Any others with you?' asked Newton Beach.

'No. They only took me, and I was the last ship they sunk.'

The Chief Officer of the Newton Beach announced, 'D'you hear that, boys? Not a kill for nearly three weeks. She must be getting hungry.'

A Chief Engineer said, 'How have they treated you?'

It was obviously an important question. Dove was able to reassure him, 'Quite all right.'

A pugnacious young Irishman said suspiciously, 'How's the Captain?'

There was a general chorus, 'Yes. What's the old man like?'

'He's a gentleman,' said Dove stoutly.

By now the Master-at-Arms had joined the group round Dove and was listening tolerantly to their talk. The Irishman gave him a dirty look and said, 'A gentleman is he? Not like our fellow Dahl on the *Altmark*! He was a proper swine – a real b – .'

Another voice chimed in: 'It's a floating ruddy Hell! Our men are like cattle in the hold! Just four walls and a stinking bucket!'

There was a general growl and the Master-at-Arms suddenly found himself the centre of a group of scowling faces. He said smartly, 'Auf wiedersehen!' and vanished. A wounded radio officer who had already fixed up on top of one of the tables near the door, cracked, 'This is going to be no luxury cruise, either!' The Master-at-Arms grinned, stepped outside and the steel door was slammed.

A second later, raw white lights came on. Dove's sharp eyes had noticed something when the door had slammed. 'That's a bit of luck,' he remarked. 'When the Chippy took that sign off the door, he forgot to stop up the holes.' True enough, there were four screw-holes left in the door. Dove and another man peered through them. They found they had a good view of the five-point-nine turret, with the gun's crew taking it easy. 'This might be useful later on,' said Dove, not knowing how true a remark he was making. 'We'll take turns keeping watch.' He turned and, going to the centre of the room, started to pick up his belongings. He looked around the crowded room a bit ruefully and said, 'When I was all alone, I rather fancied company . . . but now I'm not so sure.'

'We're moving, boys!' announced the Welsh Chief Engineer, 'Yes! ,Yes! We're under way!'

Everybody listened and the look-out at the door reported that, by the shadows on the deck, they were heading North-West. 'Well, who are you all?' said Dove, looking around him, and one by one each ship announced herself through her little group of officers. '*Huntsman*! . . . ' ' *Newton Beach*! . . . ' '*Ashlea*! . . . ' '*Trevanion*! . . . ' Last of all came Dove with: '*Africa Shell*! . . . '

A big map of the North and South Atlantic Ocean filled the end wall of the Flat, a relic of the midshipmen's school. With a sweeping gesture he indicated the vast expanse of ocean into which they were heading, and said grimly: 'Who's next?'

CHAPTER IV

THE HUNTERS

IT WOULD HAVE heartened Dove and his fellow-prisoners to know that, day and night, all over the world men were asking the very same question.

In London, the Director of Naval Intelligence was at that moment summarising the position to a remarkably varied group of people; some in uniform, some not; some respectable, others disreputable. There were both men and women among them. Some of them made notes as the D.N.I. talked, others smoked and stared at the ceiling. Only one or two looked at the map on which the vast area of the *Graf Spee*'s operations were marked. The D.N.I., by his tone, might have been discussing the weather instead of the chase of a hunting beast which covered half of the world. ' . . . *Trevanion* . . . *Newton Beach* . . . *Africa Shell* . . . all merchant-ships and all sailing alone. There may be one Raider or two. Probably only one, although more than one has been reported. Their Intelligence is good. They have agents ashore, of course, and new ways of passing it on. . . . '

An elderly officer in Naval uniform, whose face looked vaguely familiar – he was a well-known playright in civilian life – appeared at his elbow and handed him a signal which he glanced at before going on. ' . . . I am sending out a priority warning to all our agents, to all Naval Attachés at Embassies and Legations. What we are looking for are men who get frequent telegrams from neutral ports.' He held up the signal in his hand, 'Take this, for instance. This is from Stanley in Paris. The French police are being very helpful. . . . '

In Paris an hour or two later that same night, the Rome Express was about to leave. A nervous traveller, smoking a cigarette outside the sleeping-car labelled Genoa, suddenly turned and leapt up the steps into the coach. The fact that officials were already calling out 'En voiture!' hardly seemed to justify the extreme haste with which he went to bed; and, if his conscience was as clear as it should be, the sight of two men hurrying through the barrier could hardly explain it, as one of them was a French Police-Inspector called Lorrain. His companion, Gasset, was a well-known Inspector from the Sûreté in plain-clothes. They had a list of names in their hand, came straight to the Genoa sleeping car and, after checking the list with the conductor, climbed up into the corridor. A railway official had followed them and, although the hands of the clock had passed the official time of departure, the train remained in the station.

In the corridor of the wagon-lit, Lorrain and Gasset knocked at the door of number 9 and 10. There was no answer, so Lorrain tried the door. It was locked. Gasset drew a gun from his pocket and beckoned to the conductor, who opened the door with his pass-key, but the door proved to be on the chain. On the other side of the train, in the narrow steamy passage between the Express and a local train which was standing on the next track, the nervous passenger was scrambling out of the window of the sleeping car. He was in such a hurry that he dropped without looking where he was going, which was unfortunate for him, for he fell straight into the arms of a tall Englishman, who held him tight and said, politely, 'My name is Stanley – er – Dr Livingstone, I presume?'

In a London Club two days later, two men, in two armchairs, were reading their newspapers side by side. One paper was *The Times*, the other was a Paris newspaper. Behind this barrier of wood pulp, Stanley and the D.N.I. were conferring in low voices. Stanley was chuckling, 'His name was Evergreen. Amusing – eh? So we took him along to Gasset's office. There was nothing on him, then we saw this.' He passed over his Paris paper, and the D.N.I. handed him *The Times* in exchange. He knew that Stanley liked a bit of mystification, so he merely remarked, 'The racing-page, I see,' and waited for Stanley to explain, which he did in due course, in an exasperating drawl. 'Y – e – s. The racing-page. Old Gasset was brooding over it for a while, but the only remark he made was that he didn't understand why French breeders can't give French names to their horses. "What names?" said I. "Oh," he says, " 'Untsman, Newtong be-ach." Look there, sir . . . there. Under New Arrivals.'

The D.N.I. looked and murmured, 'Yes. We ought to have spotted this before.'

Stanley added, 'And in each case the port of sailing is printed.'

'Very neat,' said the D.N.I.

'We're holding him, of course,' Stanley winked. 'No habeas corpus in France. Gasset has put a man to sit in his apartment.'

The D.N.I. had been reading the page with attention. He said,

'There are a lot of South American ports mentioned here. Ray Martin is going to be pleased about this.'

Stanley yawned and said, 'Time for a martini. Where is Ray Martin just now?'

The D.N.I. said, 'The drinks are on me,' and then, after striking the bell, 'Montevideo.'

In Uruguay, on the other side of the world, Mike Fowler was sitting on top of a telegraph pole. There were three odd things about this particular telegraph pole: one was an odd sort of metal fork which stuck up on the cross-piece, second was a large lump of mud which looked very like a small baker's oven, and the third was Mike Fowler. He held a microphone in his hand, and he was talking with enthusiasm to the housewives of America. 'This is Mike Fowler bringing you by courtesy of the Red Meat Packing Company of Chicago his series of Real Nature Recordings of the birds and beasts of the Rio de la Plata. Today we bring you the voice of the Oven Bird. The Oven Bird is so called because of its peculiar, oven-like nest, made of mud, one of which I've got right in front of me. The entrance is cunningly curved, and the bird is inside on the nest – I hope.'

He knocked on the mud and asked, 'Anybody home?' After a pause he continued: 'Yes! Yes, I can hear the peculiar hissing noise which this creature makes when it is molested. Listen, I will bring the mike close up to the nest.' But as he did so, all other sounds were drowned by the bellowing of cattle. Mike said wearily into the microphone, 'Cut!' Then he looked down below him and said, 'Pop! Don't tell me we've got cattle again!'

The man he addressed as 'Pop' was a picturesque gaucho, lean tough and with greying hair, philosophically rolling a cigarette, as he leant against the base of the telegraph pole. All around him and as far as the eye could see along the dusty cattle track, which bordered the side of the motor road, were cattle, cattle and more cattle, heading past on their way to the stockyards of Montevideo, driven at a deliberate pace by mounted gauchos, who glanced incuriously at Mike on his post as they rode by. Some of them yelled in Spanish to Pop, who ran his tongue delicately along the edge of his cigarette paper, sealed it, and finally answered his employer before sticking it in his mouth. 'Sure! That's cattle! Plenty cattle!'

'Any use asking them to hurry?'

Pop struck a match on his thumb nail and lit his cigarette, before replying. 'No use, Mike. Cattle lose weight when driven fast. You know that.'

'You bet I know it,' said Mike. 'Who's this?'

A uniformed man carrying a repair kit, had left his motor bike and was pushing through the cattle towards them. The gauchos shouted, the dogs barked, the cattle bellowed and the new arrival shouted in Spanish at Mike. Pop translated between puffs, 'Man says you have cut telephone line to Montevideo . . . this very important line . . . carry telephone from Post Office to Radio Station.' Mike groaned. 'Man says he been watching you. Why you always say "cut"? He think we cut wire. Have we got permit?'

Mike was indignant. 'Of course we got permits.' He pulled a sheaf of papers from his pocket, 'One from the Uruguayan Government to make recordings. One from the Postmaster General to make a recording on his telegraph pole. Special permit from the United States Government to – ', but the new arrival and Pop were not listening to him. Finally Pop looked up and reported, 'Man says if you have all these permits you must be all right and the Oven Bird cut the line, not you. These Oven Birds make plenty trouble with Telephone Company. The Company put spikes on bar to stop Oven Bird making a nest. But nothing stops Oven Bird. Man says please come down and let him come up to test line.'

Mike said, sadly, 'O.K., O.K.' He climbed down and the Post Office man climbed up.

In Montevideo, in the British Legation, a rather insignificant-looking man was reading all the newspapers. He appeared to be a civilian, and was certainly a chain-smoker. The door opened, and a young and smart secretary came in, gave a doubtful look through the blue atmosphere at the newspaper reader, and picked up the telephone. She said, 'Give me that call in here, please. . . . British Embassy? Can I have Captain McCall, please? . . . Yes, the Naval Attaché.' Then, covering the telephone with her hand for a moment, she said, 'Mr Martin, the line is all right now. Buenos Aires is on the line.'

The crumpled-looking man silently held out his hand for the telephone. She gave it to him and, after another doubtful look, went out, as he said quietly: 'Is that you, McCall . . . Ray Martin here. Something important has come up. Fly over, will you?' Evidently McCall was not prepared to jump at the invitation, for after a moment of listening, Martin went on, 'No. Sorry about your daughter, but it can't wait. The *Exeter* is calling here to-morrow.'

This news had the desired effect for, in a moment, he said with satisfaction: 'Right. Then we'll see you here in the morning.' He rang off and went back to his newspapers.

In a Paris apartment, a stolid French detective sat on an uncomfortable chair in the hall, also reading a paper and smoking, while at his elbow, Radio Paris murmured the news over a cabinet radio which he had pulled half way into the hall for company.

The front door buzzer sounded. The detective got up, went to the front door, which was on the chain, and opened it. He exchanged just a few words with the messenger, took a cablegram from him, closed the door, came back to the telephone on the wall, dialled a number, turned down the radio and opened the cable. Meanwhile he said on the telephone, 'Sûreté trois cent dix. . . . Monsieur l'Inspecteur? Ici Lemaitre. Un marconigram. . . . de Montevideo. . . . addresse Evergreen. . . . "Courses Montevideo stop Exeter va courir" . . . Oui, Monsieur Gasset, oui, c'est tout. Oui . . . oui,' and he repeated the name – *Exeter*.

The cruiser *Exeter* was lying alongside the quay in Montevideo harbour, in the brilliant morning sunshine. She was a pretty ship and beautifully kept, a light cruiser of 8,400 tons, mounting six eight-inch guns. A guard of honour was drawn up on the quarterdeck and a group of officers wearing dazzling white uniform, Number Tens, with swords and medals, was at the head of the gangway to greet a distinguished visitor.

The Rolls-Royce of the British Minister glided over the tramlines and stopped at the bottom of the gangway. The Minister got out, accompanied by Captain McCall. They climbed the gangway and were piped aboard with proper ceremony. Formal salutes were exchanged. Mr Millington-Drake lifted his hat.

Mr Eugen Millington-Drake, tall, elegant, Eton and Oxford, a rowing blue, a first-class sportsman, rich, a great Hispanophile, handsome and graceful, was enormously popular in Uruguay, and at this period of history was most definitely the right man in the right place. He was generous, an excellent showman, more than a little of an actor and was on good terms with Commodore Harwood. He was dressed for a formal call, in morning coat and top hat.

Commodore Henry Harwood-Harwood, a big, bluff, and burly man, looked very simple and was not. He was a good disciplinarian, a passionate patriot, a student of strategy and of Naval history. He had a keen sense of the political and diplomatic importance to England of a high-ranking Naval officer abroad, and during the two years he had spent on the South American Station, there were very few useful officials in Brazil, Uruguay and the Argentine, whom he did not know personally. He had very keen and shrewd eyes, and he liked to talk a great deal about sport, while finding out what he really wanted to know.

Captain 'Hookie' Bell, who commanded the *Exeter*, was a taciturn and formidable officer, with a nose that would have commanded respect both from Julius Caesar and William the Conqueror. He had newly taken over command of the Flagship, and was not yet on familiar terms with his Commodore. He was a popular Captain. He was the kind of fighting man that stood beside Nelson, and he had a grim sense of humour.

Captain McCall, the British Naval Attaché at B.A., was an active, incisive man, with a high domed head, very keen dark eyes and a forceful personality.

After the salutes, Harwood stepped forward, and he and the Minister shook hands. Then presenting the others: 'Minister, may I present the new Captain of the *Exeter*? Mr Millington-Drake – Captain Bell.' The two men shook hands. Harwood turned and said, 'McCall you know Bell, don't you?'

McCall nodded and said, 'Hello, Hookie.'

Harwood said breezily, 'Well, now that all the beastly formality is over, let's go down and have a drink.'

Below, on the flat outside the Admiral's cabin, a steward was taking in a tray of drinks. Bill Roper, a young seaman, one of the Captain's messengers, accosted him: 'Get the dope on shore leave, will you?' The steward, a cynic, said, 'Don't worry. She's forgotten you.'

'You don't know Julie,' was the reply, as Bill vanished and feet came down the companionway. The steward grunted, 'Anyway – I'm in the Rattle.' He went in to the big airy cabin and put the drinks on a side table. The cabin was not empty. Ray Martin, quiet and insignificant as ever, was sitting there reading his eternal papers. McCall's voice was heard outside, ' . . . the usual programme, Sir. Formal calls upon the Admiral Commanding the Port and upon General Campos, the Defence Minister. Reception for all officers at the British Club at 17.00. Dinner with the Minister 20.30. The Admiral and General Campos will return your call this morning at 11.30 and 12.30.' Martin glanced up, as they all came in. Harwood, who had been impatiently listening to McCall's programme, said, 'Yes, yes. By the way, you all know Martin.' They all did, and Martin nodded. Harwood went on,

40

'Now what's between 15.00 and 17.00, that's what interests me?'

McCall said, 'The Minister asked me to leave those two hours free.'

The Commodore was relieved. 'I should hope so. Golf, my dear fellow, golf! They're all coming, aren't they?' he said to Millington-Drake.

'Yes. The Defence Minister, the Admiral, and Senor Guani, the Foreign Minister, are playing you a foursome.'

'Splendid,' said Harwood. 'Now, what about the men?'

The steward, who was handing round drinks, cocked an ear.

McCall said to Bell, 'Special buses will take those who wish to go to the British Brewery. A football game has been laid on at 15.00 in the Stadium. Are you giving leave to all hands?'

Bell said, with a glance at the Commodore, 'If you agree, sir. I'd like to give even men under punishment a turn ashore, in the circumstances.'

Harwood agreed, and his steward's eyes gleamed.

McCall went on, 'All the beaches will be open. Nobody in uniform will be charged anything.'

Harwood took his own drink from the steward and said, 'Buzz off, Wilkins.' Then to McCall he said, 'Now what about this other business?'

McCall lowered his voice and said, 'Well, to put it in a nutshell, the telephone line between the Ministry here and the Embassy in B.A. is tapped. Nobody but I and Martin here knew of *Exeter*'s proposed arrival, but on the same day that he 'phoned me, it was known in Paris, eh, Martin?'

Martin nodded and picked up another newspaper, and murmured, 'Might be useful if we ever want to give them false information.'

Harwood said, 'Any of our merchant ships in port?'

Martin held up four fingers. Harwood said, 'Well, they'll have to be re-routed, or better still, kept here for a few days. That's the devil of it. The mention of a leakage immobilises shipping for weeks. This is my first visit to Montevideo since war was declared. How's the feeling here, now that we're really in it?'

Millington-Drake said, 'I can tell you exactly. They will observe strictly the rules of neutrality, but there sympathies are with us.'

Harwood looked at McCall, 'How about the Argentine?'

McCall said carefully, 'They've been impressed by German propaganda, and they're backing the Germans to win. But they'll stay neutral.'

'To sum up,' said Harwood, 'we're surrounded by neutrals but some are more neutral than others.'

There was general laughter. He raised his glass in a toast, 'Here's to the enemy. May he head this way!'

Lieutenant-Commander Medley, Harwood's Staff Officer, said to McCall, 'What's the latest news, sir?'

'Nothing since that little tanker, the *Africa Shell*,' was the reply. 'Of course we don't hear of all the victims. They don't all get a chance to squeak.'

Millington-Drake said thoughtfully: 'It is very like a hunt for a man-eating tiger . . . an unknown killer at large, terrorising the Seven Seas. Do you think it's the *Scheer*?'

His question provoked a general discussion. The only thing certain was that the Raider was a Pocket battleship. Keenly interested, Millington-Drake asked, 'If she comes this way, can you handle her?'

Harwood answered promptly, 'To fight her, certainly. To finish her off, doubtful. If it's the *Scheer* or the *Graf Spee* she has six eleven-inch guns. Of my two eight-inch cruisers, the *Cumberland* is down at the Falklands boiler-cleaning. That only leaves *Exeter* and my two small six-inch cruisers, *Ajax* and *Achilles*, to police the whole coast from Pernambuco to the Falkland Islands.'

Millington-Drake said thoughtfully, 'Three thousand miles of sea. A tall order.'

'Y – e – s,' said Harwood, 'a tall order.' But he didn't seem too down-hearted. Switching the conversation, he said, 'By George, I wonder how my pack of hounds are getting on at Punta del Este. Twenty mixed breeds. You never shot over so many different tails in your life, Bell. I must take them out next month.'

Medley said, 'May I remind you, sir, that by International Law, *Exeter* can't put into territorial waters here for another three months.'

Harwood replied, '*Exeter* can't, but I can.'

All glasses were lowered. Everyone stared. Even Ray Martin put down his newspaper. Harwood kept them in suspense and then announced, 'I'm transferring my broad pendant to *Ajax*.' He sipped his drink and his eyes sparkled as he looked at the others over his drink. But he told them nothing further.

CHAPTER V

IDYLL

An empty bus flying a small British flag stood on the edge of
the Playa Pocitos, one of the golden sandy beaches of Montevideo. The local driver leant against it, and watched the bathers
through a cheap pair of glasses. At that moment, he was watching Lotte, a pretty girl in a light summer frock. which was blowing in the breeze. She was standing on a landing stage and
looking out to sea, where a diving raft was moored about a
hundred yards from the shore.

On the raft, a boy heaved himself out of the water and then,
turning, pulled up a young girl beside him. They were both very
much in love. In the distance they heard the other girl's voice
calling faintly, 'Julita!'

Bill Roper said, 'Someone's calling you.'

Julita waved and said, 'It is Lotte. She work with me in our
shop. Not in the same departimento.'

'Nice girl?'

'You want meet her?' sharply.

'Not at the moment,' lazily.

'You can meet her, if you want. She is more clever as me. She
is head of her departimento.'

Bill stroked her arm and said, 'You don't say. What is her
departimento?'

Julita, who liked being stroked, purred and answered, 'Work
clothes. You know, for the workmen, for the estancias. The
jeans, the overalls, the ponchos.'

Bill pulled her down dreamily beside him and said, 'What's
ponchos?' He didn't really care what they were. Their heads
were close together on the raft. Julita answered slowly, 'What the
gauchos wear.' They kissed. The water lapping under the raft
heard a sigh and then, 'Billy . . . my Billy. . . . ' There was a
silence, then the boy's voice said, 'I love you, Julie.'

After a time, they started to talk again. 'Last time your ship
was in Montevideo, you promised come my shop.'

'I'll come this time.'

'Tomorrow?'

'Today. We won't be here tomorrow.'

'You shall stay. Because your Commodore likes to play golf.'

'How do you know?'

'Everyone know it. He is famous man.'

Bill was genuinely surprised. 'Is he? Our old man? But in war-time, we can't stay as long as we like.'

Julita said, 'How long you like?'

He teased her, 'Oh – a week – a month – for ever – but not this time.'

'Why?'

'You don't let us.'

'Why, why, why?'

'You're neutral,' said Bill tolerantly, 'that's why. International Law says fighting ships of a country – that's us – at war with another country – that's Germany – can't stay longer than twenty-four hours in a neutral port – that's you – and then only once in three months.'

Julita let off a long string of Spanish epithets, finishing with, 'I think that International Law is – '

Bill cut her short. 'So do I.' Then he added, slyly, 'Of course, we can call in other ports in other neutral countries . . . Rio . . . Santiago . . . Buenos Aires?'

'You have girl in Buenos Aires?'

Bill nodded. 'And in Santiago. And in Rio.'

Julita leapt to her feet and walked away to the edge of the raft. She stood there with her back to him. She had a pretty figure. Bill sat up and said, 'Julie. There isn't any girl but you.' But she didn't turn round. He said, in a different tone, 'Julie! Have you got anybody else?'

Julita answered without turning, 'Yes! I have!'

There was a pause.

'Oh,' said Bill rather flatly. 'One of these galloping gauchos, I suppose?'

Julita turned and came to him and said, 'No. A silly sailor boy.'

Bill held her tight and looked in her eyes and said, 'I'll come back, Julie darling. However long I stay away, I'll always come back. Haven't I come back twice already?'

From the harbour, the siren of the *Exeter* blew a long blast. Bill stood up. 'What is it?' asked Julita. The siren blew a second blast. 'It's our ship,' said Bill. 'Three blasts means an emergency.' The siren blew a third blast. Bill said, 'I've got to go! Come on! I'll race you to the shore.'

He dived in. 'Santa Maria,' breathed Julita and followed him.

44

In the big football Stadium, the three blasts had also been heard. The game was still in progress, but among the seats little islands of British sailors were rising and hurrying to the exit.

In the cinemas, hand-printed slides were projected on to the screens: ENGLISH SAILORS RETURN THEIR SHIP PLEASE. Sailors and their girls were rising still entwined.

On the golf course, in the middle of the city, overlooking the river, four gentlemen, one of them Commodore Harwood in sporting tweeds, were on the fifteenth green. Harwood was just about to putt. The other gentlemen were looking towards the harbour, where the *Exeter* was flying the Recall signal. Harwood, addressing the ball, said, 'Gentlemen! I have to leave you, but there is just time to win this hole.'

He putted and holed out. Amid general applause, he added, 'We'll finish the match another time. Two up and three to play!'

On the beach, sailors in all stages of dress and undress were piling into the bus. The driver honked his horn, leaning in through the window to press the button. Lotte, smoking a cigarette, leant against the wing beside him. They seemed to have got acquainted. He winked at her as he pressed the horn, and she smiled back, as she asked, 'Do you always drive a bus?'

He winked again as he answered, 'Sometimes I get a car, too. I drive for the British Legation.'

'Do you like driving?'

'Sure. Why?'

'I like being driven,' she said.

He could think of nothing better to say than, 'We ought to get together.'

On the other side of the bus, close against it, stood Bill and Julie. He was dressed, his hair was still wet, and he carried his wet swimsuit and towel. She was still in her swimsuit and was fighting gallantly against tears. Bill said gently, 'I must be off now.'

She clung to him and said, 'Billy, oh my Billy. . . .'

Bill said, 'Chin up, Julie. I'll come back – soon.'

The bus honked. Sailors above looked out of the windows and laughed. Little they cared. Julie tried to smile and whispered, 'I'll wait for you . . . my silly sailor boy.'

Bill repeated, 'I'll be back. I swear I'll come back.'

He kissed her and about fifty of his friends applauded. He said, quickly, 'Adios!' The bus engine roared, he ran around and got in.

The young driver waved to Lotte and the bus backed up.

45

Inside, Bill battled his way ruthlessly through the mob to get to a window. As the bus drew away, he hung out of the window and shouted once again, 'I'll be back!'

Lotte and Julie stood looking after the bus with very different thoughts. Lotte put her arm around her friend, 'Did he say where they were going?'

Julie couldn't speak, she just shook her head. Lotte asked again, 'Why were they all recalled?'

Julie turned away, and started to walk to her clothes. Lotte went with her. Julie said in a low voice, full of tears, 'Billy said it was an Emergency.' She was too full of her own thoughts to listen to the tone of her friend's voice or to notice the expression on her face. Lotte was thinking hard. She repeated, 'An Emergency . . . do you think it could be the German Raider?'

Julie murmured, 'I'll pray for him every day.'

'You'd better pray that he doesn't meet the German Raider.'

Julie stopped short and looked at her friend, 'Why?'

Lotte answered proudly, 'It's the most powerful ship in the world.'

'How do you know?' asked Julie, staring.

'I know!' answered Lotte. 'I've seen pictures of it in magazines at home that father gets from Germany.'

Julie still stared at Lotte as if she had never seen her friend before. 'Lotte! You are German! . . . I forgot you were German. . . .'

CHAPTER VI

VARIOUS PARTIES
CONVERGING ON THE WEST

(i) *Commodore Harwood*

AT NINE O'CLOCK on the morning of December 12th, Commodore Harwood's squadron, consisting of H.M.S. *Ajax*, H.M.S. *Exeter* and H.M.N.Z.S. *Achilles*, was steaming in line ahead, approximately on the thirty-fifth parallel of latitude and about one hundred miles off Punta del Este, at the mouth of the River Plate. H.M.S. *Ajax* was flying Harwood's broad pendant of a Commodore First Class. H.M.N.Z.S. *Achilles*, ordered down from the north, had only joined the squadron that morning. For the first time since the outbreak of the war, the Commodore had three of the ships under his Command together. It was no accident.

Captain Woodhouse, the Captain of the *Ajax*, was standing in his usual position on the port side of the bridge. He was tall, fair, slow-spoken and deliberate, with an uncompromising look in his eye. At some period in his life, his nose had collided with a hard object, probably a boxing-glove. He stepped to the side of the bridge and glanced astern at the other two cruisers keeping station. It was a perfect South Atlantic morning. The cruisers gleamed white in the sunshine, and the sea was deep blue. Woodhouse wondered to himself why the Commodore had ordered this concentration at this particular time. As if in answer to his thoughts, the Commodore appeared on the bridge.

His formidable presence caused a little stir of self-consciousness as he came for'ard. Messengers stopped lounging and straightened their hats. So did the Officer of the Watch. The navigator stopped leaning on the binnacle. Woodhouse, outwardly unperturbed, started to patrol the bridge so that he could be in ear-shot. He had an instinct that things were brewing. Medley, who had been talking to the Gunnery Officer in the wing of the bridge, hastily closed up to his Chief's elbow. Harwood, after a glance around which took in everything, including the weather, made straight for his high teak chair on the starboard side of the bridge, plumped himself down in it, took off his cap and hung it on the binnacle, and said in a voice that made everybody jump, 'Staffy!'

Medley said, 'Sir?' and Woodhouse drifted across the bridge within earshot.

Harwood said, 'Make to *Achilles* and *Exeter*: I would like to see you on board Flagship at 11.0 today.'

He caught Woodhouse's eye, enjoyed his surprise, and added, 'Are the charts prepared?'

Medley said, 'All ready, sir.' He ordered the Yeoman, to whom he had passed the message: 'Put a Time of Origin on that.'

Woodhouse smiled to himself, with deep satisfaction. His instinct had been right. It was very rare indeed these days that an Admiral called a Council of Captains at Sea. It had the Nelson touch about it. But it proved to Woodhouse that Harwood had something very important to say to his Captains, something far too important and complicated to be signalled, and quite impossible to send by radio, because of wireless silence. Although he appeared outwardly calm, it was with great feelings of excitement that he came to Harwood's cabin at the appointed hour.

The three ships had come to stop twenty minutes earlier, and both *Achilles* and *Exeter* had lowered sea-boats. Woodhouse had waited to see both boats pulling towards the Flagship, and then had left the Officer of the Watch and Medley to receive the visitors. Captain Bell was the first on board. Medley announced, '*Exeter*, sir.'

Harwood was at his desk, going through a list of signals, 'Morning, Bell. D'you know Woodhouse?'

Bell said, 'Haven't seen you for years,' and Woodhouse answered, 'Not since that famous game at Twickenham.'

At the same time Bell's eyes were saying, 'What's up?' and Woodhouse was answering in like manner, 'We'll soon know.'

Harwood coming up, with a signal still in his hand, said, 'I'll take care not to leave you two together. Bell can tell you too much about my bad habits when I flew my flag in *Exeter*.'

Medley announced, '*Achilles*, sir.'

Captain Parry was very tall and slim, and was older than the other two Captains. He was shrewd, with an easy charm of manner, and a great gift for handling all sorts and conditions of men. Harwood said heartily, 'Glad to see you, Parry.' To Bell, he added, 'Hookie! I don't think you know Parry.' They shook hands.

'Well,' said Harwood. 'How are your New Zealanders shaping?'

Parry thought a moment, smiled, then summed it up with 'Five hundred individualists.'

Harwood put down the batch of signals and said, out of the blue, 'Hookie!' Bell jumped. Harwood went on, 'What about that defect list and list of spares for *Exeter* that I asked you to get out and send to base? Has it gone?' He knew that it couldn't possibly have gone and Bell knew that he knew, and this was the second time he had asked for it in the last three days.

Bell answered tactfully, 'No. Not yet, sir.'

Harwood didn't let him off so lightly. 'What's the delay?' he asked.

The other two Captains studied the ceiling or the pictures. Bell said, 'Sorry, sir. It's not completed. I'll get it finished today.'

'Please do so,' said Harwood, his eye still remorselessly fixed upon his junior Captain. 'Please do so, and put it aboard the first merchant ship that can take it to Simonstown.'

Jove having spoken, he said to everybody, 'Well. Let's start.'

The three Captains and Medley sat down around the big table, and Harwood said, 'Please smoke if you want to.'

He himself remained standing at the head of the table with his pipe in his hands.

There was an historic pause. The fans whirred in the ceilings. The ship, with her engines motionless, was strangely quiet. They could hear the water lapping around the stern. Parry and Bell very carefully took cigarettes and lit them. Woodhouse, just as carefully, refused. Medley watched his Chief.

Harwood gave a little self-conscious laugh and said, 'I've — er ; . . . I've taken the rather unusual course of sending for you, because I wanted to see you and to give you, personally, my appreciation of the situation. I have ordered this concentration here, off the River Plate, because of news that I have received of the latest movements of the German Surface Raider which is at large in the South Atlantic. I would like you to look at the charts. The Admiralty have good information that this Pocket battleship — it may be the *Admiral Scheer* or the *Graf Spee* or the *Deutschland* — sailed from Kiel on August 21st. She took up position somewhere in the South Atlantic well before war was declared. Up till September 30, she attacked no shipping. I can guess why not. Hitler thought that, after the fall of Poland, Britain and France would make peace. However . . . on September 30th she sunk the *Clement* . . . here . . . off Pernambuco. She immediately left this area for mid-Atlantic, where between the 5th and the 10th her victims were the *Newton Beach*, the *Ashlea* and the *Huntsman*. Then she left hurriedly, to proceed to the west coast of Africa, where she sunk the *Trevanion*. Once again she moved to a new hunting ground and rounded the Cape into the Indian Ocean, presumably to attack the Cape-India-Australia routes, but she only sank a small tanker, the *Africa Shell* . . . here! . . . in the Mozambique Channel. She then presumably doubled back, because some days ago she sank the Blue Star liner, *Doric Star* . . . there! . . . As she knows that the *Doric Star* managed to get off a signal, it is obvious that the Raider will be anxious to get out of that area as soon as possible. . . . Now, in my opinion, she will do one of three things. One – she will double back again into the Indian Ocean. Two – she will try and slip back to Germany as she came out . . . through the Denmark Strait . . . or three – before returning home, she will come over here to our part of the world – where she should have been all the time – to make a last killing among the grain ships and the meat cargoes from South America . . . and it's my opinion, that that is exactly what she will do!'

There was a pause as he finished speaking. Each Captain was solemn with his own thoughts, the thoughts of Action for which he had trained during the whole of his professional career. Harwood's appreciation had carried complete conviction to all of them. They believed him, and they believed that, at this moment, the enemy was steaming towards them.

Harwood sat down at the head of the table, and resumed in a different tone, the tone of a man who is dealing with immediate problems, 'Making a guess at her probable speed, I estimate that if she were making for Rio she would be there this morning – December 12th. If she is making here . . . for the River Plate . . . and that is what I believe, then she will be here twenty-four hours later.'

Bell heard his voice saying, 'Tomorrow,' without realising that he had spoken. Harwood repeated, 'Yes, tomorrow.' Then gathering them all together with his eye, 'My object is destruction of the enemy. My intention is to attack at once, day or night. She can out-gun and out-range us. So, as soon as we sight the Beast, we will close at maximum speed and divide her fire, by attacking on separate flanks. *Ajax* and *Achilles* will attack in close company. *Exeter* will attack on her own.'

Parry and Bell accepted this order philosophically. Bell, being younger, couldn't conceal a slight grin at the thought of independent action. Harwood continued, 'In this way, besides splitting the enemy's main armament, we can also report each other's

50

fall of shot.' He noticed Bell's grin and said, 'Search for any defect that might reduce fighting efficiency, and have it dealt with.' He waited until Bell's grin had vanished and been replaced by the expression of a wooden idol, and then went on speaking generally, 'I wish I had the *Cumberland*. I could do with another eight-inch cruiser. But she's still re-fitting in the Falklands. She won't rejoin us for a fortnight. Tell your ships' companies to be on their toes for the next few days. We will exercise my tactics for engaging a Pocket battleship, both in daylight and after dark today.'

He had said these last words in the voice of a Commander on the eve of battle. Nobody spoke or stirred. The smoke curled up from their cigarettes and was whirled away by the fans in the ceiling. Their eyes were fixed upon the square resolute figure at the head of the table in the white uniform, the powerful blunt hands drumming on the table, the thick grey hair, and the cunning eyes.

Harwood turned to Medley, and without altering his tone, said sharply, 'Staffy! Where's the sun?'

Startled out of his trance, Medley stared at his Chief, saw the twinkle in his eyes, grinned and answered smartly, 'Well over the yard-arm, sir!'

'Good,' said Harwood, 'then open the gin!'

At 04.50 on the morning of the 13th December, the three cruisers were steaming in line ahead at Dawn Action Stations. This was common practice before the days of radar as it had been since Nelson's day, as you never know what you will see when the sun comes up. They were proceeding on a north-easterly course at cruising speed, i.e. fourteen knots, with all boilers connected, ready to go on to full speed if dawn should reveal the enemy to be in sight.

The stars were fading, but it was still very dark. On the bridge of the Flagship you could only see dim forms, blue and red lights, and silent muffled figures. A dull glow came from the hooded chart table. It was cold before the sun rose, and everyone was in all sorts of mixed rigs. Harwood strolled up and down looking supremely confident, a pipe gripped between his teeth. Woodhouse nursed a cup of cocoa in his two hands, and looked astern. The looming shapes of the following ships coud be felt rather than seen, but already in the east there was a glow in the sky.

In *Achilles*, which was next in line, two look-outs were talking

51

in low tones. One of them called Archer, with an oilskin buttoned up to his chin and a black stocking hat pulled down to his eyebrows, so that only his mournful eyes and melancholy mouth could be seen, yawned and said, 'What a lovely dream I was havin'.'

His pal said sympathetically, 'Who was she?'

'It wasn't a *She*,' explained Archer, 'it was –'

A bulky figure passed by, growling, 'No talking, you, Archer, Barnes.'

After a safe interval, Archer resumed in a low voice, his lips hardly moving, 'It was him I was dreaming of.'

'*Him!*'

The ghostly voice of Archer went on, 'Yes, him. I was staying at the Ritz Hotel in London –' with a jerk of his head ' – our Chief Buffer was the Hall Porter. I was sending him out in rain for a taxi, and when it came, I'd say, "Fetch me another one, my man. I don't like the colour".'

His friend sniggered. Archer was the accepted wit in his Watch. And even the feeblest joke helps to pass the long hour standing-to before the dawn.

In *Exeter*, last in line, Bill Roper handed Captain Bell his cup of cocoa and said, 'Your cocoa, Captain, sir.'

Bell accepted the thick sweet beverage and said politely, 'Thank you, Roper. Do you approve of the weather this morning?'

'Command Performance, sir,' ventured Billy. 'Full of stars.'

A light breeze was humming overhead. Bell stepped up beside the navigator and glanced into the binnacle. 'Watch your station, Pilot,' he said, 'the Flagship's altered course a few points. The Commodore's probably done it on purpose to make sure we're keeping our eye's open.'

Already the two ships ahead could be clearly seen, black shapes against the grey-green sea. The line of the horizon was beginning to appear.

Bell said, 'Roper's right, as usual. It's going to be a fair day.'

His navigator nodded, thinking of what they might see and do before the sun went down – he was never to see another dawn – and answered, 'Should be good visibility, sir.'

In *Ajax* the shape of the little Seafire aircraft was now clear against the sky, standing upon its catapult aft. The stars had gone. The observer, Dick Kearney, a big solid young man, was already in his seat. The catapult officer was chatting with him. The pilot, Drunkie Lewin, grumbled under his breath as he swung easily into his seat. He fiddled a little, sighed and then said, ' 'Morning, Dickie – 'morning, Monk.'

The night before had been a thick one in the wardroom. Kearney and Monk grinned at each other, and said sympathetically, ' 'Morning, Drunkie.'

Lewin's name was Duncan, Duncan had become Drunken, and Drunken had become Drunkie, very early in his Navy career. It was to stay with him all his life, but there were some mornings when the nickname was harder to bear than others. The mechanic started his litany, and he gave the responses half-automatically. 'Switches off.'

'Switches off.'

'Petrol on.'

'Petrol on.'

'Throttle set.'

'Throttle set.'

'Contact.'

'Contact!'

The mechanic swung the propeller, and at the third try the engine leapt into roaring life.

On the bridge of *Ajax*, Harwood and Woodhouse stood side by side, looking towards the east. Each conned a chart of the South Atlantic in his hand, and came to slightly different conclusions. Both were convinced that somewhere, out of that waste of water, their enemy would sooner or later appear. It was going to be a rose dawn. After a long interval, Woodhouse said, 'Well – today's the day.'

Harwood answered, 'Y – e – s.'

The words were only an outward sign of their inner communion. Both men were perfectly in tune.

In *Achilles* every figure was on the alert. By now the horizon had become a clear cut line between dark sea and lighter sky. Everyone knew the Commodore's conviction that the Pocket battleship would appear that morning. Night glasses were sweeping the vast expanses of the sea. Every cruiser-class was manned. Parry said, 'Tell the Gunnery Officer to sweep the horizon.'

The gunnery control-tower is aft of the bridge and above it and, with the exception of the masthead look-out, is the highest point in the ship. It is lightly armoured and holds about a dozen men. It can turn 360 degrees upon its axis. The Gunnery Officer sits highest of all in his chair, by voice-pipes leading to the bridge and to the lower compartment, looking out through armoured slits. It is the best spotting position in the ship and, consequently, one of the most exposed.

Lieutenant Washbourn, the Gunnery Officer of the *Achilles,* was popular with his crew, whom he had trained to a high pitch of efficiency. He had also taught them to regard their jobs as interchangeable, a fact for which he was to be thankful later on that day. He was a big, dashing, handsome officer, outspoken and highly coloured.

The voice of the Officer of the Watch came up the voice-pipe, 'Guns! Sweep the horizon both sides.'

Washbourn acknowledged and gave the order, 'Train right.' At the same time he noticed that his own messenger, who should have been on the telephone behind him, was, as usual, not at his post but was chatting and laughing with a pal in the lower compartment. He bellowed, 'Dorset!' and scowled at the boy as he scrambled to his seat. Boy Dorset was a very young, very good-looking boy and rather spoilt by the rest of the ship's company. Washbourn liked having him around, and felt that it was his duty to sit on him hard and frequently.

The control-tower started to sweep the eastern horizon, turning smoothly on its bearings, all five binoculars and periscopes intensely on the watch. Any moment now the sun would appear.

The bearded look-out in *Exeter,* who was on the big cruiser-glass, sucked his breath and said, 'Here she comes! The old tiddy-oggy!' (Etymologists will be glad to know that tiddy-oggy is Royal Navy for that repellent object, a cold fried egg.)

A light morning mist restricted visibility to about twenty thousand yards, but there was no sign of any other ship. The control-tower on *Achilles* finished the sweep and Washbourn reported, 'Captain! Sir! Horizon clear.'

Parry, sitting relaxed on his chair on the bridge, leant over to the speaking-tube and said, 'Thank you, Guns.'

The tension had slackened. There was a murmur of voices and someone laughed. Lieutenant Cowburn, the Navigating Officer, said interrogatively, 'Fall out from Action Stations, sir?'

Parry answered equably, 'Better wait for the Flagship.'

On the bridge of *Ajax,* there had been a similar relaxing of tension. Everyone was waiting for Harwood, but that worthy was a long time making up his mind. He remained glaring out to sea, with his back pressed against the binnacle and every eye upon him. The sun had risen that morning at 05.56, and there was a good half-hour before the normal stand-to. On active service at sea, an extra half-hour in your bunk or your hammock means a good deal.

Captain Woodhouse, respecting Harwood's instinct, but conscious of reproachful looks around him, finally reported, 'Maximum visibility, sir. Nothing in sight.'

Harwood grunted, and continued to look towards the East.

After a further pause, Woodhouse ventured, 'Third degree readiness?'

Harwood stirred restively and then nodded, reluctantly. Woodhouse stood up and said, 'All right, Pilot. Cruising Stations.'

The bridge broke up into an orderly bustle. The Navigating Officer ordered, 'Bosun's mate! Sound the Disperse. Sound off Cruising Stations.'

The Chief Yeoman moved to the flag-deck voice-pipe. The Commodore's and the Captain's secretaries went thankfully below. Woodhouse moved around his chair and picked up his duffle coat. The Midshipman on watch folded back the canvas top of the Navigator's chart-table.

In *Achilles,* the Chief Yeoman, his glass to his eye, reported, 'Signal flying: Assume thaird degrree rreadiness.'

Parry ordered, 'Close up the cruising watch,' and the Officer of the Watch called, 'Bugler!' in the tone of a man who does not expect to be answered. It is a peculiar but well-known fact that no Boy Bugler is ever there when called. At the second shout, the boy appeared smartly and said, 'Sir?' in a tone which implied that you could always count upon the Marines.

'Sound the Disperse! Sound off Cruising Stations!'

In a moment, the thin sound of the bugle was heard passing from ship to ship.

The mist was clearing rapidly. Captain Bell wrote in his diary: 'It was one of those perfect South Atlantic days, a warm sun with hardly a cloud in the sky, a gentle breeze and calm sea, and such a crystal clear atmosphere that one could see as far as the earth's curvature allowed.'

Lieutenant-Commander Smith was the Officer of the Watch. Bell said to him, 'I'm going down for a shave and a bath. Keep an eye on everything.' He walked aft then turned and added, 'And two eyes on the Commodore.'

Smith grinned and nodded. He was an alert, highly competent officer.

On the bridge of the Flagship, Harwood still stood looking eastward, as if he would conjure his enemy out of the sea. Woodhouse stopped by him before going below and said, 'To quote Shakespeare freely: "The Ides of December are come".'

'Aye, Caesar,' replied Harwood emphatically, 'but not gone.'

55

In *Achilles,* Cowburn looked reproachfully at Parry and said, 'Six ten, sir.'

Parry looked at his watch, stretched, took off his cap, rubbed his eyes and finally said, with a yawn, 'I'll be in my cabin.'

All three Captains were slightly restive for as Parry hung his glasses on the side of the chart-table, he said quite unnecessarily, in Cowburn's opinion, 'Keep a sharp look-out.'

Cowburn replied, 'Aye, aye, sir!'

Parry added before he disappeared below, 'And especially on the Flagship.'

As a matter of fact, Harwood was still on the bridge with everybody devoutly wishing he would go below. Drunkie Lewin was Officer of the Watch, and was dying for a chat with his Observer, Kearney, who was hovering near him. The Duty Commanding Officer was Pennefather, the Torpedo Officer. The leading hand in the Port Watch was an efficient lynx-eyed Borderer named Swanston. Harwood's eye kept falling upon them as he strolled about deep in thought. Each examined his sins as that awful eye came to rest upon him for a measurable space of time. The little Boy Messenger, whom Harwood had probably never noticed before, came in for one of these stares, 'Where's your belt?' he demanded. He took a step away, then turned back, just as the boy was in the middle of a grimace of relief, and added, 'And get your hair cut.'

He strolled round to the binnacle, stepped up beside Lewin and gave the instrument a totally unnecessary tap. He completed the circuit of the bridge back to the chart-table, and settled down as though he were going to stay there for ever. Medley had been hovering in the background, and eventually thrust his head into the lion's jaw by saying, 'Shall I bring those papers for you to sign after breakfast, sir?'

He got away with it. The lion growled assent, and Medley ducked below. To the others' great relief, Harwood, after another growl, said, 'Torps!'

'Sir?' came the immediate answer.

Having made up his mind, Harwood was already leaving the bridge. He said over his shoulder, 'Let me know immediately you see anything!' and went aft, adding to the look-outs as he passed, 'You fellows! Keep your eyes skinned!'

Swanston answered smartly, 'Aye, aye, sir,' and then with the voice and manner of a minor prophet to his other look-outs, 'Well – you heard!'

Torps sighed with relief and walked to the front of the bridge.

Lewin and Kearney fell chatting. Everything seemed normal. It looked as if this were going to be just another day.

Swanston remained upon the alert. The mantle of Harwood's uneasiness seemed to have fallen upon the minor prophet. He prowled up and down once or twice, fetched the big leather-covered telescope from its resting place and mounted it in its socket for'ard of the bridge, did another prowl, then approached Lewin who was discussing torpedo attacks with Kearney, and reported to him in a tone which indicated that he, Swanston, was the only man in the ship with two eyes open, 'Look-outs of the Watch closed up, sir.'

Lewin said casually, 'Very good,' and went on with his technical discussion.

Dissatisfied with this offhand treatment of his keenness, Swanston went to the nearest pair of cruiser-glasses, mounted the step and proceeded to sweep the horizon with his own eyes. Virtue was not immediately rewarded. The sea was empty. Visibility was extreme. His glass swept slowly from north to south and back again. He straightened up, rubbed his chin and then bent again to the glasses. This time he swept steadily around to the north-west.

Suddenly he paused and checked. There was smoke on the horizon.

(ii) *Captain Langsdorff*

He was desperately tired. Dove had been right in guessing that the Captain's gaiety when they met the *Altmark* a week ago, was the result of nerves stretched to breaking point. He was sleeping badly and smoking far too much. The strain of more than three months' ceaseless vigilance had told on him.

He ground out the butt of the cigar he had been smoking and looked down at his big chart. There was the long line stretching from Hamburg to the Indian Ocean and back again, which marked his incredible voyage. There, too, on the chart before him were the counters representing the ships he had sunk: eighty thousand tons of British shipping sent to the bottom, but still not as many as the German Admiralty had hoped when he had been given his secret orders. He looked at them one by one: the *Clement*, the *Ashlea*, the *Newton Beach*, the *Huntsman*, the *Trevanion*, the *Africa Shell* – he paused and gave an involuntary smile as he remembered Dove's honest indignant face. His cigar was going nicely. He looked back at the chart again: the *Doric Star*, the *Tairoa* and last of all, on the 7th December, the *Streonshalh*.

How many times during those weary weeks at sea had he crossed and re-crossed his own course. . . . How many leagues of sea had he covered, always pressed by the necessity to conceal his tracks, and after each kill to confuse the scent and move his precious ship a thousand miles away from the hue and cry. That long dash to the Indian Ocean had proved a waste of time and fuel. He would never have sunk Dove's little tanker of the mist and rain of the African coast had not magnified her to ten times her actual size when she was first spotted. Why, the seven hundred tons of fuel that the *Africa Shell* carried would hardly take him a thousand miles. . . . His very humanity had been against him. Who knows? If he had ruthlessly destroyed all who crossed his path, perhaps he would not have had these powerful Hunting-Groups, of which he had been warned, scouring the seas for him now. He looked again at the chart and his tangled course, up to the sinking of the *Streonshalh* five days ago, when he had made his decision. Now it was the 12th December, and the line of his course upon the chart, stretched straight as a die for the last five days, straight as the line of his destiny – westward.

Somewhere in the ship, the voices of young sailors could be heard rehearsing a Christmas carol, 'Stille Nacht, Heilige Nacht.' Langsdorff sighed and picked up a leather frame from his desk, which held a photograph of his wife and children. The distant carol-singing went on, and he murmured the familiar words as he looked at his wife and family. The door opened. (He hated his officers to knock and they had orders to come straight in.) He put the photograph down carefully and turned. It was the Master-at-Arms, who announced, 'Kapitan Dove von der *Africa Shell*, Herr Kapitan.'

Dove stepped in with his cap in his hands. It was a semi-official visit for he came to state a grievance. The Master-at-Arms prepared to stay, but Langsdorff dismissed him. He went out and closed the door. And it was in the friendliest way possible that Langsdorff said, once more, 'Well, Captain Dove.' He motioned to a chair. 'You wanted to see me. Come and sit down. What's the trouble?'

Dove had come as spokesman for the others but, as usual, the charm of Langsdorff and his own genuine friendship for the Captain disarmed him. He sat down and said, 'The others asked me to come and see you, sir. I speak for us all. We're very cramped in our quarters and that's a fact! And we hear that there is some intention to stuff a few more in as well. There are already over fifty of us. I sleep on top of a table – and that's a privilege!'

Langsdorff offered him a cigarette and said sympathetically, 'I'm sorry, Captain. I am the last man to wish to ill-treat my prisoners.'

'I know, sir,' said Dove hastily: 'That's why I've taken the liberty to come and . . . '

Langsdorff interrupted him. 'Captain Dove, you are not the only one with troubles. Something has happened recently off the coast of Iceland which has altered all my plans.'

He got up and walked restlessly back to the chart table. Then he turned and said, 'Did you ever hear of the *Rawalpindi*?'

The name struck a chord with Dove. He said, '*Rawalpindi*? – yes . . . P. & O. Liner. . . . Haven't they armed her with a few old guns? She's doing guard duty on the Western Approaches.'

Langsdorff, staring at the chart, said, 'She's been sunk.' After a pause he went on: 'She encountered two of our heavy cruisers off Iceland a few days ago, and joined action. Dusk was falling and she closed to ten thousand yards. Her Captain – a Captain Kennedy – perhaps you knew him – fought his ship most gallantly. The fourth salvo from our cruisers carried away the bridge and the radio cabin. Her guns were put out of action, and the whole ship, except her fo'c'sle and poop, was ablaze. She sank without striking her flag. It was a most gallant action.'

In the silence which followed his words, Dove heard the fresh young voices carol-singing below. He had listened spell-bound to Langsdorff's words. Langsdorff himself was deeply moved, as any serving-officer would be. He repeated: 'It was a most gallant action.'

Dove said thickly, 'It was a massacre.'

Langsdorff nodded. 'Yes. It was a massacre.'

Dove said bitterly, 'What a waste of good men. . . . '

Langsdorff, still staring at the chart, said: 'I don't agree with you, Captain. To take the offensive is never a mistake. That action revealed the presence of our ships in the North Atlantic. They had to turn back home. And now the sea between us and our home port is swarming with British and French warships and aircraft. So instead of going home for Christmas, we are going – in another direction. . . . '

Dove absorbed this information and said reflectively: 'So that's why they are practising Christmas carols.'

Langsdorff nodded. 'It keeps the younger boys going. Some

of them are very homesick. I sent you, too, some Christmas decorations. I hope you got them.'

Dove said, 'Yes thanks. We were surprised at getting them so early. It's just like the shops back home. After all – it's only the 12th of December.'

Early on the morning of the 13th, Langsdorff arrived off the coast of Brazil, slightly to the north of the River Plate. Harwood had exactly divined his intentions. He had decided to cruise up and down at a safe distance from the shore, until he sighted a prize worthy of his attention. He knew that some very rich convoys were sailing, under escort, from Buenos Aires and Montevideo. Before he could be reported, he could do appalling damage which would amply repay his venture westward! – and he could then escape back into the vast spaces of the South Atlantic, and so home at his leisure.

At 05.02, his radar indicated the presence of ships to the south-west. He altered course directly towards them, and presently sighted four thin masts which he soon identified as H.M.S. *Exeter*. A little later the *Graf Spee*'s look-out reported two low-built ships which they hastily identified as two destroyers. Langsdorff gave the order to close at full speed. He believed that his moment had come, that these two destroyers and the *Exeter* were escorting the rich convoy for which he was looking. In a few minutes he realised his mistake. At the precise moment when Swanston spotted his smoke upon the horizon, Langsdorff found that he was heading, at twenty-eight knots, directly towards three enemy light-cruisers. A paralysing moment of indecision followed. His orders were to avoid an engagement and to bring his ship back home. But if he had identified the three small ships, it was just as certain that they had identified him by now: If he altered course and tried to escape, it was unlikely, with their greatly inferior armament, that they would attack him. But he would be reported and his whereabouts would be known, and there was no telling whether or not one of the Hunting-Groups were near at hand. These thoughts flashed through his head as the ship rushed on at fifty feet a second. He realised that he was committed to battle. His only chance was to destroy the three small cruisers and to disappear again into the Atlantic. The die was cast, His moment had indeed come. He altered course to bring all his guns to bear upon the enemy, and gave the order to open fire.

(iii) *The Prisoners of the* Graf Spee

After the *Graf Spee* had parted with the *Altmark* on the 29th November, she headed north. The rendezvous had been very far south, a long way out of the normal area of shipping, so for some days no incidents occurred, and Dove and his fellow-prisoners had time to settle down. They were all emphatic about the change for the better since they had left the *Altmark*. Captain Dahl of the *Altmark* seems to have been a petty tyrant, both towards his own officers and ship's company and towards his prisoners. Nobody had a good word to say for him. The contrast of their treatment in the *Graf Spee* was all the more marked. They were prisoners, it was true, and in pretty cramped quarters, though they could not expect much else in a modern battleship. But they were treated properly; an officer attended every day to hear complaints and to deal with them, if it were possible. The food was good and plentiful and, most important of all to English sailors, they had as much tea to brew as they wanted. The kettle in the pantry was hardly ever off the boil. The screw-holes in the door had never been stopped up, and it was surprising what a difference those little holes, with their glimpse of the sun and the blue sea, the guns' crews chatting and sun-bathing, made to the men in the steel prison.

The Alarm to Action Stations was sounded for the first time on the afternoon of the 2nd December, just after the mid-day dinner. The loudspeaker had been blaring a series of gramophone records, mostly German dance tunes and, of course, tea was being brewed. Men were sleeping or playing cards, writing up their diaries or reading. Some fanatics for keeping fit were doing exercises. The alarm buzzer brought everybody to their feet, and there was a rush for the screw-holes. Captain Dove and the Chief Officer of the *Huntsman* got there first and, since they were both large men, it was impossible to dislodge them from their vantage points.

They could see the guns crew manning the turret of the five-point-nine which was immediately outside, and very soon another of the five-point-nines fired a shot, no doubt a warning to the merchant ship which they were chasing. The listening seamen, who had all been through this experience, waited in suspense. The next thing they expected to hear was the engines slowing down, followed by the orders over the loudspeaker to swing out the boat with a boarding party in it. But this time the pattern was not the same, and hopes began to run high. The popping of a distant gun was heard, and the *Graf Spee* altered course, and presently fired again. All sorts of fantastic theories were offered as to what might be happening out there. Some optimists hoped the *Graf Spee* might have met a destroyer, but those with more experience said that the gun they had heard could not be more than a three or four-pounder. Excitement, frustration and anger worked up to fever pitch during the afternoon, as the chase went on. The thought that one of their comrades was putting up such a gallant resistance out there, made the imprisoned men mad. Men strode up and down cursing, insults were flung at the steel walls and the wildest threats were made by even the mildest men when Dove reported that the gun's crew he could see outside, were sky-larking about and acting very cocky indeed.

At last, towards sunset, there was no more firing. The engines went to Half Speed and then to Stop. 'They've sunk her,' said somebody and there was a most extraordinary noise from the band of men, a mixture of a groan of dismay and a roar of anger. The long-expected orders were given and half an hour went by. Tempers were on hair-triggers by the time that the Chief Officer of the *Huntsman* reported from his lookout at the door, 'Stand by, everybody! Here come old Zoonk.'

This was the name by which the Master-at-Arms was known to all the prisoners. He was not a bad fellow. He was their main contact with the outside, and he could usually be drawn into a chat. His favourite topic of conversation was the triumphant cruise of the *Graf Spee:* the ships she had sunk and the ships she was going to sink. Since he was shaky about the past tense of his pet verb, he was naturally known as 'Zoonk'. He now appeared in the doorway, with a broad smile on his face. Ignoring the scowls which greeted him, he stepped into the room and announced, 'The fight is finished.'

He was a thick-skinned man. Somebody growled belligerently, 'Fight? What fight?'

'We have zoonk her,' was the reply, which was automatically greeted, all over the room, by a chorus of 'Zoonk her! Zank her! Zonk her! Won't you ever learn? Etc.' But today the fellow was not to be cheated of his triumph. He brushed his tormentors aside with a, 'Nix, nix.' Then he announced with a significant gesture, '*Doric Star* kaput!'

His news caused a profound sensation. The *Doric Star* was a Blue Star boat, one of the big modern refrigeration ships, anything between twelve and fifteen thousand tons, a real prize. They all knew her, and more than half of them knew William Stubbs, her Captain. Suddenly the blind running fight which had been going on all afternoon, came alive. They could imagine the big, handsome ship defying the Hunting Beast which had surprised her. They could picture old Stubbs on the bridge, ignoring the order to heave-to, turning away under Full Speed, whilst his radio operator broadcast their position and the news of the attack, and his solitary little gun, mounted aft, barked sturdily at the huge pursuer. Yes! That was Stubbs all right. Probably he had intended to keep on the run until nightfall. And he had only surrendered at last to save his men's lives. . . .

Someone said, 'Poor old Stubbs.'

A Sparks, who could never get enough to eat, said practically, 'Well, if she's a perishing meat boat we might get a good feed out of this.'

Other realists agreed with him, but the Chief Officer of the *Ashlea* seemed to voice the general opinion when he bellowed at the Master-at-Arms, 'Wait till the Navy catches up with you!'

But, of course, that was just the sort of remark the fellow liked. He chuckled blandly and said, 'We wait.' His calm superiority was maddening.

The Captain of the *Trevanion* said morosely, 'Well – at any rate, I hope you remembered about the cruet!' And the Captain of the *Newton Beach* added, 'And the pack of cards!' When you are in prison it is the little things that count, and Lieutenant Hertzberg had promised to get them one or two small comforts from the battleship's next victim. The Master-at-Arms, enjoying himself, said, 'Soon you shall see. Soon you have many more friends with you.'

'More!' shouted Dove. 'Where are you going to put them?'

But it was like water off a duck's back, 'Plenty of room here,' was the reply.

English voices were heard outside, and Captain Stubbs of the *Doric Star* stepped over the threshold followed by his officers. They were greeted with a roar of welcome and applause. The other Captains hastily formed a Reception Committee, although the Captain of the *Newton Beach* rather spoilt the effect by saying, 'Welcome to the Arab quarter!'

One or two of them had superficial wounds from shell splinters, and the radio operator had an arm broken. It was a direct hit by one of the five-point-nine shells which had decided Captain Stubbs to give in. He himself was in his pyjamas, with a uniform coat and cap put on over them, and his feet thrust into mosquito boots. He apologised for this get-up, explaining that he had not been allowed to bring any of his gear as a punishment for using his radio.

'Good for you! . . . Well done!' came from all over the room, and a number of voices asked eagerly, 'Did you get through, Sparks?'

He nodded and gave the thumbs-up sign.

His fellow Sparks who had been edging his way up to Captain Stubbs, said hungrily, 'Excuse me, Captain. I suppose they boarded you?'

Stubbs replied grimly, 'We didn't give them time to do any looting. We scuttled her.'

There was a murmur of admiration. He was surrounded by symphathetic faces. The graceless Sparks whispered to a neighbour, 'Another meatless day.'

The Captain of the *Newton Beach* said formally, 'Captain, you are very welcome here,' and a dozen hands were extended to confirm the greeting. Even the Master-at-Arms was impressed and said, 'Yes. Very brave! But very foolish!'

The words were hardly out of his mouth, before he found a face glaring at him about six inches away, while a deep voice said, 'You, laddie! You're lucky you didn't get zoonk!'

He took the hint, said smartly, 'Auf Wiedersehen,' and vanished amid a roar of rather savage laughter. The door closed.

Indicating the only unoccupied table, Dove said to the new arrivals, 'We reserve table tops for Captains.' Then to the Chief Engineer he said, pointing to the space under the table, 'Engine room staff below.'

The tall, curly-headed Chief grinned and held out a worn pack of cards, saying, 'These any use to you?'

There was a cheer from the card-players, and Stubbs turned to his officers: 'Where's the cruet?'

The second Officer had it. It was passed over and formally presented by Captain Stubbs to the President of the Mess. There was no doubt about it. The new arrivals had started well.

Ten days later, by the morning of the day upon which Patrick Dove had his interview with Captain Langsdorff, the *Tairoa,* (Captain Starr), the *Streonshalh,* (Captain Robinson) had both been added to the bag, and the Midshipmen's Flat, with more than fifty prisoners in it, was uncomfortably crowded. Meals had to be taken in three shifts: one shift drew the rations from the galley, while the second shift ate, and the third washed up. It was breakfast time; breakfast consisted of weak coffee and black bread, and was the worst meal of the day. The last arrivals ate with poor appetite and looked with amazement at the old hands, not only gobbling up their own breakfast, but offering to finish theirs for them.

Passing his plate over, Stubbs said, 'I don't understand how you people can eat that ersatz muck.'

The only answer he got was, 'You should have tasted the food on the *Altmark!*'

He said sceptically, 'It couldn't have been worse.'

But half a dozen voices assured him that he didn't know what he was talking about.

The Chief Officer of the *Tairoa,* who was fond of his coffee, put down his cup violently and said, 'I'd give a year's wages to have one of our battle-wagons turn up right now!'

His Radio Officer cracked, 'You'd be tickled to death to have the Navy sink us, wouldn't you, Chief?'

'You bet!' was his answer.

'That's what I call patriotism,' said somebody.

'Anyway, what is the Navy doing? These beggars seem to go where they like and do what they please.'

The Captain of the *Streonshalh* said, 'I can tell you something about that.' He lowered his voice, and spoke as if he might be overheard: 'Two days before I picked up with you, I passed through one of the strongest concentrations of Allied warships I've ever seen.' He paused to see the effect upon his listeners and went on: 'You know our Navy and the French have formed Hunting-Groups? They did it as soon as this Raider was reported in the South Atlantic. I believe there are several of them – these groups, I mean. Battleships, carriers, the whole works. . . . Any one of them could handle a Pocket battleship.'

His listeners looked impressed, but Stubbs asked: 'With all that lot of ships, how do you explain they haven't found us yet?'

Dove answered, 'Because Langsdorff never stays in the same place. He makes a kill off Portuguese East Africa and then off he goes. When he makes another kill, he is hundreds of miles away.' He spoke with authority, remembering the chart he had seen on Langsdorff's table, but the Captain of the *Newton Beach* was not satisfied. 'But how does it pay off? He sinks a potty little tanker in the Indian Ocean and then he sails for a thousand miles – '

'A potty little tanker!' said his outraged listener. 'You mean my ship?'

Somebody said cheerfully, 'Well, it was a potty little tanker, wasn't it?'

'Seven hundred and six tons,' said her Captain, emphasising every ton.

Stubbs said, 'I think I can tell you how it pays off. It isn't even so much the tonnage which the Raider sinks, but her presence out there in the Atlantic. When a Raider is reported in the shipping lanes, all merchant ships, hundreds of them, are kept in port. That's what the enemy wants. If a hundred ships are stuck in harbour, it's the same as if they were at the bottom of the sea.'

A voice said, 'Oh, is it, Captain?'

Stubbs gave a wry smile and said, 'Well – nearly the same. . . . Hello! What's that?'

They all listened. They could hear singing. They were used to hearing records of all nations blared over the loudspeakers, but this was different. 'It's a Christmas carol!' said Dove.

The sound came closer. Several voices were singing in unison. By now everybody's attention was on the door. It opened and the Master-at-Arms appeared. 'Why!' said a voice, 'it's old Zoonk-Zink having a Zing-Zong!'

The Master-at-Arms was smiling and beating time to the singing. He wore a false nose and a paper hat. A number of young sailors followed him in, singing and smiling, carrying in their arms baskets of Christmas decorations and carnival favours. The prisoners gazed at them with open mouths as they put down the baskets and the Master-at-Arms started to make a little speech: 'Kapitans and Officers! A present from Kapitan Langsdorff. Christmas decorations. We have only one Christmas tree, that is for our own men, but have plenty decorations! Kapitan Langsdorff ask me to tell you that – ' The alarm buzzer cut him short. Loudspeakers started to blare all over the ship. For a moment even the Master-at-Arms was taken aback. The smiles froze on all their faces. The Chief Officer of the *Travanion* said grimly: 'Another little ship for Uncle Adolf's stocking!'

The spell was broken. The Master-at-Arms barked, 'Achtung!' and the young sailors ran out to their posts. He took off his false nose and said, 'Excuse please! You will soon have more company.' Then, stopping the third shift who were about to go out to the galley to draw their rations, he announced: 'Everybody here in! Back please everyone. The door shall be locked.' He was obeyed sullenly. The other shift who were washing up, protested angrily. They had had no breakfast. Meanwhile, Dove was following up

66

the Master-at-Arms protesting: 'You can't dump any more in here! We're sleeping on top of the lockers now! D'you hear, you slab-sided son of a Hamburg sea-cook!'

The door was locked without a reply. Dove took up his old position at the screw-holes and reported, 'The gun's crew look very jolly, so it can't be the *Renown*.....'

The Chief Engineer of the *Ashlea* joined him at the other screw-holes and said, 'We're slowing down.'

'Same old stuff,' said Dove bitterly.

'Boarding party. . . . 'Guten Morgen, Kapitan – Mind if we sink your ship? . . . Kapitan and officers step this way please. . . . ' That smooth pirate Hertzberg! I'd like to tell him what I think of him! . . . '

An hour went by. There had been no firing, and now they were moving again. The All Clear was sounded. 'Do you think they've sunk her?' the Chief asked Dove.

He shrugged his shoulders. Stubbs joined them and said, 'We ought to hang out a sign "House Full".'

Dove said, doggedly, 'I'm going to complain to Captain Langsdorff.'

'Stand by,' said the Chief from his look-out. 'Here comes Santa Claus!'

They stepped back from the door and waited belligerently for it to open. The Master-at-Arms appeared, blandly smiling as usual. 'All in order,' he said, 'the galley is open again.'

The waiting men hurried to get their breakfast, but Dove stayed confronting the Master-at-Arms. 'Well,' he said, 'who was it this time?'

The Master-at-Arms was in a good humour. He said, 'False alarm! It was a neutral, but we have news of a big ship. We go after it. The *Highland Monarch*.' He pronounced the first word *Higland*.

Dove said, '*Highland Monarch*? She's a passenger ship.'

The Master-at-Arms shook his head. 'Not now!'

'She is then,' said the Chief Engineer of the *Streonshalh*, 'we spoke to her three weeks ago.'

The Master-at-Arms answered, his smile vanishing, 'It is not my business. And it is not yours.'

'Well, you're wrong there, laddie,' was the reply. 'Her Chief owes me half a dollar.'

Dove took no notice of this. He was an easy-going man but once he had got an idea into his head, it was difficult to get it out. He said, 'I request to see the Captain.'

The Master-at-Arms replied, 'The Kapitan will not see you now.'

Dove told him straight. 'You tell the Captain that Captain Dove requests an interview. If you don't, I'll tell him, next time we exercise on deck, that you have refused to convey my request.'

The two men looked each other in the eye. The Master-at-Arms was plainly irresolute. Finally, he nodded and said, 'I will tell the Kapitan.'

And, as we know, he did.

On the morning of the 13th December, when the Alarm to Action Stations started ringing, the prisoners were all asleep. It was an urgent series of five staccato bursts, repeated for several minutes. Everywhere men were sitting up sleepily, and looking at each other in surprise. They had never heard anything like it before.

Stubbs, wrapped in a blanket on his table, sat up like a heathen idol and said, 'She's bought something this time.'

They all listened in silence to the rush of heavy boots up ladders and along the deck. They heard the shouting of orders and the clang of steel doors, then the whine of power-operated turrets. The Chief of the *Tairoa* and Dove raced each other for the screw-holes, treading on several faces as they went. They arrived there together and reported in great excitement that working parties were unloding shell from the hoists.

Dove reported, 'No more sky-larking . . . they don't look so cocky now!'

Everybody was listening intently. The petty officers could be heard, bawling orders. The loudspeakers were screaming out commands in hysterical German. The Chief said happily, 'It's no merchantman this time!'

Stubbs, still sitting on his table in the blue light, said fervently, 'I hope it's one of our big fellows. We'll blow this tin-can right out of the water!'

'And us with it!' said a fellow Captain.

Stubbs said, 'You're right! I hadn't thought of that.'

At that precise moment, the *Graf Spee* opened fire. The sound was tremendous. The whole ship shuddered. Crockery started to rain down on the men in the pantry corner, and clouds of dust came down the air-vents and filled the room. people yelled, coughed and cried out: 'We're hit, we're hit!'

Only Dove and Stubbs kept their heads and, from their vantage points at the door and the table, they both roared, 'We're not hit! Get down on the floor. That was her first eleven-inch salvo!'

CHAPTER VII

THE BATTLE OF THE RIVER PLATE

(i) H.M.S. *Ajax*

WHEN SWANSTON spotted the smoke on the horizon, he reported in a loud and virtuous voice, 'Smoke! Bearing Red 100.'

The Chief Yeoman came over to him and looked at the smoke with his own glass. Swanston said, 'D'you see it, Chief?'

The smoke was still a long way away, and there was some mirage. The Chief answered, 'Aye. Some merchantman.'

Meanwhile, Drunkie Lewin who, it may be remembered, was Officer of the Watch, went to the voice-pipe connected with the Captain's and the Commodore's sea-cabins and reported first to Woodhouse, 'Captain, sir. Look-out reports smoke bearing Red 100.'

Woodhouse acknowledged this for the routine report that it was. Lewin then repeated it to Harwood. They were in the main area of shipping and, beyond the necessity for increased alertness that morning, there was no reason to suppose that this would be the expected enemy, especially coming from the north-west. Harwood said, 'Tell *Exeter* to investigate.'

The signal was passed by S-P, and was crossed by a flag signal from *Exeter* saying that she had sighted the smoke. In obedience to Harwood's orders, she altered course to 320 degrees. A moment later, Harwood's voice came up the voice-pipe again, 'Officer of the Watch!'

Lewin answered, and Harwood said, 'Make to *Exeter;* "If this is a British merchant vessel bound for the Plate, and due to get into harbour soon, transfer your defect list and list of spares to her".'

Lewin said, 'Aye, aye, sir!' and grinned at the Chief Yeoman. There had been at least one signal a day on this subject ever since Harwood flew his broad pendant in *Ajax*. Meanwhile, the smoke was getting rapidly clearer.

Exeter had left the line and gone up to twenty knots as she headed towards the smoke. She looked very fine as she came up fast on the Flagship's quarter. The gap between them widened steadily.

Swanston, who had started all this activity, suddenly reminded everybody of his remorseless presence by saying, from the cruiser-glass where he was still stationed, 'Mr Lewin, sir. Can you see those upper works? She looks like a Pocket battleship.'

The slight extra suspense during the early morning stand-to, had been dissipated by the sunshine and by the day's routine. At that very moment, the Chief Yeoman was clicking out the Commodore's message to *Exeter*. Lewin will always remember how Swanston's conscientious pessimism had got on his nerves so that he answered, scoffing, 'You see Pocket battleships everywhere, Swanston. That's the third since Sunday,' and went on discussing catapult technicalities with Dick Kearney. The Duty Commanding Officer, Lieutenant Pennefather, took Swanston's foreboding more seriously, but there was still little to be seen. The latter crossed grumbling, to the big telescope and looked through it. He announced, 'I can see a control-tower. I'm sure I can. I've been in big ships. . . . '

Kearney said tolerantly, 'So you're always saying.'

At that moment, Captain Woodhouse came on deck, saying, 'Well, Pennefather? Can you make her out?'

Pennefather answered that there was too much haze, and at an order from Woodhouse he went up the mast to identify what was under the smoke. From that moment, events moved quickly. The Chief Yeoman reported, '*Exeter* signalling, sir.'

A light was signalling from *Exeter*'s flag-deck, as Pennefather scrambled up into the mast-head. The Yeoman read out: 'I – think – it – is – a – Pocket – battleship.'

Simultaneously a yell from Pennefather and a roar from Swanston confirmed the news. The Chief Yeoman and two look-outs shouted together that *Exeter* was flying Flag Five: Enemy in Sight. Woodhouse ordered, 'Sound the Alarm!'

This called every man on his Action Station. Kearney left the bridge in a hurry, and was followed by Lewin as soon as he had handed over to the Navigator, who came rushing up, half-dressed and half-asleep. Pennefather had fallen rather than climbed down the mast, and was already on the telephone to his torpedo crews. Woodhouse, his glasses to his eyes, ordered, 'Connect all boilers!' Commodore Harwood, in a strong line of orange pyjamas, struggling into his uniform coat, came on deck followed closely by Medley. All over the ship, men were running to their stations, most of them straight from their hammocks, in pyjamas or just a pair of shorts. Harwood's face was an inspiration to see, as he buttoned his coat and stared towards the rapidly approaching enemy, whom he had conjured out of the sea.

'Hoist Battle Ensigns!' ordered Woodhouse, and as the order was repeated to the flag-deck, Harwood said, 'Pilot! Alter course straight for her! Speed twenty-eight knots.' Then to Medley, at his elbow, he said, never taking his eyes off the enemy, 'Make to Admiralty from Commodore South Atlantic: "Am engaging Pocket battleship" ... Give them our reference position!'

The Chief Yeoman, who had his glass on *Achilles,* reported, 'Your speed signal answered, sir.'

'Execute!' replied Harwood focusing his glasses upon the Pocket battleship.

'By George!' said Woodhouse, 'Just look at *Exeter*'s battle Flags!'

Harwood swung around and looked. *Exeter* had swung off to attack according to plan and was already going at 25 knots. Chance had favoured Harwood's battle tactics. She would soon be within range of the enemy. Her Battle Ensigns were going up at mast-heads and yard-arms – four or five of them – and her turrets were swinging around in unison. Woodhouse, his eyes sparkling, counted aloud, 'Three, four, five! She's dressing ship!'

At that moment, at 06.18 local time, 14.18 G.M.T., the *Graf Spee* opened fire with full broadside: three great black mushrooms of smoke with vivid orange-red centres, an awe-inspiring sight. By now all three cruisers were going over twenty knots, and were heading towards the enemy to close the range as quickly as possible. The foaming wake swirled higher and higher from their sterns as the ships gathered speed. The wind was whistling through the stays and the increased roar of the boiler-room fans could be heard above the wind. A few seconds later the *Graf Spee*'s first salvo arrived. Great fountains of water went up into the air near *Ajax* and stradled *Exeter* as well. She was firing at *Exeter* with her two forward turrets, and at the Flagship with her after turrets, Harwood, who had his glasses on *Exeter* said, 'We've split her fire all right! Their gunnery is very accurate.' He turned his glasses back on to the enemy and remarked, 'She'll soon be in range. Can't understand what her Captain's doing. If you've got a longer reach than the other fellow, why get in close?'

In the gunnery control-tower, the Gunnery Officer ordered, 'Broadsides!' He leant over and watched the lights come up in the Gun Ready Lamp Box. As usual, the Marine turret won the race. He said, 'Well done the Royals!' Then announced over the speaking-tube to the bridge, 'We are opening fire, sir.'

71

'At last!' exclaimed Harwood thankfully.

The Firing Bell went ting-ting. They all involuntarily held their breath, or screwed up their eyes. Then the whole bridge shook as the six-inch turrets fired. An orange glow lit every face. There was a crash, as if a huge steel door had slammed, and the smoke of the discharge drifted across the bridge. This continued at an average interval of fifteen seconds during the next hour and a half.

The range was about eighteen thousand yards, so the next broadside was on its way before the first salvo landed. Everyone had their glasses to their eyes. The midshipman reported to Woodhouse, 'Aircraft ready, sir.'

Harwood said, 'The *Exeter*'s straddling her . . . got her range. By gad! So have we!'

Woodhouse ordered, 'Prepare to catapult aircraft!'

The catapult platform was situated aft, in a very unpleasant position. Lewin and Kearney were in their seats, and the engine was roaring. At intervals, the Firing Bell would ring out . . . then the guns crashed, shaking the whole ship and enveloping her in clouds of drifting orange-brown cordite smoke. Woodhouse was steering as near as he could to the enemy whilst keeping all his guns bearing, with the result that the after turret was firing forward so close to the catapult platform, that they were half-blinded by the red flash of the guns and could feel the heat of the cordite explosions. It seemed extremely likely that, as soon as they became airborne, they would be blown out of the sky by their own guns. But Drunkie Lewin couldn't have cared less. He waved his arm airily to the catapult officer and yelled, above the roar of the engine, 'We'll have to stooge off between salvos! Stand by!'

Monk shouted back, 'You've only got a twelve seconds gap!'

Kearney leant forward and tapped Lewin's shoulder. 'With a six-inch shell up our tail, we'll really get some speed out of this old string-bag!'

It was a spectacular take-off. They were enveloped in swirling smoke, the wind was whistling and shrieking through the stays and halyards. The aircraft roared, the guns crashed out, Lewin gave the signal. There was a flash and a bang from the catapult machinery and they were airborne! Lewin banked steeply. He had no time to gain altitude, and a few seconds later the after turret fired again. He nearly went into a side-slip, straightened out and started to climb. He headed towards the *Graf Spee,* and soon the whole battle area lay beneath him.

The four ships were at maximum range, although the *Exeter* was closing with the enemy rapidly. She was already several miles away from the two six-inch cruisers, who were gathering speed to the northward. At this stage of the action, *Ajax* and *Achilles* had not concentrated their gun-fire. On the alarm being given, each ship had gone into action independently with all guns at highest elevation, and they were firing rapidly and accurately at the enemy, who was replying with equal accuracy. His ack-ack guns opened up on Lewin, who was by now close enough over-head to see, with some discomfort, that the Pocket battleship had two fighter aircraft and that one of them was already about to be catapulted. Without even a six-shooter to defend himself, Lewin felt as naked as Icarus. He watched the fighter aircraft drawn back on the catapult, ready to be launched into the air against him, and decided, like the man who met the grizzly-bear on the mountain path, that even a folded newspaper would come in handy.

At that very moment, one of the six-inch cruisers scored her first hit, right on the catapult platform. The aircraft was wrecked. Lewin reported the successful hit to the Flagship and drew a deep breath. By now the ack-ack guns had found his range and he climbed higher. He looked around for cover. There was a thin ceiling of cloud at about 3,000 feet. According to his own account, he cruised along six feet under it, ready to pop through and put it between him and the enemy at the slightest encourage-ment, although it would have provided about as much protection as a transparent nightdress to a persecuted heroine.

From his vantage point, Lewin could see that the big battleship was seriously worried and puzzled by Harwood's tactics. Langs-dorff had been trapped into dividing his fire, and his small antagonists were shooting very accurately. Evidently he appreci-ated his situation, for while Lewin watched, the *Graf Spee* altered course and all her turrets swung round on the same bear-ings. She was concentrating her main armament on *Exeter*. Lewin at once reported this to the Flagship.

On the bridge of *Ajax*, Swanston had just reported, 'Enemy altering course towards us, sir,' In answer to which, Harwood exclaimed, 'That suits us!' But a second later, Woodhouse got the spotter's report from the G.C.P. that *Exeter* was now the main target. Harwood's expression changed. 'The devil she is,' he said. 'We can't have that! Alter course to bring all guns to bear. That'll make him take some of his guns off *Exeter*.'

Woodhouse said calmly, 'Bring her round, Pilot.' And the

order was given, 'Starboard twenty.'

Both Harwood and Woodhouse put their glasses to their eyes and looked anxiously towards *Exeter*. The Chief Yeoman reported, '*Achilles* following round, sir.'

About ten minutes had passed since the start of the action, and *Ajax* and *Achilles* were now concentrating their fire as originally planned by Harwood in the Orders of the day before. Concentration of gun-fire means that two or more ships act as one. One Gunnery Control passes all the necessary orders, the range, the deflection, and the firing signal, to the consorts. The consorts do as they are told, applying what is known as 'the position in line' correction for their distance and bearing from the Master Ship. All good Gunnery-Officers like to control their own guns, and naturally hate Concentration (unless they happen to be the Master Gunner), but it increases the hitting rate and prevents confusion in spotting the fall of shot and, in theory at any rate, all the shells from all the ships should fall simultaneously and in much the same piece of water. We shall hear more about Concentration from Washbourn, the Gunnery-Officer, in *Achilles*.

By now the din was tremendous, with both small cruisers hammering away as hard as they could to disract the *Graf Spee* from *Exeter*. A look-out reported, '*Exeter* hit for'ard, sir. A lot of smoke.' And very soon afterwards he reported a big explosion and a sharp turn to port by the wounded ship. Harwood groaned. If the *Graf Spee* had the wit to concentrate on any one of them, she could destroy her by sheer weight of armour. The horrified voice of Swanston was heard above the din, shouting: '*Exeter* completely disappeared in smoke and flames, sir.'

Woodhouse said, between his teeth: 'That last one seemed to be very near the bridge and the forward turret.'

The Gunnery-Officer's voice came up the voice-pipe saying: 'Aircraft reports the enemy putting one turret back on to us again, sir.' Harwood received the news with relief. Half a minute later the salvo arrived and straddled *Ajax* uncomfortably close. Woodhouse, who was still watching *Exeter* through his glasses, suddenly yelled, 'By gad! She's firing again with her other two turrets! Good old Hookie!'

There was something like a cheer from the port look-outs. One of them reported, 'Enemy altering course away, sir.'

Harwood said, 'I see he's beginning to make smoke too. That's a good sign.'

Another salvo arrived and Woodhouse reported, 'She's firing at

74

Achilles with her five-nines now, sir.'

Harwood grunted, 'And stradling us with her eleven-inch. Swing off to starboard for a couple of minutes and then come back to port again. That ought to throw her gunnery out.'

But in spite of all that they could do, *Exeter* was still the main target, and the enemy was pounding her relentlessly. The look-outs reported, 'Direct hit on *Exeter* . . . *Exeter* altering course to starboard . . . *Exeter* hit again . . . and again. . . . Only one turret firing now, sir!'

This was at about 06.40. *Exeter*'s change of direction had been made in order to fire torpedoes and she was hit on the turn. It brought her end-on to the Flagship, so that on *Ajax* they could see she was listing to starboard, although she was nine miles off. This was the most desperate time of the action. A salvo of eleven-inch shell, high explosive, fell a few yards from the port side of *Achilles* and detonated on the surface of the water. Splinters peppered the ship, causing several casualties and damaging communications by knocking out the radio in the gunnery control-tower. Concentration of gun-power naturally ceased and this, coupled with *Graf Spee* making herself a very difficult target, for she was nearly end-on to the two six-inch cruisers and was making small alterations of course, made the British fire ineffective for some time. The fact that *Graf Spee* did not appear to have suffered damage was bad for morale. *Exeter* seemed to be out of the battle and out of control. She was already listing and another direct hit might finish her off. Harwood knew that it was now or never. This was no time to husband resources, the battle might be lost or won in the next few minutes. The disparity of size between his own small ships and the enemy no longer mattered. There is one thing that can never be taught to any nation or Navy, but can only come from a hundred years of tradition and discipline, and that is the Offensive Spirit. Men can build, equip and train a modern Navy in twenty years, but they cannot endow their ships with battle honours nor can they create that spirit. It was with three hundred and fifty years of battle experience behind him that Harwood exclaimed, 'What's our range?'

Woodhouse recognised the tone and, glancing at the indicator, answered, 'Eighteen thousand, sir.'

'In we go! Woodie!' was the reply. 'To hell with battle instructions. We've got to draw his fire. At this range we might as well bombard the Beast with snowballs.'

He couldn't have said anything that would have pleased

Woodhouse better. He answered: 'Aye, aye, sir. Steer straight for her, Pilot!'

The *Ajax* turned like a destroyer about forty degrees towards the *Graf Spee*. Woodhouse stepped to the port side of the bridge and watched *Achilles* come foaming round after her consort. He ordered: 'Alter course to 60 degrees to port' (this to cover the *Achilles* course). When both ships were heading directly towards the enemy, Harwood gave the order, 'Make to *Achilles*: 30 knots!' He was flinging his cruisers at the Pocket battleship like two destroyers. The after guns no longer bore on the enemy and ceased firing, but both ships continued to load and fire their forward turrents as they rushed towards the enemy.

Several minutes went by. The range was down to 13,000 yards, yet still their fire was not effective in turning the *Graf Spee* off *Exeter*. She was closing in to finish her. Salvo after salvo battered the eight-inch cruiser. All her guns were silenced by now and she was on fire in several places. It was obvious that she was out of control. Her engines were evidently intact, for she was still travelling at full speed with a twenty degree list to starboard. She was pouring out black smoke from her funnel while the smoke and flame of fires on board made her deck and superstructure almost invisible. At 07.06 Harwood ordered a swing to starboard to bring all guns to bear on the enemy, but the range was still too long. Round they went again, their forward turrets firing all the time, and rushed once more towards the Pocket battleship. The range shortened rapidly. Harwood stood facing the enemy. Woodhouse stood beside him, every now and then glancing at the range indicator and reporting, 'One three two . . . one oh seven . . . nine two five . . . eight two six. . . .'

It was magnificent. They were practically at point blank range. Now their fire was beginning to have an effect upon the enemy. Several hits were seen on the superstructure. She started evasive action and turned away from *Exeter*. She began firing at the two small cruisers with both the five-nines and eleven-inch. Woodhouse gave the order to 'Snake the line'. And, still closing the range at full speed, the two ships started to twist and turn. The *Graf Spee* seemed bewildered. Her firing became ragged. Once again, Harwood gave the order to swing to starboard and brought all guns to bear. At this deadly range they could hardly miss. Hit after hit was made upon the enemy. With their six-inch shells, they could hardly hope to deal a crippling blow on the heavily-armoured battleship, but tremendous damage was being inflicted upon the superstructure and decks, and at least two of the five-point-nine guns were knocked out. It was like a destroyer action. Harwood was shouting: 'Take that you beast! . . . And that! . . . And that!' Then as a great orange flash and cloud of black smoke followed a hit on a five-point-nine gun turret, he dashed his cap against the side of the bridge and shouted in exultation: 'What price snowballs now!'

Woodhouse said, 'We've done it. She's altering course!'

The *Graf Spee* had turned away from the *Exeter* and put all her guns on to the two small cruisers, except her five-nines which continued to fire at *Exeter*. *Ajax* and *Achilles* opened the range slightly but went on firing with all guns and snaking the line. By now the morale of the two cruisers was so high, that they would have cheerfully taken on a Pocket battleship apiece.

'D'you think she's going to stand and fight, sir?' asked Woodhouse, his eyes gleaming.

'Looks like it,' said Harwood.

'Torpedoes ready for firing, sir,' reported Pennefather eagerly at his elbow.

'Well, get on with it,' was the answer.

'Right, sir! Swing 40 degrees to starboard necessary, sir.'

Woodhouse gave the order. Pennefather ran to his station and said over the telephone, 'Stand by port tubes. Long range, deep setting.' The Navigator reported, 'Ten degrees to go, sir.' Woodhouse ordered, 'East to five.'

Pennefather, his eyes glued to his sights, said, 'Stand by.'

The Navigator said, 'Midships . . . steady. . . . '

There was a pause of suspense. Pennefather said, 'Fire one . . . fire two. . . . '

The telephone rating reported, 'Torpedoes away, sir.'

Woodhouse at once ordered, 'Port 20.'

At the same moment, the voice of the Gunnery-Officer came over the voice-pipe, 'Captain, sir.'

Woodhouse said, 'Yes, Guns.'

'Aircraft reports torpedo approaching! It should pass ahead of us.'

The *Graf Spee* had evidently fired her torpedoes at the same time as *Ajax*. Harwood was a torpedo expert, so Woodhouse said to him, tentatively, 'Turn to port, sir, to comb the tracks?'

Harwood assented reluctantly, 'Yes. Can't be very near. A few points will be enough.'

Woodhouse said cheerfully, 'Hard a-port, Pilot,' and blandly avoided Harwood's glance. In a minute or two the masthead look-out reported over the voice-pipe, 'I can see a torpedo-track, sir. Just one and it's well clear.'

Harwood gave a triumphant look at his Captain and said, 'Back we go again!'

A moment later, at 07.25, when the range was down to about four and a half miles, *Ajax* received a direct hit from an eleven-inch shell, putting X-turret out of action and jamming Y-turret. At that range, with no trajectory, it went through the armour as if it were paper. It was a most eccentric shell for it ricochetted all over the ship, doing appalling damage, before it burst. It infuriated Harwood, who roared at the Gunnery-Officer down the voice-pipe when the latter reported the two turrets out of action: 'You've still got two left!'

His midshipman appeared at Woodhouse's elbow, reporting, 'Captain, sir. From X-turret, fire in ammunition hoist.'

Woodhouse said calmly, 'Well, nip down and see if it's under control.'

The turret was jammed by the base of the shell penetrating the armour. Blacksmiths were already working on it. In X-turret the men were lying about sweating, grimed and in every stage of nakedness. They were all Royal Marines. They could get neither in nor out, and smoke and fire was coming up the ammunition hoist. The Lieutenant of Marines had ordered the hoist spraying system to be switched on, but it was dead. At that moment a torrent of water came from above, like a miracle from Heaven. A marine had got a hose in from the upper deck.

A breathless messenger arrived at Harwood's side on the bridge and reported, 'From Commander, sir. It was a direct hit on X ammunition lobby, sir.'

Firing was still going on from the forward turrets. Woodhouse asked, 'Any casualties?'

'Yes, sir,' was the answer, 'I'm afraid so, sir. Shell passed right through the Commander's and Secretary's cabin, sir. Went down to the next deck and did no good to X lobby, sir, and came up again and burst in the Commodore's cabin, sir.'

The Gunnery-Officer remarked over the voice-pipe, 'Quite a whimsical brick!'

The Snotty, who had returned, reported to Harwood, 'Commodore, sir! Report, sir, eleven-inch shell went clean through your day cabin. Exploded in your sleeping cabin, sir.'

Harwood asked, 'Any casualties?'

The Snotty said, 'Yes, sir. Took all the heads off your golf clubs, sir.' The little beast had actually brought them up on the bridge with him.

Harwood looked at them, then remarked: 'Very unsporting.'

Woodhouse said, 'Bad luck about your cabin, sir.'

The Snotty piped up, 'It went through your cabin, too, Captain, sir.'

The Chief Yeoman said, 'Message from *Exeter*, sir.'

Harwood hurried across to where he stood by the voice-pipe. He snatched the signal from him and read aloud to Woodhouse: 'All guns out of action. We are still sea-worthy.' He looked at Woodhouse and said, 'She must be in a pretty grim condition. I wonder if she can make the Falklands?'

The message was sent, and in a few minutes the answer came back, '*Exeter* to flagship: Can reach Plymouth if ordered. Request permission revise list of spares.'

Harwood blinked. There was a silence. Both men could picture the conditions on board the cruiser. She was plainly visible away to the southward, still burning. A messenger came to Woodhouse, who reported to Harwood, 'Ammunition getting short, sir.'

Harwood started out of his reverie and said, 'Eh! What? Well – scrape the bin!' Then his thoughts returned to Hookie Bell and he said to the Chief Yoeman, 'Make to *Exeter*: "Proceed Falklands. God speed".'

He turned to Woodhouse and said, 'Well. Let's get on with it.'

It was now 07.40, and the pace a bit too hot to last. Both ships had lengthened the range. The *Graf Spee* could not break off the action, of course, since the other ships were faster than she was, but it was obvious that she had had enough. Firing had been continuous for a hundred minutes and was still going on. Harwood paced up and down once or twice, then said to Woodhouse, 'We must open up the range, Woodie. I'm going to break off the action and take her on again after dark. Turn stern on to her and make smoke.' Then to the Chief Yeoman he said, 'Make to *Achilles*: "I am breaking off the action".'

Woodhouse gave the order, 'Port 30.'

At that moment, there was a tremendous crash aft. A shell had carried away the main top-mast. It was one of the last shots of this phase of the action. Woodhouse remarked resignedly, 'That means wireless aerials gone. Pass the word to rig a new lot.'

Harwood, who had his glasses on the enemy, said: 'He's not turning after us anyway. We'll shadow him from either quarter.'

Woodhouse, thinking of his new main top-mast, added viciously: 'Yes. And give her one for herself now and then.'

79

(ii) H.M.N.Z.S. *Achilles*

When the *Graf Spee* first revealed her presence in the South Atlantic some twelve weeks earlier, the *Achilles* was working up in her home waters. As a ship in the New Zealand Division of the Royal Navy, the majority of the crew were from those Islands. On the other hand, most of the officers and petty officers were British. Of her four six-inch gun turrets, three were manned by New Zealanders and the fourth by Royal Marines. Discipline and morale were very high. Captain Parry was extremely popular, and deservedly so, with his ship's company. They were enthusiastic, and he had succeeded in working them up to considerable efficiency during their training period in the South Seas. He then received orders from the Admiralty to join Commodore Harwood's squadron off South America. After the long voyage across the Pacific, *Achilles* first contact with the mainland had been at Santiago in Chile. Subsequently she had proceeded through the Straits of Magellan to join the Squadron and to patrol the long coastline of the Southern Continent.

Immediately prior to the concentration ordered by Commodore Harwood, *Achilles* had been off Pernambuco. Parry proceeded thence to the River Plate area and arrived on the 10th December. *Exeter* made her appearance on the 12th. Captain Parry was proud of the high morale of his ship's company. He felt that the unruly elements properly controlled, would add extra pepper in time of action. Parry was a man of vision and imagination, who fully appreciated the romance of our far-flung Dominion sending one of its ships from one end of the world to the other; and he took pride that she had no difficulty in immediately working and fighting with Royal Naval ships. The battle of the River Plate was the first occasion that a ship of the New Zealand Division of the Royal Navy was in action. It is for this reason that, in conversation with any one of the two million inhabitants of those Islands, it sometimes seems that there was only one ship in the action.

Lieutenant Washbourn, the uninhibited and efficient Gunnery-Officer of the *Achilles*, whom we have already met in the gunnery control-tower at Dawn Action Stations, was Principal Control Officer on the morning watch of the 13th December. The P.C.O. is in charge of the ship in the absence of the Captain. When the order was given to close up the cruising watch at about 06.10, all quarters fell out, as on *Ajax*, except the small numbers who were kept at instant readiness during daylight hours. It was still Washbourn's watch, so he returned to the bridge and stood talking with Captain Parry about the gunnery exercises that they were to do later on that day. In view of what was to happen shortly, there was a certain irony in the subject of discussion. Harwood had announced his intention the night before of continuing his tactical exercises, which meant that there would be more practising of Concentration of gun-power and of Flank-Marking Communication exercises. It has already been said that no Gunnery Officer likes the control of his guns taken away from him, and Washbourn was no exception. Being Washbourn, he was frankly outspoken about it. Parry, being Parry, smiled indulgently and said little.

Flank-Marking Communication exercises were quite a different thing, and were an important part of Harwood's scheme for dividing the attack and the enemy's fire. If the two attacking forces could keep the enemy in such a position that their individual lines of fire were at right angles, then each ship could report how far 'short' or 'over' the other's division's fall of shot was. Before radar and without aircraft spotting which, naturally could not always be depended upon, this was very important. Otherwise, all that the gunnery control officer could do was to correct on those salvos which fell in line with the enemy. If the enemy was obscured by splashes, you were 'short' and went 'up' If the reverse, then you came 'down'. If some splashes were in front of the enemy and some behind him, then you were 'straddling' him and all was well. But keeping line was always difficult with an enemy who was as mobile as you were, and so range-information on salvos which were not in line could be most valuable. Washbourn was fully aware of this, of course. What irked him was having to fire in concentration. Somebody must be better than the other fellow, and Washbourn was always sure that it must be he. So he grumbled good-humouredly to anyone who would listen, which included his Captain pacing to and fro across the bridge, and the Navigator, Lieutenant Cowburn, a tall, thin, rather taciturn type whom absolutely nothing could perturb, not even at that hour of the morning.

At about fifteen minutes past six the look-out reported, 'Smoke, bearing Red one double-oh, sir.'

At the same time, they saw *Exeter*, who it will be remembered was last in the line, fall out to investigate. Parry and Washbourn strolled unhurriedly to the port wing of the bridge. There had been a thousand such reports before and, in spite of the Commodore's intuition, nobody really expected to encounter the Pocket battleship which, when they had last heard of it, was about three thousand miles closer to home and Christmas than at present. Parry raised his binoculars to his eyes and looked. Washbourn used the mounted cruiser-glasses.

It was instantly obvious to both of them that it was a Pocket battleship. Visibility was extreme and all that was visible was a control-tower, a range finder and a fairly thin feather of orange-brown smoke, but to both men it could not have been anything else. They turned to each other and Parry said, 'Good God! It's a Pocket battleship. Pilot, sound the Alarm. Warn the Engine room that we will be increasing to full speed shortly and are going into action.'

Washbourn nipped up into his control-tower by the shortest route, which was the outside ladder and the emergency door. He took one more look from the highest position. It was unmistakably a Pocket battleship. He swung into his seat, gave the order to train left, donned his headphones and waited for the reports to come in. Meanwhile, the Alarm Rattlers were sounding, followed by the bugle. The ship's company knew at once that it was a real Alarm by the bugle call which had no 'G-s' preceding it. Washbourn could hear everything that happened on the bridge through the voice-pipes. The Chief Yeoman reported, '*Exeter* hoisted Flag Five, sir. Enemy in Sight.'

Cowburn had taken over Officer of the Watch. Parry said to him in a matter-of-fact voice, 'Open out to about three or four cables from *Ajax*, Pilot, and keep loose formation. Weave when she fires at us, but don't use too much rudder.'

Meanwhile, Washbourn's own crew were arriving, out of breath, straight from their bunks in many cases, and sliding into their seats or positions. Considering the size of a gunnery control-tower, there are a surprising number of men in it. All three control-towers of the cruisers were more or less identical; so if this one is described in detail the others can be imagined.

The Gunnery-Officer, Washbourn, sat aloft and conducted the orchestra.

The Rate Officer, Mr Watts, rotund, placid and very competent, watched the enemy and constantly estimated his speed and course.

The Plotting Officer, Sergeant Trimble, was large-ish, red-faced and rather slow in speech. He was an Ulster man. It was he who watched the fall of shot around the enemy and passed it to the transmitting station to be plotted.

Close behind these three officers, were two telegraphists and Boy Dorset, who was on a direct line to all four turrets. His opposite numbers in the other turrets were all Boys too, and were usually exasperating everybody by chattering amongst themselves. This morning they had something else to chatter about.

Even higher than these three officers, was the Position-in-Line Range-Taker (P.I.L.), Shirley, who, in order to get a better view, stood on a stool and had his head out of the top of the G.C.T., from which position he could see *Ajax*'s movements clearly for correction of position when gun-fire was being concentrated.

On a lower level in the tower were the director-layer and the director-trainer, who laid and trained the guns vertically and horizontally, respectively. The director-layer fired all the guns. Close to them were two operators who wound handles, applying corrections for range, elevation and cross-levels, to all the guns; their names were Shaw and Rogers. They were both New Zealanders. So were Shirley and Boy Dorset, and the director-trainer, Petty Officer Stacey. The Gunnery Officer, of course, had a direct voice-pipe to the Captain on the bridge.

On arrival in the G.C.T., Washbourn had ordered all quarters to be closed up, which took a few minutes. He then gave the order for all turrets to load the guns with armour-piercing shell, 'All quarters with C.P.B.C. – load!'

This order, which made it quite clear to the gunners that it was the real thing this time, was bellowed out in the gunhouses of all turrets and caused meaning glances to be exchanged. At this point *Ajax* opened fire. Captain Parry, on the bridge, glanced at Range-Finder-Receiver which indicated the fighting range as two-four-three-oh-oh (twenty four thousand three hundred yards), and observed, 'Maximum range.'

'Not for long, sir,' answered Cowburn. As if in reply the weird wooh-wooh-wooh of a salvo of eleven-inch shells approached and passed overhead, like huge invisible birds, followed by a crash and three great fountains of water. The *Graf Spee*'s first salvo had arrived. It fell on *Achilles*' starboard bow and Parry said sharply, 'Alter course to starboard, Pilot.'

After a startled look, Cowburn answered, 'Aye, aye, sir. Starboard 20!'

Parry, over the voice-pipe, called, 'Guns!'

Washbourn's voice answered. Parry said slowly and clearly, 'I shall always steer towards the last fall of shot. So be prepared to correct accordingly.'

Up in his tower, Washbourn grimaced and answered obediently, 'Yes, sir.'

Parry walked back to the centre of the bridge and turned suddenly to Cowburn, who was still gazing open-mouthed, 'Understand, Pilot?'

Cowburn gathered his wits together and answered, 'Yes, sir. Hope the enemy doesn't.'

Parry gave a dry smile. It was quite true that this manoeuvre is always a little risky. At the same time, to turn towards the enemy if his fire was falling short and away if falling over, was a dodge with some sense in it. Of course if the enemy spotted these tactics, he had only to leave several salvos uncorrected and you ran right into them. In discussing the battle, Parry always attributed *Achilles'* invulnerability to Cowburn's skill in following this plan.

In the control-tower, Washbourn gave the order, 'Broadsides!'

Once again the order echoed through the gun-house as the signal to bring the loaded guns to the ready. Beside Washbourn the lights in the Gun Ready Lamp Box started flickering on irregularly.

Parry's voice came over the voice-pipe, 'Open fire as soon as you can, Guns.'

Five lamps were already lit, so without taking his eyes off the lamp-box, Washbourn put his mouth to the voice-pipe and said, 'We are ready to open fire now, sir.'

'Open fire,' was the answer. All eight lamps were lit. Washbourn said into his microphone, 'Shoot!'

Almost at once there was the ting-ting on the firing-bell. A second later there came the c-r-u-m-p of a full broadside. Instantaneously all the lamps went out. Then, as the men reloaded, they started flickering on again. In less than twenty seconds another broadside was on its way, and then another.

At the opening range of the action, the time of flight was about fifty seconds. The lengthy time of flight in naval gunnery is probably something that the lay man doesn't appreciate. Washbourn glanced at his watch. The long wait while his bricks were travelling at their best speed towards the target, three broadsides of them in the air at once, was a little trying for his patience.

One of the gadgets in the tower was a machine which made a series of vulgar noises at the end of the time of flight of each broadside. It now gave a pattern of short grunts which indicated that the first salvo was about to reach its target. Washbourn and Trimble glued their eyes to the binoculars. A second single belch

84

announced the moment of the splash. Corrections were given over the microphone and rapid firing continued, most enjoyably so far as Washbourn was concerned, until the telegraphist behind his right shoulder nudged him and said in his ear, 'Ajax calling. Master Ship Control.' He then leant over and wrote on the pad by Washbourn's right hand, so that he could read it, the Range and Deflection ordered by the Flagship and continued to do so for the next fifteen minutes. Ajax and Achilles were now concentrating their fire. We know what Washbourn thought of having the control of his own guns snatched from him, so what he felt on this occasion is, perhaps, not for the record and implied no reflection on the competence of Desmond Dreyer, the Gunnery Officer of Ajax.

At 06.40, as has already been described, one of Graf Spee's salvos detonated on the surface of the water, a few yards from Achilles and sprayed the port-side with splinters, the bridge and G.C.T. getting most of it. 'Splinters' is, of course, a generic term and it would perhaps be as well to state that a 'splinter' can range from a genuine sliver to a large and angry lump of jagged steel. Several of these penetrated the light bullet-proof plate surrounding the bridge bringing down Captain Parry with a hole through the calf of both legs, and Chief Yeoman Martinson with a shattered knee. Parry blacked out for a very few moments and then, recovering consciousness, found that he was lying on the deck and wondered how he got there. Curiously enough he felt no pain in his legs. The first thing he heard was the moaning of the Chief Yeoman as he was removed by the first-aid party. He pulled himself up and seat down on the edge of Monkey's Island, the foot-high platform around the two compasses. Something was wrong. He couldn't tell what it was. Suddenly he realised that his guns were no longer firing.

In the G.C.T., about six splinters of varying size had penetrated the one-inch armour bringing some of it in with them. From Washbourn's point of view, there was a loud noise and a momentary black-out. He looked around. There was a lot of ventilation that hadn't been there before and a number of prostrate bodies.

Parry pulled himself up to his feet and stepped to the front of the bridge. He still didn't know he had been hit until a first-aid man told him so. One glance at the forward turrets told him that his guns were no longer trained on the enemy at all. And glancing back over his shoulder, he could see the punctured gunnery control-tower. He knew that something was seriously wrong and, moving to the voice-pipe, he said, 'Bridge – G.C.T. Captain speaking. Are you all right, Guns?'

In the control-tower, Shirley had fallen back and was lying across the stool upon which he had been standing, bleeding heavily from wounds in the thigh. Both telegraphists were sprawled dead upon the floor with multiple injuries. One of them had partially fallen through on top of the range-takers in their little compartment below. Washbourn had received two or three scalp wounds and was still a bit dazed. Mr Watts was saying calmly into his microphone, 'G.C.T. has been hit. After-Control take over!' Then he stood up and said to Washbourn, 'Come on, sir. Running repairs.'

Washbourn stammered, 'What's up? I'm all right. . . . ' He put his hand to his head and it came away sticky with blood. So he meekly climbed off his stool and submitted to bandaging.

At about this time, the Captain's enquiry came over the voice-pipe, and he answered that the After-Control was now in charge and requested first-aid parties to be sent up. After a minute or two of Mr Watts' ministrations, he was himself again. He climbed back into his seat and took stock. Looking down into the forward half of the tower, he saw that both the layer and trainer were all right. Shaw was still seated at his instrument, although leaning forward against it. Gunfire was, however, very slow and ragged. The After-Control position was not at all effective. The two men who manned it were no longer fit to carry on, for they had been subjected to the continuous blast of X turret which was firing on a close forward-bearing. They were both as deaf as posts, stupid with the concussion and vomiting from time to time. In fact, at the end of the battle some of the most visible damage caused to *Achilles* was on the after super-structure from the blast of her own guns.

Washbourn decided to regain control and asked, 'What's out of action?'

Petty Officer Headen turned round from his telescope and answered, 'Director seems all right, sir.'

Washbourn said, 'O.K. We'll see what happens. Switch to G.C.T. controlling, Stand by, Shaw!'

Headen acknowledged the order, 'Switched to G.C.T., sir.'

Washbourn repeated sharply, 'Shaw!'

Stacey, who was seated beside Shaw, answered quietly over the voice-pipe, 'Archie's had it, sir.'

Washbourn looked down quickly. Shaw was still seated at his

86

sights, stone dead. Washbourn ordered, 'Rogers! Take over Shaw's job.'

Rogers moved over without a word, got Shaw's body clear and took his place. About this time first-aid parties had arrived and were banging on the door. But they were unable to get in for it was jammed by splinter damage to the hinge. So with three dead men for company Washbourn took control, and he and his men fought the rest of the action.

With aerials shot down and his telegraphists dead, Washbourn was not slow to realise that he was once more his own master, and could control his own fire. *Achilles'* gunfire became regular and accurate once more. No occasion arose to inform *Ajax* that *Achilles* could no longer be her consort in gun-fire. Washbourn was himself again.

Parry, whose legs were beginning to stiffen, sat down on a blue cushion on a high chair on the bridge and conducted the remainder of the action from there. A sick-bay Petty Officer saw to his legs without him paying much attention. This was the time when *Exeter* was getting so badly damaged, and all his attention was on her. He was just saying to Cowburn, '*Exeter*'s turning south, she'll soon be out of it,' when the P.O. finished bandaging his right leg and said, 'Now the other leg, please, sir.'

He said impatiently, 'What's wrong with that?' Then looked down and appreciated for the first time that both his legs were holed.

There are single-minded men in every job, particularly in ships. Whilst this incident was occurring on deck, a stoker is said to have approached Lieutenant Jasper Abbott, the senior Engineer on duty, a small, efficient and precise officer with a neatly-trimmed black beard, saying, 'I want to state a complaint, sir.'

Every time the ship's fired a salvo, the flames from the furnaces leapt out several feet. Sometimes the burners were knocked out altogether. After each flash, the stokers on duty would move up and look into the boilers to make sure that they were all burning. It was usually the top ones that were blown out. If they were, they would re-ignite them by pulling out taps on either side and pushing them back quickly. The roar of the furnaces was deafening.

Abbott kept his eye on his gauges and said, 'Well. What is it?'

The stoker had a grievance! 'Sir. I have tried for five minutes to pass the revolutions for the last hour to the bridge for the

Logs, and they told me they weren't interested. And when I insisted, sir, the navigating officer came to the phone and told me to stuff – ' His last words were lost in the next broadside. Abbott nodded and said, 'Never mind. Perhaps they have other things to think about on the bridge just now.'

The *Achilles* fought on for the next forty minutes in company with the *Ajax*, first at about sixteen thousand yards and then, after closing up on the enemy at maximum speed, at about eight thousand yards. As in *Ajax*, everyone in *Achilles* was bitterly disappointed by their apparent failure to inflict any serious damage to either the enemy's main armament or his engines. They had been firing everything they had at him for over an hour, with no visible result. What they perhaps failed to appreciate was that the very ferocity of their attack had bewildered him and put him on the defensive from the beginning. After the first few minutes of the action, *Graf Spee* had shown no inclination to come to grips with the two small cruisers. After his one savage attack upon the *Exeter*, he had been moving steadily westward during the whole of the battle. It was the smaller ships which had done the pressing. Except for the brief period when his control-tower had been knocked-out, Washbourn had been directing the firing continuously, and was under the impression that *Achilles* had delivered about fifty broadsides. The actual number was two hundred and ten.

In *Achilles* both A and B turrets fired considerably more rounds than X and Y, which could fire no further ahead than about thirty-five degrees. The guns of A and B turret were so hot that all the paint blistered off, they began to expand inside their jackets and failed to 'run-out' after firing. In other words they recoiled and stayed back. Eventually, the crews learned that a good concerted kick in the hot breach started the guns running out again.

Once, in B turret, there was a temporary delay in the ammunition supply, so the gun-house crews took the ready shell from the racks and continued to feed the guns. When they ran out of armour-piercing shell, they came to the two dummy practice projectiles which were kept in the racks. B turret was manned by New Zealanders and they were men of action. The Sub, 'Slim' Somerville, who was Officer of Quarters, said, 'What are you waiting for? Stuff them in, too.'

So off they went and Washbourn learnt, from a chance meeting with the Gunnery Officer of the *Graf Spee* in Hamburg after the war, that one of them passed through the wardroom of *Graf Spee* and came to rest finally under a Warrant Officer's bunk, greatly puzzling the recipient.

At about 07.40, as we know, Harwood broke off the action and led *Achilles* and *Ajax* off under smoke, much to Washbourn's disappointment. For the last ten minutes he had had the impression that they were hitting the enemy hard. What he overlooked, though, was that very soon they would have nothing left to hit the enemy with. While he was still cursing, Captain Parry called him up and said, 'How much ammunition have you remaining, Guns?'

'I've no idea, sir,' was the answer. 'I will report as soon as possible.'

He telephoned all quarters and then, as the replies came in, scribbled them on a match-box and added them up. It was in a more subdued voice that he reported finally, 'Captain, sir.'

Parry's patient voice said, 'Yes, Guns?'

'We have fired nearly twelve hundred rounds. About one-third of the outfit only remaining. The Commander has got stokers' fire-parties humping ammunition from the After group to the Forward turrets now. They volunteered for the job.'

Parry said, 'Thank you, Guns. Are you all right?'

Washbourn answered, 'Several casualties, sir, and it's a bit draughty, otherwise it's all right.'

The blacksmith had been working for some time on the jammed door of the control-tower and it now opened with a crash. The first-aid parties got in and started to remove the dead and wounded men. For the first time Washbourn realised that Sergeant Trimble, sitting immediately on his right, was looking pale. He had said nothing during the action. Washbourn asked, 'What's up with you, Trimble?'

The big man answered, 'Nothing much, sir. I'll go and get it attended to now. I got a bit of a scratch where I sit down.' He stood up, gave a little nod and walked out unaided. His bucket-seat was full of blood and there was a jagged hole where a splinter had passed along it.

All over the ship everyone was in fine heart. Dozens of scouts came up to the bridge and to the G.C.T. to find out what the firing had looked like and what damage had been done to the enemy. The upper deck was a bit of a shambles, not so much from enemy splinters, but from the fire of her own guns A messenger came running up to Cowburn, his pockets bulging with toffee and chocolate and his mouth full, and reported, 'From the Paymaster, sir. All action breakfasts ready for issue.'

Cowburn answered, 'Very good. Where did you get all that chocolate? Stolen the key of the canteen?'

'No, sir,' was the cocky reply. 'Legitimate, sir. The door was blown off.'

A little while later, a signal was received from the Commodore ordering: 'Splice the Mainbrace.' (The difference between 'Splice the Mainbrace' and the ordinary rum issue is that, in the former, every officer and man in the ship gets his whack.) It was a welcome order, and Washbourn was most impressed during the next three hours by the unusually mellow state of mind of his Chief Gunner's Mate, who came to see him in his G.C.T. at about quarter of an hour intervals to ask if there was anything he could do for him. He later found out the reason. The Chief, Joe Mosford, short, rather rugged and slow, West country, had been walking along the waist in the course of his duties, when he came upon a small and innocent ordinary seaman carrying a 'fanny' with a fair quantity of rum, in the wrong direction. 'Here, son. Where are you taking that?' he said.

'Back, Chief,' was the answer. 'We've had all we want.'

The Chief was outraged. 'All you want! You can't do that. Here, give it to me,' and he finished it off.

Of such stuff were the men of the *Achilles* made.

(iii) *Hookie Bell*

It will be remembered that just after dawn, Captain Bell had left the bridge, with Lieutenant-Commander Smith in charge. He had, of course, been informed of the smoke sighted to the north-west and of the Commodore's two messages, but there had been no reason to come on deck. He was lying on his bunk reading. He had his jacket and shoes off, but otherwise was dressed as he had been on the bridge, in white flannel trousers pulled on over pyjama coat and a scarf.

The alarm buzzer by his pillow went off like an angry bee. At once he sat up and started putting on his shoes as he listened to the report. Smith's voice came down over the speaking-tube, clear, steady and unhurried. 'Captain, sir. I think the *Scheer* is on our port beam.'

Bell answered, 'Very good! Sound the Alarm.'

He carefully finished tying his shoes, grabbed his coat and went on deck. He was on the bridge in a few seconds. His sea-cabin was directly underneath it.

On his way up the ladder, he heard the shrill of the bosun's pipes, the cries of the bosun's mates and the call boys shouting, 'Hands to Action Stations!' as they pattered along. The Boy Bugler on the bridge was sounding off 'Action', followed by the 'Double'. All over the ship, Bell could hear feet running along decks and up and down ladders; the excited, cheerful voices of the men; the Officers and Petty Officers giving orders to clear away guns and instruments.

On the bridge, there was a subdued and orderly bustle. All glasses were levelled on the enemy. Clear and concise orders were being passed by telephone and speaking-tube, as if it were another exercise. Bell passed through all this to his station in the front of the bridge, and, through his glasses, took a hasty look at the enemy, who was now clearly visible. He ordered, 'Hoist Battle Ensigns. Speed 28 knots.'

The Chief Yeoman said, 'Aye, aye, sir.' and ran aft to the voice-pipe. The Navigator ordered, 'Two-four-oh revolutions.'

Bell glanced again at the enemy and said, 'Port 20.' To the Gunnery Officers he said, 'Guns! Open fire as soon as you are ready,' and to Smith, 'Pass the word to all parts of the ship that we are engaging a Pocket battleship.'

At that moment, Commander Graham came running on to the bridge, buttoning his coat. He glanced at the enemy and exchanged a look with Bell who said, his eyes dancing, 'Well, Commander. There she is!'

Graham nodded and replied, 'I'll go around all quarters, sir, and ginger them up!' He ran off.

By now the ship was travelling at about 25 knots and increasing speed all the time. The mounting roar of the boiler-room fans was even louder than the wind, and the ship was swinging to port to engage. Bell stepped up close to the Navigator, glanced at the compass and ordered, 'Steer as near as you can for the enemy, but keep our A-arcs open.' To the Midshipman on Watch, he said, 'Time?'

'6.18, sir,' was the answer.

At that moment their share of the *Graf Spee*'s first salvo arrived. There was a piercing whistle and then a c-r-r-u-m-p! Great columns of water shot up into the air on both sides of the ship. Bell remarked. 'They've straddled us with their first salvo. Better put your umbrellas up.'

Jennings, in the G.C.T., announced, 'We are opening fire, sir.'

Bell answered, 'Good,' and a moment later bells rang and the first salvo crashed out.

Smith suddenly remembered the depth charges in their racks on the quarter-deck. Like torpedoes, depth charges are uncomfortable passengers when you are being shelled by the enemy. A direct hit might blow the ship's stern off. He asked permission to jettison them; and was told: 'By all means!'

By now firing was continuous. *Exeter* had only three turrets, but they were eight-inch, and the whole ship shook each time she fired a broadside. The *Graf Spee* was well within range and *Exeter* had already scored two hits. She was steaming at 30 knots with the wind whistling and shrieking through the stays and halyards. From her closeness to the *Graf Spee* and her superior size, it was obvious that she would soon be the main target. Bell and his companions moved calm and busy in the middle of the drifting smoke. Every twenty seconds or so the firing bell rang out followed by the crash of a salvo. Suddenly, it became clear that they were now the principal object of attack. Shell splashes were shooting up all around them. Bell ordered evasive action. The *Graf Spee* altered course and brought all her main armament to bear on the cruiser. One salvo after another straddled them. The sea was a mass of foam. They could not go unscathed for long. Then there was a sudden crash and a sheet of flame from the bows.

Smith shouted above the din, 'Direct hit on the paint shop!' And down the voice-pipe, he ordered, 'First-aid party for'ard.'

There were shouts below on the fo'c'sle. Sub-Lieutenant Morse appeared at the head of a fire-party. Black smoke and flames were pouring out of a great hole in the bow of the ship. While his men dragged a hose, Morse ran ahead of them with a fire extinguisher. He had got half-way to the fire when there was another explosion, fiercer than the last. A sheet of flame hid Morse from view of the bridge. When the smoke cleared, he had gone and in his place there was a gaping hole in the deck, wide enough to lower a bus into. The forward turret fired, as if in defiance. Bell was very grim as he said, 'Pass the word to all parts of the ship that we are hitting the enemy as hard as they are hitting us.'

Another salvo arrived, short this time. The fire-party were dealing with the two fires. Bell was on the point of telling the Navigator to alter course when there was an ear-splitting detonation and a sheet of flame, right in his face. A wave of hot air hit him and he thought his head had blown up. He threw up his hands to protect his eyes and staggered back. All around him, men were falling and slumping to the deck. Cries and groans filled the air. The whole bridge had been swept by a blizzard of lumps of steel and splinters of shell. Where everything a moment ago was all calm, ordered efficiency, there were now only broken pipes, twisted metal and gaping holes. Bell himself had been thrown back against the compass, his hands still covering his eyes. His cap was missing. There was a second of complete silence.

He took his hands away, covered with blood, and said, 'Are you all right, Pilot?'

There was no answer.

He asked, 'Are you there, Chief Yeoman?'

No one replied.

They had all been killed or wounded. Men were lying sprawled on the long, narrow bridge. Bell heard the moans of the dying and the seriously wounded. It was a miracle he was alive. Probably only his forward position on the bridge had saved him. When the shell burst the rain of splinters shot straight up into the air past his face, hit the roof of the bridge above his head and ricochetted backwards to kill everybody behind him. He had been in a hailstorm of hurtling steel. He had lost his cap, his face was blackened and there was a cut on his head from a splinter. There were also minute shell splinters sticking in the iris of each eye, but he only found that out later.

Bill Roper, the Captain's messenger, had been standing about six feet behind him and was wounded in the groin. He now staggered to his feet. Bell was trying to get either the Helmsman or the Lower Steering Position on the voice-pipes, but all communications seemed to be cut. He said, ' Good man, Roper! Are you all right?'

Roper jammed his hand into his pocket and nodded.

Bell tried again. It was no use; nobody answered. The Navigator was dead, the Chief Yeoman badly wounded. The ship was out of control and doing up to thirty knots. She was doing figures of eight but was still firing. At intervals the eight-inch guns crashed out, shaking the whole ship and enveloping the bridge in clouds of drifting, brown cordite smoke. Bell said, 'Come on, Roper,' and hurried aft calling, 'First-aid parties on the bridge!'

Commander Graham met him at the top of the ladder. 'Thank God you're all right, sir! There's a big fire between decks. We're coping.'

Spray from shell-bursts swept across the bridge. Bell asked, 'B turret?'

'Out of action. Nearly all killed. Direct hit ripped off the armour. You seem to have caught most of it.'

Bell nodded and said, 'If the fire spreads, flood the magazines.'

It was an inferno of sound and action. First-aid parties were at work. The Padre was kneeling by the dying. The ship was careering at maximum speed, like a bolting horse, while the wind screamed and whipped the smoke overhead. Bell shouted, 'I'm going to the after conning position. Good Lord! What's that?'

Graham turned to look where he was pointing and, as he turned, Bell snatched the cap off his head and put it on his own. For a moment, the Commander thought his Captain must have gone mad. Bell grinned at him and said, 'Sorry, Bobby. Captain must have a hat. You'll have to use your Sunday best! Come on, Roper!'

He made his way aft with difficulty. The deck was a shambles. With the forward gun turret destroyed, smoke and flames were pouring from her decks for'ard blinding everybody. Fires were raging. Bell had to clamber over masses of wreckage and past fire-parties who were fighting the flames. With no one at the helm, the ship was careering at high speed, out of control, but her two after turrets were still firing. In spite of the desperate position, or perhaps because of it, there was cheerfulness and energy shown everywhere.

Bell passed rapidly on his way to the after conning position and Billy toiled along behind him. He felt himself getting weaker, but nothing would have persuaded him to leave the Captain. By the starboard torpedo tubes, Bell met Smith. Both men were grimed and bleeding and strangely cheerful. Bell said, 'Hello, Smith. The bridge has had it! I'm going up to the after conning position. How are things?'

He started to climb the vertical ladder. Smith reported, 'Nearly all torpedo crews killed or wounded, sir.'

Roper followed Bell, who said over his shoulder, 'Got any spare hands?'

Smith shouted, 'They're on the job now sir,' and hurried off.

For a moment, Bill Roper hung on the ladder. He thought he could never get to the top. A first-aid party hurried by and one of them said, 'All right, chum?'

Billy gritted his teeth, nodded and followed his Captain up the ladder.

The after conning position was an open platform above the upper-deck, between the aircraft catapult and the main mast. Men were already working feverishly to re-establish communications. A Petty Officer was in charge. The wind was howling and shrieking all round the platform, the black smoke was rolling from the funnel and. hiding the sun, while loose wireless aerials, cut by shell-fire, were whipping about into men's faces. Once an enormous seven-pound insulator fell with a crash at Captain Bell's feet. Swinging up on to the platform, Bell announced, 'I'll fight the ship from here.'

'All communications are cut, sir.'

'Gyro-compass?'

'Failed, sir.'

'Get a boat's compass!'

The Petty Officer said to a Rating, 'Get one out of the port whaler,' Bell added, 'One up here! One down below with the stand-by Helmsman! I'll transmit orders by a chain of men. Jump to it!'

The Petty Officer jumped, and in a few moments could be heard shouting, 'You there! Form a chain of men to the lower steering compartment. Get some of the four-inch gun crew.'

Graham appeared, climbing over the rail on to the platform, saying, 'You sent for me, sir?'

A fine mist was sweeping over them. Bell said, 'Yes, I did. What the hell is this?'

'Petrol from the punctured aircraft. We're trying to get the blasted thing over the side.'

Just then the after turret fired, with a great orange flash. Bell said, 'I should hope you were! One more flash like that, and we'll go up like Joan of Arc.'

There was a tremendous explosion quite near. The *Exeter* was hit twice in quick succession. She was already listing to starboard. But still she fired with what guns she had left. Men were appearing, as if by magic, all round Bell, rallying around their Captain in this new centre of command. A Yeoman of Signals announced that he had taken over from the Chief. Lieutenant McBarnett arrived with a boat's compass in his hand to take over navigation. By now the chain of men was formed. Bell said, 'Pass your orders through my messenger. Stand by, Roper!'

The little band of men took up their positions and faced the enemy. There was Control again. McBarnett reported, 'Enemy coming straight for us, sir.'

Bell ordered, 'Starboard 20.'

The order was passed from McBarnett to Bill Roper, from him down on to the deck, then through the chain of men along a hundred feet of deck, across the quarter-deck, down a hatchway and so down three decks and along to where half a dozen men, stripped to the waist, man-handled the wheel directly over the rudder. It was a heart-breaking job; however switfly the order was passed down the line, inevitably by the time it arrived at the straining men in the hold, another order was on the way. But it was the only means of controlling the ship.

At the time when *Ajax* and *Achilles* were rapidly closing upon the Pocket battleship, the situation on *Exeter* had become desperate. The enemy was determined to finish the cruiser and was scoring hit after hit. Yet they still fought on. Another turret was knocked out, but the after turret still went on firing, with the Gunnery Officer, Lieutenant Jennings, standing on the top of the turret and directing the fire! Smith reported four torpedoes left in the port tubes and was told by Bell to fire them if he had a chance. Standing on their little platform, in the teeth of the wind, they were continually shaken and scorched by the blast of their own gun-fire, or half-drowned by the shell-splash of near-misses. And still they fought on, and still the orders flew down the eager line of men.

Suddenly, there was an extraordinary pause in the noise and racket. The after turret – the last of them all – had ceased firing, just as the Chief Engineer came to the after conning position to report. Bell caught sight of him and said, 'Hello, Chief. How are things down below?'

The Chief had been appalled by what he had seen on his way up, but he answered, 'Engines and boilers still intact, sir.'

'Enemy closing rapidly, sir,' reported McBarnett. And Bell, for the first time losing his calm, exclaimed, 'And not a gun or a torpedo left! Port 10!'

The order was passed on. Bell turned and looked at the approaching enemy. He had still one projectile of six thousand tons travelling at thirty knots, so he moved to Graham's side and said, in a low voice which only the two of them could hear, 'Well, Bobby. There seems to be only one thing left to do. She means to finish us off, so – if she gives us half a chance, I shall try and ram the beggar.'

He heard Graham give a little gulp, and remembered that he was a married man with a family; then he answered in a perfectly steady voice, 'Yes, sir!'

96

Bell said cheerfully. 'It means the end of us, but it will be the end of her also, and that's all that matters. . . . '

McBarnett said, in a startled voice, 'Enemy altering course, sir.'

Graham shouted, 'It's *Ajax* and *Achilles* – they've closed the range! They're drawing her off!'

They all turned to look at the *Graf Spee*. Suddenly the great ship was surrounded by leaping fountains as the salvos fell. All three ships had been astounded during the action, at the speed with which *Graf Spee* could turn and manoeuvre. Now, under this relentless attack from the smaller cruisers, she started to make smoke and turned and twisted to avoid them. Bell gripped the rail and said, 'By George! They're pounding her! They've drawn her off. We'll open the range. Port 20.'

They were no longer being fired at. Listing, on fire, and defenceless, they limped away to the southward, while the *Graf Spee* turned West. It had been a very near thing.

They were like men who have woken from a nightmare. Lieutenant-Commander Smith was sitting on one of the wrecked torpedo tubes, eating something green. Graham looked down from the after conning and asked incredulously, 'Are you eating?'

Smith said cheerfully from below, 'Cabbage. Have a piece. Here's a nice piece of heart!' He threw it up. And suddenly they all realised that they were famished. The cabbage was crisp and fresh and green. Graham caught it and said to Bell, 'Have a piece, sir?'

Bell took it, and soon they were all munching. It seemed to Bell that it was one of the best things he had ever tasted. He mumbled, 'Good . . . it must be nearly lunch-time. . . . '

Bill Roper answered, '7.30, sir.'

His voice was very weak and he swayed where he stood. Bell was astonished. 'Good Lord! Only 75 minutes since we sighted her.'

For the first time he had a chance to notice Bill and see his colour. He said gently, 'Roper – are you wounded?'

Billy answered, 'Yes, sir.'

Bell ordered him, 'Go below to the doctor. One of you go with him.'

Bill gathered all his strength and said in quite a strong voice, 'I can go alone, sir.'

'Off you go then,' said Bell. And as he went, he turned to Graham, 'A good boy, that!'

Billy felt his way down the ladders to the deck. He was think-

97

of Julie. Of Julie and mumbling to himself over and over, 'Must get back.'

All at once he felt so tired that he couldn't move another step. His legs gave way, there was a roaring in his ears, and he sank to the deck.

On the after conning, the Signalman handed a message to Bell, 'From the Flagship, sir: "Report condition".'

Bell held the message in his hands and said, 'What is our condition, Bobby?'

'All guns out of action, sir,' answered Graham. 'We're getting the fires under control. We're making water fast. We have a fifteen degree list to starboard and are down by the bows. About a hundred killed and wounded. Engines and boilers still intact.'

Bell nodded and said, 'Make to Flagship: "All guns out of action. We are still seaworthy!"'

This was the message which Harwood received in *Ajax*. It was a thousand miles to the Falklands, but Harwood knew that if anybody could do it, Hookie Bell would. When the final order came, Bell nodded. All around him men were working hard. The Chief reported, 'Flooding now under control, sir. Getting the ship upright.'

At the same time, a petty officer reported that communications had been re-established and that the gyro-compass was working correctly. McBarnett, pointing to the boat compass, said ungratefully, 'Then you can take that damned thing away.'

Bell said, 'All right, Pilot. Due south, eighteen knots.' He turned to Graham and said, 'Well Bobby. We'd better start cleaning up.'

(iv) 'They Also Serve . . .'

The prisoners of the *Graf Spee*, who were all active men, were in a very unpleasant position during the battle. They were blind and they were defenceless. They were in danger of their lives and could do nothing about it. They knew that the *Graf Spee* was being attacked by one or more ships, but they didn't know who the attackers were. Patriotism, inspired them to believe that they were British. But all of them agreed that the most terrible part of the experience, while the battle raged over their heads and during the long chase which followed, when minutes seemed like hours and hours like days, when time ceased to matter and night and day became interchangeable, was their complete uncertainty of the outcome of the battle coupled with their anxiety to know the fate of their own ships and their complete helplessness during the game of cat and mouse which was being played over a vast area, beyond the steel walls in which they were imprisoned.

We abandoned them to their fate as they were taking cover when the *Graf Spee* fired her first eleven-inch salvo, their only contact with the outer world being the tiny screw-holes in the door, to which Dove still clung, reporting what he could see, while choking dust rolled down from the ventilators. A minute later, the *Exeter*'s first salvos arrived, and soon all three of the British cruisers were straddling the Pocket battleship, which started evasive action even while she replied with all her armament. The din was tremendous in the confined space of the prison and the great ship seemed to be turning, rolling and jumping continuously. Dove reported fountains of water shooting into the air all around, and getting closer every time. Suddenly as he watched, a whole salvo burst upon the water and swept the side of the ship with jagged splinters. Dove dived for the deck and found himself sharing the underneath of a table with Stubbs and two other Captains. Overhead, great pieces of jagged metal could be heard rattling about the superstructure and showering on to the deck. There was a rending crash as part of the radar mast was carried away, a lucky hit in the early stages of the battle, which did a great deal to destroy the accuracy of *Graf Spee*'s gunnery.

Stubbs said, pushing Dove's knee out of his ear, 'That was a near one.'

Dove agreed, 'They've got the range. We'll know when we get a direct hit all right.'

As he spoke, there was the father and mother of an explosion overhead. Debris came raining down on the roof of the prison. They could hear yells and feet running. And orders were bawled over their loud-speakers which were still connected to the main system. Something serious had obviously happened, but there was no time to guess what, for in quick succession the *Graf Spee* was hit half a dozen times on the superstructure directly around and above the prisoners. Each time that a hundred-pound projectile from the six-inch cruisers, or a two-hundred-and-fifty-six-pound one from the *Exeter*, struck the Pocket battleship, there was a sudden shudder followed by the gashing and rending of metal, the screams of the wounded and the bellowed orders on the loudspeakers mixed with the thunderous concussion of the eleven-inch salvos and the crashing of the five-point-nines, one of which was right outside their entrance door. Behind and beyond these stunning noises, they could hear the chatter of the ack-ack guns, the high-pitched whine of the diesels at full speed, and they were constantly clutching tables, chairs, stanchions or one another as the ship twisted and turned and snaked the line.

Add to all this the noise that the prisoners themselves were making. They was a babel of yells, guesses, prognostications, curses and prayers, threats and jokes. Already, there were two clear parties: the Patriots who yelled, 'Hurrah! Hit him again'; and the Realists who had as much objection to being sunk by their friends as by their enemies. These last were very bitter about the Chief Engineer of the *Doric Star* and the Chief Officer of the *Newton Beach*, who were lying with their heads in the pantry, singing, 'There's no place like Home!'

Those who couldn't find the coveted protection of tables, chairs or lockers, wedged themselves into corners, covered their heads with blankets or put their caps on for added protection. It is common experience that one feels much safer if one can put anything, no matter what, between oneself and the enemy's guns. In the British ships, the four-inch guns' crews lay down behind canvas screens as a shelter from the eleven-inch salvos; and a Paymaster Sub-Lieutenant is reported, after looking at the enemy for a little while out of his scuttle, to have pulled the curtain across because it made him feel safer.

Suddenly 'a gentle dew from Heaven' started to rain down, and everybody started to sniff. Dove said, 'What's that smell?'

There was soon no doubt what it was. There was a chorus of 'It's petrol . . . it's octane spirit . . . put out that cigarette, you damned fool.' Dove bellowed, 'The spotting plane's been hit. It's right overhead.'

They heard concussion after concussion and the rending of metal. The Captain of the *Newton Beach* said gloomily, 'They've got the range now. If that petrol goes up we'll be burnt to a crisp.'

'Like that Yorkshire pud you made last Sunday,' remarked a friend of his.

The Radio Officer of the *Tairoa*, who had been wounded in the capture of his ship and still had a leg in plaster, said, 'Mr Murphy. When I'm done one side, will you turn me over?'

Anyone who has been in a civilian air-raid can picture the scene for himself. It was a continuous bombardment on both the giving and the receiving end, for over a hundred minutes. In

Dove's own words, 'It was no picnic.'

When Harwood finally broke off the action, the *Graf Spee* headed Westward at full speed. As we know, Harwood was content to let her get out of range but not out of sight. He had given orders to *Ajax* and *Achilles* to keep outside the enemy's gun-range which was far longer than their own. Of course, when the range was shortened, either side was liable to let fly. This indeed was what happened and desultory firing went on all day during the long chase, the *Graf Spee* warning her pursuers not to come any closer, while on the British side there were impulsive characters, like Washbourn, who were only too ready to hurl a brick at the enemy if they got the chance.

In the *Graf Spee*, the prisoners were still taking cover. Dust, broken crockery and personal belongings littered the floor and the bodies of the prostrate men. Nobody spoke. The ship was travelling at full speed and they listened in silence to the furious song of the diesels. There had been no firing for nearly half an hour. The comparative quiet was extraordinary after tl.e continuous racket of the battle. Dove was, of course, the first to speak as he stretched himself, 'D'you think it's all over?'

Stubbs said politely, 'Would you mind getting off my legs? There's been no firing for a quarter of an hour.'

'More like half an hour,' said another, 'I checked it on my watch. Hullo! It's stopped.'

By now all the men were sitting up, stretching cramped limbs and crawling out of their various funk-holes. The Captain of the *Newton Beach* said, 'I'd give a lot to know what happened. Do you think our ships are sunk?'

'Not likely!' said half a dozen voices.

The Chief of the *Trevanion* said, 'Listen! We're going full speed. We shouldn't be in such a hurry if our boys were sunk.'

Dove said loyally, 'Anyway Langsdorff would have stopped to pick up survivors.'

Slowly the place was getting back to normal activity. Men began to realise that their stomachs were rumbling. It was time for breakfast. There was a chorus of, 'I'm stiff! . . . I'm hungry! . . . I'm starving! . . .'

'I'm alive!' announced Dove, 'and that's all I care about.'

Stubbs felt his broad cheeks and said, 'I'm going to have a shave. I won't feel right until I've had a shave.'

'Chief! I'm starving too,' said the Radio Operator of the *Tairoa* in a pathetic voice. 'Wouldn't you like to go and see if there's anything to eat in the pantry?'

'Why don't you go yourself, Ralph?' growled Murphy.

'What – in my condition?'

Murphy grinned and went towards the pantry. At that moment there was a tremendous explosion. The lights went out and stayed out. Debris showered down into the room, while dust and fumes made everybody choke. They dived back under the tables or into the funk-holes, some held life-jackets over their heads. Slowly the dust and smoke cleared and daylight showed through bent and twisted steel. There was a gaping hole in the deck above. Dove and Stubbs roared, 'Anyone hurt?'

Nobody was.

They all sat looking up at the mass of twisted steel eight feet above their heads. Dove said solemnly, 'It must have struck the deck beam. Well! That's about the luckiest thing ever. But for that beam we'd have had it.'

The Chief of the *Trevanion*, full of patriotic pride, said, 'Who said the *Graf Spee* had sunk our ships? We're right on her tail.'

'They are right on our tail, you mean,' said someone sourly.

The Welsh engineer, his voice soaring, said fervently, 'My soul is out there with the boys!'

'I wish I was,' said the Sparks of the *Tairoa*, one of the Realists.

Dove, by now, was standing on a table and could reach the beam. He announced, 'I'm going to take a look-see! Give me a hand up, some of you.'

He was boosted up and, with his head sticking out in the open air, he made his report, 'My word! What a mess! Another five-nine has been hit. First-aid parties coming up. There's a lot of damage from shell-bursts and splinters. The port side of the bridge is just a mass of wreckage. Steel doors have been blown off and there are hoses pouring water all over the deck. My goodness! They have done some damage. There are bits of twisted rail and steel bulkhead everywhere. Hullo! We're altering course. Our guns are all trained aft. That looks as if Longsdorff is on the run. I can't see any of our ships. The sea is like a mill-pond. We are going – '

A blinding orange flash made him jump and his words were drowned by a tremendous concussion. He lost hold of the beam and fell back into the room, where he was caught by his friends. He reported breathlessly, 'She was firing aft with the forward turret. She's not done yet. But it looks as if her after turret is out of action.'

Although Dove could not know it, keen eyes on the pursuing

102

ships had already drawn the same conclusions from the *Graf Spee*'s action. The warning salvo fell short. It did not seem as if the *Graf Spee* had deliberately aimed at her pursuers. It had been like a wounded tiger growling. Harwood gave orders to open the range to twenty-two thousand yards. There was no point in damaging his two small ships until he had to. The enemy was still heading steadily westward, that suited him. He was quite content to keep his distance. Everyone in *Ajax* was drinking tea and eating enormous bacon sandwiches. Morale was very high in both ships. The hunt was up. Harwood summed up, 'We'll close in and finish her when the light fails. We'll keep her between us and the after-glow. She'll be silhouetted against the western sky. We'll be in the cover of the dark.'

So the long day passed. The Tiger of the Sea slunk nearer and nearer to the land. The Hunters followed at a cautious distance. When they closed disrespectfully the hunted beast growled, and great fountains of water sprung up between it and its pursuers. They would answer in their turn. And excited watchers on the distant shore declared that a great Naval Battle was raging somewhere out at sea. Already radio amateurs had picked up some of the signals during the battle and the rumour was spreading that, somewhere out at sea off the River Plate, British and German forces were fighting. From Rio to Bahia Blanca, peaceful merchantmen were hurrying into the nearest port and the cables were humming with long coded telegrams from the Admiralty to Naval Attachés in the Argentine, Brazil and Uruguay.

When the last rim of the sun on that momentous day of Wednesday, 13th December, was vanishing behind low purple hills, the lighthouse keeper at Punta del Este made out the dark shapes of naval ships, saw flashes like summer lightning and heard the thunder of the guns.

In the prison, the day had passed like a bad dream. The few Germans with whom they had contact refused to answer questions. Food had been cold and mostly out of tins, as, apparently, the galleys had been destroyed. The electricity was still cut. Only the distant rumble of the pursuers' guns and the concussion of their own guns answering told them that the chase was still continuing. Gradually the day died. Through the hole in the roof, they watched the sky pale, turn pink and go dark. Still the *Graf Spee* moved westward. For a long time, nobody had spoken nor moved. They had matches. A few pipes and cigarettes glowed. They heard, as if in a nightmare, the splashes of shells falling near the hunted ship, the shudder of the hull and the rattle of flying

103

splinters on the deck. Dove stirred and said, 'Sounds as if they're moving in for the kill.'

Stubbs grunted, pulled on his pipe and said irritably, 'Chief! Can't you get that light going?'

He was assured for the tenth time that there was nothing to be done, that the cable aft must be cut. Murphy suggested in a gloomy voice, 'What about the Christmas decorations?'

'That's right,' said someone, 'there's some paper lanterns among them and candles. Here, give us a match!'

Dove was already rummaging in the cardboard boxes. Several matches were struck and the candles lit. One by one the flames burnt up in the incongruous Japanese lanterns. Curling dragons, demons and jasmine flowers uncoiled in the darkness, revealing the weary, strained faces of the prisoners. Murphy lit a small one and hung it in his corner, saying, 'I'm lighting this one to my guardian angel.'

Another hour went by. There had been no fighting during the whole time. The *Graf Spee* seemed to be going much slower. The colourful forms on the lanterns were vanishing as the candles flickered and burned out. The strain was telling upon the weary men. Nobody spoke. Everyone listened as if his life depended upon it. Suddenly the Welsh Chief Engineer said, almost in a whisper. 'She's easing down, boys.'

The tension grew. Some men were at the door with their ears pressed against it. A group stood below the shell-hole and gazed up at the starry sky. Some lay with their ears to the steel decks trying to catch the slightest sound. The forms of men could be felt and their breathing could be heard, but only the occasional glow of a pipe or a cigarette indicated a face. The Welsh Chief said again, in a louder voice, 'She's stopped!'

It was true. They could no longer hear the steady heart-beat of the engines. They were sliding soundlessly through the water under their own momentum. Dove suddenly cursed aloud and said, 'That's the game! Langsdorff is going to let our chaps dash past him in the dark, then he'll turn in his tracks and slip out to sea again!'

Men started to growl and curse aloud. Stubbs shouted, 'Dove's right! By morning he'll be miles away!'

The growling and cursing rose to a shout as men raved, hammered on the steel and on the doors, filled their lungs with air and expelled it in great roars of hatred, exasperation and helplessness. Suddenly, the look-out at the door called out,

104

'Quiet. Quiet everybody. Pipe down, can't you. Somebody's coming.'

Gradually the noise subsided and steel boots could be heard marching along the deck. Then an order was given, and through the tiny holes in the door there came pin-points of light from an electric torch. By now the men were quiet and drew back from the door in a semi-circle, like a herd of wild bulls facing a stranger. In the general hush they could hear the clang of the clamps being withdrawn outside, and a blacksmith with his tool wrenching at the door, which had been damaged by splinters. Suddenly it flew open with a clang, and a ghostly beam shone in from a shielded blue flash-light carried by Lieutenant Hertzberg who entered, followed by the Master-at-Arms and two armed sentries. Dove stepped forward and stammered, 'Hertzberg! You've got to – '

He was stopped by Hertzberg putting his hand on his shoulder in a friendly manner and addressing everybody in the cabin. First he said, 'All right, Dove.' Then, raising his lantern so that everybody could see his face, he said, 'May I have your attention, please, gentlemen.'

He got it.

Then measuring every word he said, 'Gentlemen! For you, the battle is over. We are now in the outer harbour of Montevideo – '

For a moment his voice was drowned by a babel of exclamations, as the full meaning of his statement started to dawn upon the seamen. He raised his voice and dominated the others: 'So Captain Langsdorff has told me to tell you . . . that as we are in the neutral country of Uruguay . . . according to International Law . . . you will be set free – tomorrow!'

He was hardly allowed to finish his set speech. At the news, everybody seemed to have gone demented. Hertzberg himself seemed quite pleased at the turn of events. Half a dozen people shook him by the hand, Dove amongst them. Some were cheering, some were singing, two were crying. Dove pushed his way through the shouting, rejoicing men and stepped out of the doorway into the night air. He wanted to see for himself. Yet he could hardly believe his eyes when he saw, only a short distance away, the sky-line of Montevideo with the lights and the sky-scrapers. The ship was still drifting slowly. He could hear distant automobiles honking. There was no doubt about it. They really were in the outer harbour of Montevideo.

CHAPTER VIII

THE PURPLE LAND

WHEN THE LONG-DISTANCE connection of the Red Meat Packing Company of Chicago, U.S.A., with the beef-producing country of Uruguay sent Mike Fowler to Montevideo, he knew as much about South America and the River Plate as the average American or Briton: he knew nothing. Rare moments of attention at High School had given him a hazy impression of a large parsnip-shaped continent, tò the South of The Land of the Free, containing a number of countries easy to confuse with one another, without the blessings of democracy, producing gauchos, Indians and hot-tempered dictators in large quantities, and exporting coffee from Brazil. They also exported the dictators. Presumably somebody on the Board which employed him had read W. H. Hudson. It was quite certain Mike hadn't. Perhaps some middle-aged executive possessed a well-thumbed copy of 'The Birds of the Rio de la Plata', or had indulged in romantic dreams after reading 'Green Mansions' or 'The Purple Land', and had envied Mike his youth and his chance of adventure. But Mike had no dreams when he agreed to go; he only had dreams after eating hot lobster. For him it was just another job.

When he arrived in Montevideo, which he had been told to make his base, he didn't even know where it was on the map. Why should he? His ticket had been bought for him. So it was with mild surprise and approval that he discovered Montevideo to be a large, modern city on the north bank of the Rio de la Plata (at that point fifty miles wide), with one of the finest and largest natural harbours in the world, with miles of bathing beaches only a stone's throw from busy streets, with luxury hotels and sky-scrapers, and even with those highest products of modern civilisation: bars and night-clubs. There was one particular bar down on the beach, Manolo's, which opened late and never seemed anxious to close, where Mike really felt at home. He ate there, he made appointments there, they took messages for him, and Manalo cashed his cheques. The band was good and the singer who led it, Dolores, with the horr-glass figure and paprika in her voice, was even better. Yes, there was no doubt that Mike had practically gone native; and if what he had not known about Uruguay before he came would have filled a large quarto volume, it had now shrunk to an octavo. For most of this information he had Pop to thank.

Pop's real names were Manoel Herrera McTavish, and he had adopted Mike on his first trip to an *estancia* to make recordings. Mike was under the impression that he had adopted Pop. Like so many Americans, he had found it a great time-saver to model his personality upon one that already existed, rather than to create his own. In December 1939 he was modelling himself upon Spencer Tracy. It is doubtful whether Tracy would have recognised the imitation, but it successfully interposed a shield between young Mike and the world – and that was all that mattered to him. It had taken Pop about fifteen seconds to realise that Mike was playing a part, and the same number to recognise that the American had three months' work ahead of him, a liberal expense account, and was paid regularly every Friday. The McTavish in Pop was stirred and he moved in. Actually he was not a gaucho at all, although an excellent horseman: he was handling the *remuda* for his friend, the ranch-foreman, when he and Mike first met. Uruguay is a civilised country and a pastoral one, where every man thinks that legs are something to wrap around a horse – and the horses think so too. To make things easier, besides millions of cattle, there are at least two horses per head of the population and everybody, man, woman and child spends his holidays in the Camp.

Pop styled himself 'retired' (one can live on very little in Uruguay if one has friends – Pop had thousands – and there is an excellent scheme of State pensions to cover everybody which would be the anathema of both the Conservative and the Labour Party in England, but which, strange to say, works in Uruguay), but he also had a small job which was connected in some vague way with the Administration of the Port. It can't have been a very exacting job for, as has been said, he adopted Mike and stuck to him closer than the Angel to Tobias. He realised that, having captured Mike's childlike wonder as a gaucho, he must continue as one. So when they returned together to Montevideo, instead of changing into his normal city clothes, he went everywhere with Mike in full gaucho outfit, thoroughly enjoying the open stares of the few people to whom he was a stranger and the rude questions of the thousands who were his friends and, in most cases, his relatives. The only thing that he lamented (and Mike listened with sympathy to his complaint) was that Police Regulations forbade him carrying his big gaucho knife hooked in the back of his belt. 'Not to feel my knife right there,' he said, patting the naked part, 'give me lumbargo'. He was such a good actor that it probably did.

Mike had bought a powerful and battered station-wagon to transport the equipment, and had hired an enthusiastic young man from one of the local radio stations to run it. It was the very latest portable set, fully equipped with gadgets and spares, and the youth spent all his waking hours in wrapt contemplation of it. He usually had it in pieces when Mike wanted to record. He never spoke, seldom ate and drank two litres of red wine a day, never less and never more. He was called Tony and was a second-generation Italian immigrant. Pop reported that when he opened his mouth only Spanish came out of it. 'So he's Italian, you're Scotch and the hotel-keeper is German,' said Mike, 'the night-porter is Hungarian, the fellow across the Square who runs the restaurant is a Czech, Mr Svensson, the radio engineer, is a Swede, and the owner of this *estancia* is an Englishman. I thought you were all Spanish or Indians here. Why, it's just like America.'

'No, Mike. You got it wrong,' said Pop, rolling one of his eternal cigarettes. 'No Indian in Uruguay now. Indian here very fierce, fight like mad when first white man come. Many, many fight. No use to talk peace, Indian no want peace. Indian want to kill. Either kill or he kill you. So – ' he made an expressive gesture, 'no Indians.'

'I see,' said Mike, 'then what about the Spanish? What happened to them? I suppose when the Clan McTavish moved in, they moved out.'

'Sure, there Spanish, plenty Spanish,' replied the Clansman calmly, 'Urugay was Spanish colony just like all other Latin America countries.'

'Except Brazil,' his pupil reminded him. 'You told me Brazil was Portuguese.'

'That right,' agreed Pop. 'But in the old days, Mike, Uruguay not so important country as now. More like one big farm. Montevideo, she a town, but she a small town. Then much *estancias*, some few forts, many Missions, much cattle, just like now. Men mostly soldier or gaucho or priest, but most Spaniards live up River, at Buenos Aires.'

'I suppose B.A. was a big town even then?' asked Mike, looking through his field-glasses. They were sitting in a 'hide', in a clump of eucalyptus near the *estancia*, waiting for the evening-song to start.

'Sure B.A. big city, always been big city. Then when we fight the Wars of Liberation all these colonies, you understand Mike, become countries. Uruguay fight too, so become country too. First very few people, but then good land, good water, nice weather, so many people come. My great-grandfather, Hector McTavish, was Staff Officer with General Gregor McGregor. You heard of General Gregor McGregor?'

'No,' said Mike simply.

'He one of the great liberators,' said Pop enthusiastically. 'He Staff Officer to Simon Bolivar.'

'I've heard of him,' said Mike. 'He's a cigar.'

Pop looked sharply at him, then caught Mike's grin and grinned back.

'Did your great-grandfather liberate this country, Pop?' enquired Mike, 'or did he just liberate a piece for the McTavishes?'

But Pop refused to be drawn: it was too serious a subject.

'This one good contry, Mike,' he said. 'Take two great men to liberate it. My great-grandpop pretty good man, too. But San Martin great man. José Artigas great man. These two men liberate this country. I not laugh at Jeff Davis, Mike. You not laugh about them.'

But Mike was irrepressible.

'You can laugh at Jeff Davis if it's any help,' he offered. 'We don't take our democracy as seriously as you do. It just comes naturally.'

Pop, however, was in a fighting mood.

– 'Some thing you must take seriously. In South America liberty very serious matter, something to fight for and watch out for each new day. In America is different. Your great men invent democracy – '

'You're wrong there,' interrupted Mike. 'The Greeks invented it. We just took out the patent.'

Pop nodded, 'O.K We take out patent too. We take it out every day.'

'So I gather,' said Mike drily, 'but don't get me wrong, Pop. This is a swell country and a real democracy. Maybe you've got something in this idea of minting it fresh every morning. This José Artigas, is he the guy up on the horse in the middle of the Plaza Independencia?'

Pop nodded vigorously, 'Sure, that's him. That's José Artigas.'

'Right,' said Mike, 'next time we're in town I'll go and give the old boy a salute on behalf of Jeff Davis.'

ɪ ne next time that Mike and Pop were in Montevideo was on the morning of the 13th December. They had been up at Concordia, beyond Colón, and had left the ranch at dawn. It had been a terrific orange sunrise, followed by light rain and haze, very different from the clear dawn which the British ships had seen that morning. Mike had been glad of the rain, it laid the dust. The road lay through broad, rolling country with occasional ranges of hills not more than six hundred feet high, but sometimes very rocky. Great herds of Hereford cattle were grazing over the plains and occasionally a mountain gaucho would trot by on his horse, with a dignified wave of his hand, his poncho flapping in the wind. By the time they got to Minas, a busy little market town of broad streets and white square houses, the sun was high and the haze had vanished. They stopped for coffee at the Espresso on the corner. Cheerful Italian women were marketing and chattering as they passed Mike. It was like an Italian toy town, brand new, set down in the middle of the pampa. It was only about eighty miles to the capital and Mike rattled along, singing lustily a gaucho song which the men had taught him, while Pop beamed and chain-smoked, and Tony sat in the back nursing the most delicate parts of the apparatus in his lap. The day was glorious. The brown and white Herefords shone with health and went on steadily grazing – ('Just imagine browsing every day on miles of bacon and eggs. I'd look contented, too,' said Mike) – clouds of green parakeets flew up before them, and oven-birds sat with determination on every telegraph pole.

'This is a swell country,' said Mike again. 'There's room to breathe.'

He glanced at his watch. It was seven-thirty; the *Exeter* was already out of the battle and had started on her thousand-mile voyage, full of tragedy and heroism, to the Falklands.

It was nine o'clock when they got to their hotel. After breakfast Mike walked round to the Plaza Independencia to fulfil his promise. It was a very large square in the centre of the city, lined with palm-trees, musical with the constant hootings of automobiles. There were no restrictions in Montevideo, and everyone blew his horn from morning to night. The Square was surrounded by long, low buildings and vaulted arcades, except on one side where the Palacio Salvo, Montevideo's only sky-scraper, rose twenty-seven storeys into the air, its grotesque bulk ornamental with towers, cupolas, balconies and other unlikely features. One of the ugliest buildings in the world, from its

110

upper floors it commanded a magnificent view over the River Plate and on clear days, when the pampero blew, the inhabitants claimed to see the coast of Argentina. They could even see the haze of smoke rising from the great city of Buenos Aires, one hundred and twenty-five miles up-river.

Mike bought a paper at his favourite kiosk, walked past the building where the President lived and worked, and approached the giant equestrian statue of Artigas in the centre of the Square. Mike never wore a hat, but he was carrying one in his hand. Arrived in front of the Liberator he put it on, and then formally took it off in salutation, with a slight bow as between two democrats. He was watched with interest by four postcard sellers and two depressed photographers lounging by black cameras like concertinas with an obscene bulb hanging down over tripods with rickets. Before they could close on him Mike turned his back, and walked swiftly away towards the Palacio Salvo. On the way he met a fellow-countryman, who covered B.A. and Montevideo for the United Press, in a high state of excitement.

'Heard the news?' he panted. 'There's been a big Naval battle out at sea early this morning. And it's still going on. The British and Germans. They can hear the guns from Punta del Este. Nobody knows anything yet, but the *Exeter* is in it. They broke wireless silence at about half-past six and the air has been full of stuff ever since.'

He was racing across the Square as he spoke, and Mike ran with him.

'Where are you going?' yelled Mike.

'Punta del Este! It's a running fight. They may be coming this way. You ought to get your firm to let you cover it.'

He leapt into his waiting car and roared away.

Now for the first time Mike noticed that there were little clusters of people taking in excited tones. Suddenly the usual newspaper van fetched up at the corner of the Square with a most unusual screech of breaks and was mobbed by a crowd of excited newsboys, who grabbed their parcels and ran away at full speed. Certainly there was something happening. Mike began to get as excited as everybody else. Suppose that one of the ships was running for shelter and that the battle did come into the River Plate; he would be the only American radio reporter on the spot. . . . It would be the chance of a life-time. . . . He could scoop the world. . . . His firm would go crazy. . . . If he pulled this off they would send him to Europe. . . . He could become another Quentin Reynolds! Mike knew a man who had an

apartment on the twenty-fifth floor of the Palacio. He took the
elevator and woke him up. Together they went out on to the
wide balcony. There was nothing to be seen, except that every
ship in sight was heading into port as fast as they could go. Not
one was outward bound. Then, as they stared towards the eastern horizon, they heard it for the first time: a dull mutter, a
rumbling like distant thunder, the sound of the guns.

The telephone rang and Mike's friend answered it.

He said, 'It's the German News Agency report.'

He listened for a minute, then said, 'Ring me back if you hear
any more,' rang off and turned to Mike. 'It's big,' he said, 'the
Germans are claiming a big Naval victory. And the British are
denying the whole story. The Germans claim that one of their
Pocket battleships came up this morning with the *Exeter* and two
smaller cruisers, which they identify as the *Ajax* and the *Achilles*.
There was a running fight and the *Exeter* was knocked out and
sunk. The two small cruisers were badly damaged and broke off
the action and the whole shebang is heading this way. The British
haven't issued any statement yet. Usual Admiralty stuff: "lie
low and say nuthin". But there's obviously some truth in it.
You'd better get on to your firm and nail the job for yourself,
before they start sending down one of their high-powered,
golden-voiced, ace reporters!'

But Mike was already racing down twenty-five flights of stairs.
The lift was a local job and not worth waiting for. It was eleven-
thirty.

By noon the whole world had heard the German news-story,
and the Admiralty realised that there was no further point in
preserving secrecy. The truth had to be told, although the running fight was still going on. So an official story was put out,
briefly stating that there had been an engagement with a Pocket
battleship which was still continuing and denying that the
Exeter had been sunk. By now the whole Western Hemisphere
was ablaze with excitement. The war had come to their very
doors. New reports and rumours were pouring out from every
city on the Atlantic sea-board of South America. By the afternoon, it was plain that the battle was moving into the area of
the River Plate. Buenos Aires and Montevideo were in a ferment
of excitement. The true facts had become general knowledge and
the neutral States were full of admiration for the gallant fight
which the three small cruisers had put up against their huge
adversary. The *Exeter*, still listing to starboard, a smoking, battered wreck, had been sighted from the coast of Argentina, pro-

ceeding at slow speed, for Captain Bell, anxious for the safety of his ship, had come in close to the coast so that, if necessary, he could beach her. The coastline down to Mar del Plata and far beyond was lined with watchers, and mounted parties from the *Estancias* with English sympathies organised a kind of coast-guard watch which went on day and night, in case they could be of some help to the wounded vessel. The whole of Argentina, which was by no means pro-British, was full of admiration for the proud and silent voyage of the *Exeter* southward. So deeply were they stirred that the Argentine Government radioed Captain Bell in courteous and chivalrous terms, offering the use of all their facilities at Bahia Blanca, including the Naval dockyard and the hospitals. The signal was intercepted by the Admiralty, who sent out a gentle, but unnecessary, reminder of the Inter-national Laws relating to internment. Hookie Bell, although grateful for the offer, had already refused it.

He was still at the after conning position where he had been all day. He had fired his last shot and fallen out of the action, but he was still in the battle area. Like Harwood, he had no idea as to the intentions of the enemy and could only guess them by what he would do himself. When the *Graf Spee* fled westward none of the British imagined, for a moment, that Langsdorff would be making for neutral waters, let alone for a neutral port. To her pursuers, the *Graf Spee* did not appear to have been badly damaged. They were quite certain that Langsdorff would break seaward, either to the north-east or to the south-west. If he could lose himself again in the wide Atlantic, he could repair his dam-age and eventually make his way back to Germany, and that is what Bell, a simple, blunt man, imagined he would do. The *Graf Spee* might easily blunder into the *Exeter* again and since Bell had nothing but hard words to throw at the enemy, he was slightly worried and had an additional reason for staying near the coast. The ship was straining and creaking and still making water for'ard, and men everywhere were working feverishly to put in hand temporary repairs. Bulkheads were being shored up, holes were stopped with anything that came to hand, fires were still being extinguished and other damage was being isolated as much as possible. The foretopmast continued to be a source of anxiety. The *Exeter*'s masts were the old-fashioned pole ones, with very high wooden topmasts and, since the stays had been shot away, each roll of the ship whipped them about like saplings. It seemed impossible that they would not snap off at the base and come crashing down on the deck causing more damage. Bell had

113

sent the Gunnery Officer to see what he could do. Under normal conditions, men would have been sent aloft and, by receiving a suitable rope, the topmast would have been housed or lowered down. Since this proved impossible, they had to stay it as well as they could. It still whipped about in an alarming manner, but to Bell's relief it stayed where it was.

Just before the Argentine message was received, the Engineer-Commander had made his report on the condition of the ship. Although damage and casualties had been appalling, and it would be twenty-four hours before they could get the ship upright, it was reassuring. Naturally Bell had kept his doubts about ever reaching the Falklands to himself, and a great weight was lifted from his mind. He ordered speed to be reduced to about ten knots and went to visit his wounded men.

The sad and terrible task of identifying the dead and tending the wounded had been going on all day. A roll-call had revealed the numbers of the dead though in many cases identification was impossible. Where an eleven-inch shell had burst it was like a charnel-house. But the task had to be done and it is amazing how human pity and a sense of stern duty can nerve men to the most dreadful task. The remains of men were collected and sewn into hammocks, and the decks and bulkheads were washed down and disinfected to wipe out the stench of death. Bell had sent for the chaplain, and it had been arranged that the dead should be buried before sunset. A silent working-party carried the sailors' hammocks one by one to the quarter-deck, where heavy fire-bars and other weights were lashed to them in preparation for the funeral.

Bell's own harbour-cabin, in the stern of the ship, was large and airy and he had told his steward to strip it of furniture so that it could be used as a hospital, since the Action Medical Stations were still busy with operations and blood-transfusions. It was to this cabin that Bell now went for a brief visit to the wounded. They were laid out in rows, some fatally wounded who were to die later, others with minor injuries, but all comforting one another. The first person that Bell spoke to was Bill Roper. The boy lay flat on his back in the corner nearest the door. He was very weak and a ghastly colour, but fully conscious. Bell knelt beside him and said, 'How's it going, Roper?'

Billy whispered, 'All right, sir. I'm sorry to let you down.'

Bell said roughly, 'Don't talk nonsense. You were invaluable. I'm mentioning you in my report.'

They boy's eyes flickered and then he gave a little smile.

Bell asked, 'Anything you want?'

Billy shook his head, gave a very weak grin and said something which was lost in a gasp.

'What?' said Bell, leaning closer.

Sweat was standing on the boy's face but the grin was still there, as he managed to whisper, 'Just go on living, sir.'

Bell could hardly trust himself to speak, but he answered confidently, 'Don't worry. You'll be all right,' and stood up.

He gave a few seconds to each man. Some were barely conscious and other were in great pain, but how stoical and cheerful they all were! There was not one complaint; only questions about the battle and whether there were any news of the enemy. Bell came away uplifted.

Towards sunset, the burials were held. To the westward the low line of the purple land stretched as far as the eye could see north and south. The long row of hammocks, more than sixty of them, were laid out on the quarter-deck, their feet towards the sea, and all covered with the Union Jack. The chaplain in his white surplice, the officers, and all the men who were able to be there, gathered around. It had been arranged that each man who wished would stand by the body of his friend and at the words, 'We therefore commit his body to the deep,' the hammocks would be pushed over the side. When it came to this moment, the Reverend George Groves' voice faltered for a moment but when it was all over, and the last hammock had vanished into the blue waters of the South Atlantic, his voice rang out as he said, 'Their bodies are buried in peace, but their name liveth for evermore!'

Once or twice during the service, Commander Graham glanced at his Captain. Bell stood beside the chaplain, his cap under his arm, the breeze ruffling his hair, his eyes on the far horizon. He looked a grim figure, sad, formidable and undefeated. The service over, he returned to the after conning position.

From the small, high, isolated platform, he watched the sun sinking over the land. He was in great pain from his eyes. He had said nothing about them. He felt that the Surgeon-Lieutenant, who never slept during the whole voyage to the Falkland Islands, had more urgent cases on his hands. As we know, Bell had a minute steel splinter in the iris of each eye. At first he found relief in closing them but it was such agony to open them again, that it seemed better on the whole to try to keep them open. As night fell, he ordered a mattress to be brought up and lay down on it at intervals during the night. Slowly the ship rolled southwards. He could not sleep nor close his eyes, but the

115

stars comforted him.

When the incredible fact became clear to Harwood that the *Graf Spee* was entering the River Plate, he ordered the *Achilles* to go round the north end of Lobos Island, while the *Ajax* followed directly after the Pocket battleship, which appeared to be going straight for Montevideo. He still couldn't believe the truth that the *Graf Spee* was fleeing into a neutral port.

The River Plate, at its mouth, is a hundred miles wide and divided into two channels by a large sandbank, known as 'The English Bank' – in the strange way that sandbanks, landfalls and ocean-currents crop up all over the globe, tagged for ever by seamen with Anglo-Saxon names. Heaven and the Admiralty know who named the English Bank. Sebastian Cabot passed that way and Sir Francis Drake singed the King of Spain's beard at Maldonado. Two hundred years later, Admiral George Anson also flew his flag there against the Spaniards and Captain Cook charted its shores. Charles Darwin in the *Beagle* sheltered there from a pampero. The Bank had been as familiar as the Goodwins to generations of British seamen before Commodore Harwood flew his broad pendant there. And now guns were heard again at sea off Maldonado.

Punta del Este is the south-eastern point of Uruguay. It is a long, low spit of land. On one side the river presses past the golden sands and rolling dunes on its way to the sea. On the other, the Atlantic surf comes rolling in almost to the doors of seaside hotels. A tall water-tower dominates the peninsula, which is covered with little white houses, and at the tip where jagged reefs dun for half a mile out into the sea, a small lighthouse stands by the harbour looking across to its big brother on the Island of Lobos, across the channel. There are many exposed reefs and two Islands, one of them low and wooded, the other exposed and rocky upon which the lighthouse stands. A seal rookery covers the rocks below the lighthouse and, at the first sound of the guns, dozens of the great animals hurled themselves off the low cliffs and were shattered on the rocks below, adding their casualties to the follies and heroisms of men. For, as darkness fell and the shape of the fleeing ship became more and more indistinct against the darkening western sky, the pursuers shortened the range and pressed the Hunted Beast so closely that he snarled in reply. With only two ships to block the whole river, Harwood was determined not to lose touch with his quarry and to give him no opportunity to double round the English Bank and so out to sea again. The battle continued thus with sharp

116

attack and sullen reply up to the very doors of Montevideo.

By now the whole north bank of the River Plate was in an uproar of excitement. The road from Punta del Este to Montevideo was crowded with automobiles tearing from one vantage point to another, guided by the flashes of the guns. Every rocky hill, every roof-top and every church tower was crowded with people straining their eyes out over the broad expanse of the river. Then darkness fell. None of the ships was showing any light and there was no more firing. A hush of expectation fell upon the coast and upon the world. In Montevideo, the life of the city seemed to be going on as usual. The trams roared and clanged and screamed their way through the streets, the tireless automobile horns created their usual cacophony, and innumerable neon-lights flashed and glared, but everywhere there was a feeling of excitement and anticipation. It is difficult to convey so many years later what it meant to the Western Hemisphere, and particularly to the neutral countries of South America, to have the war brought so dramatically to its doors, in this, the first important battle of the War. The English Club was crowded, with half a dozen radios going at once. Everywhere that they could, men got together and asked each other questions they could not answer. Many of the offices stayed open and the office buildings were brilliantly illuminated. Lights burned in the President's Palace, in the building of the Port Authority, and in the Foreign Ministry. The British and French Legations and the German Embassy were humming with activity. Yet in spite of it all, or perhaps because of it all, the cinemas and restaurants, the night-clubs and bars, were all full. People felt too restless to stay at home and sit by the radio. Manolo's bar on the waterfront was crowded. People would dance and drink, eat and flirt, rush outside to look over the dark water and rush back in again to start new rumours. Mike, with a cable from his firm burning his pocket, giving him full powers to report on a world-wide hook-up, prowled to and fro like a panther. Where was the *Graf Spee?* Not even Commodore Harwood could have been more anxious to know the answer. And where was Pop? He had sent him down to the harbour to clear some new equipment, which had come by flying-boat from Buenos Aires, with strict instructions to return at once. He was more than a half an hour overdue. He wandered about the bar impatiently clicking his fingers. Dolores, singing at the microphone beside the band, followed him with her eyes as she led the band in the rapid beat of guaracha:

117

'Como lejana tormenta
Que avanza con su tronar,
El horizonte refleja
Caballos al galopar.
Son los gauchos
En su frenesi
Que por la Pampa
Van sin reprimir. . . . '

('As the distant storm
Thunderously approaches
The horizon echoes
To galloping horses.
Here come the Gauchos!
Furiously riding
Over the Pampa
Carrying all before them. . . . ')

The words couldn't have been more apt. Here they came indeed!
Pop and two friends, wild with excitmeent, yelling, and carrying
all before them. . . . 'Mike! Señor Mike! Quick! Come quick!
The German Pocket battleship is anchoring in the Outer Harbour!'

CHAPTER IX

WEDNESDAY NIGHT

AFTER THE EXCITEMENT and suspense of the day it was to be expected that a large battleship, wearing no flag, showing no lights and groping her way into the Outer Harbour of Montevideo, was at once reported to the Port Authority, who telephoned the Head of the Government and the Naval Command Headquarters. Capitán de Fragata José Rodrigues Varela, accompanied by Capitán de Corbeta Fernando Fontana, on board the corvette *Lavalleja*, was instructed to investigate. His orders were to find out what ship this was, why it had come into port, what her requirements were and the number of dead and wounded on board. The *Lavalleja* already had been alerted, for ever since news of the westward-chase had reached Montevideo from Punta del Este, and when it became clear that the running fight had already infringed neutral territory and might very easily go much further Uruguayan Naval Headquarters, with the approval of their Government, had prepared to resist any further encroachment, by force if necessary. The fact that the entire Naval force, plus shore-batteries, that Uruguay could muster was about knee-high to either Commodore Harwood's or Captain Langsdorff's command was beside the point, as any seaman knows. The principle is the thing. Ships and the men in them are great respecters of law and of that which is right. No man can command a ship who doesn't respect custom and tradition, and who does not expect as much of others as he does of himself. So it was with a beating heart, a high spirit and the full authority of a Sovereign State that Captain Varela, standing on the bridge of his tiny corvette, approached the enormous dark shape of the Pocket battleship, which was not yet anchored but was still slowly moving through the Outer Harbour, like a blind giant groping for a resting-place.

When the corvette was about a hundred yards away from the bigger vessel, Varela ordered the searchlight switched on and hailed her: 'This is the corvette *Lavalleja* of the Uruguayan Navy. Where are your lights? What ship is that?'

After a short pause a voice answered him from the bridge high above. It was Captain Kay.

'We are a German warship. Is the holding ground good here? Can we anchor?'

Although he had guessed that this was the German ship, the answer took Varsela's breath away. Captain Fontana was quite as impressed and counfounded as he was. So it was in rather a wavering voice that Varela shouted back: 'Yes. You can anchor here. The holding ground is good!'

An acknowledgement came back and orders were shouted to the men in the bows, who were already standing by the anchor-chain. Flashing torches could be seen, waving high in the air. Then there was a sudden transformation and the fore-part of the ship showed lights. The after-part was still in darkness. The two Uruguayan officers were conferring together in excited voices while the corvette kept pace with the battleship. Then Kay's voice was heard from the bridge again, 'The Captain asks you to come on board! We are lowering a ladder on the port side.'

Varela acknowledged and gave the orders to come round under the battleship's stern, by the quarter-deck. Suddenly, high up in the air, on the bridge of the battleship a new voice was heard. It dominated without effort all other voices, as a single instrument can dominate an orchestra. It was the voice of Langsdorff and Varela realised at once that it was the Captain who was speaking. It could be no other. He hardly seemed to raise his voice and yet the tired, effortless commands were heard in every part of the ship. The ship herself seemed to listen and to be cured of her blindness and uncertainty. Varela had the impression that the voice would ride a storm as easily as it dominated the calm evening in the Outer Harbour. Suddenly there was that tremendous and thrilling sound, the roar and rattle of the anchor-chain of a big ship, followed by the plunge of the anchor into the water. Red and white torches flashed in the bows and on the bridge. Langsdorff paid out fifteen fathoms and then gave the order to stop. There was silence. For the first time for nearly four months, the *Graf Spee* rode at her anchor. Imperceptibly she started to swing round. Her cruise was at an end.

The after-part of the battleship was still in complete darkness for, as we know, the electric cable had been cut. As the corvette approached the stern, they could see the flashes of torches where men moved to and fro. When they came alongside the quarter-deck, a naked electric bulb at the end of a cable was lowered by a German officer, revealing a rope ladder. Ordering his men to hang on and wait, Varela scrambled up the ladder, followed by Fontana. Hertzberg was waiting for him at the top, accompanied

120

by a Quarter-Master and two armed sailors. A hasty attempt had
been made to greet the Uruguayans with proper formality, but
the Germans looked exhausted and dishevelled, and the Quarter-
Master had his head bandaged. As their feet touched the deck,
Varela and Fontana saluted formally and the salute was returned.
Hertzberg apologised for their appearance and for the lack of
electric light, and asked them to follow him to the Captain's
cabin. All four men carried powerful torches. Varela could see the
shapes of men lying about on the quarter-deck, exhausted after
the long day's battle. By now it was eleven o'clock at night.
Hertzberg led them along a passage lit by an occasional naked
bulb. The passage, and the cabins adjoining it, appeared to be
the first-aid quarters. There was a smell of chloroform and
disinfectant. A man wearing a red-cross band on his arm was
kneeling on the floor, operating on the stump of a sailor's leg
with a pair of scissors. The sailor was lying on a sheet and there
was a first-aid kit open by his side. Hertzberg led the way quickly.
It was difficult to walk along the passage for the floor was
covered with dead and wounded men. The impression of the
recent battle was so great that Varela hardly took in any details.
But he always remembered a glimpse that he caught through a
doorway where a dining room was being used as a surgery; a
big Christmas tree, brilliantly-lit, stood at one end of the long
table upon which a man was lying, while surgeons operated on
him by the light of the Christmas decorations. In the armchairs
and on the floor there were other bandaged sailors.

Hertzberg was hurrying them along. The end of the passage
was closed by a steel door which refused to open. The Quarter-
Master and sailors came forward and wrenched and kicked it,
but it was of no use: Shell-blast had twisted the hinges and the
door was completely jammed. So they returned along the passage
and came out on to the deck. They stumbled across the waist of
the ship with difficulty. There was debris all over the place, and
the biggest tangle was formed by the wrecked aircraft, over and
around which they had to scramble. But now they were near
the lighted forward part of the ship, which threw the wreckage up
in strong silhouette and helped them to arrive safely. They
entered the forward superstructure and crossed a small flat
where a sentry was standing. Hertzberg opened the door of the
Captain's cabin and motioned them to enter.

There was only one officer waiting in the cabin, in the uniform
of a Lieutenant. He was there to act as interpreter. He spoke good
Spanish, and Varela and he recognised each other at once; he was

121

the First Officer of the *Cap Polonio*, which was on a regular run to South American ports before the war. He had obviously been acting as Navigator and Pilot for these waters, and Varela complimented him on bringing the ship into Harbour so skilfully. He avoided the compliment with an embarrassed laugh – he had clearly been told not to say anything that could be quoted – and informed the Uruguayans that the Captain would be coming down from the bridge at any moment. As he spoke, there was a sharp order outside and steps rang on the steel ladder.

Langsdorff entered. He had never left the bridge all day and his clothes, beneath his uniform coat, were a sweater, pyjamas and sea-boots. He had received a splinter wound on the scalp and his face was covered with dried crusts of blood. Dirt and sweat had caked on his skin. He had also been wounded in the left arm and the sleeve had been torn off it whilst he had been given first-aid. A first-aid Petty Officer followed the Captain in, and during the interview which followed he put a proper bandage and sling on the wounded arm which had just been dressed with a field dressing. The two Uruguayans bowed in silence. Langsdorff gave a little bow in reply and said: 'Good evening. Captain Langsdorff, Commandant of the *Graf Spee*.'

He sat down and the Petty Officer bandaged his left arm.

Varela so far forgot his manners as to ask in an astonished tone of the interpreter: 'Is this the Pocket battleship *Admiral Graf Spee?*'

The officer nodded and Varela felt his head whirling with excitement and confusion. Things were happening too fast. He pulled himself together, and made a formal speech stating that they were representatives of the Uruguayan Government and had orders to find out the reason of the arrival of the foreign battleship. He also asked the number of casualties and offered help. Langsdorff replied that there had been a battle since early that morning between his vessel and three British ships. It had continued until only an hour ago when, just after dark, a shell had hit the bridge and he had received his wound. At that moment the Medical Officer, sent for by Langsdorff, came into the cabin covered in blood. After a very short conversation he left, and Langsdorff informed Varela that the *Graf Spee*'s casualties were more than thirty dead and very many wounded. One of them was blinded and needed urgent medical attention. Varela at once offered to take this man off with them to the hospital. Meanwhile, arrangements would be made to receive the others in hospitals ashore.

Langsdorff went on to say that he wished to see his Ambassador as soon as possible. He needed time and facilities from the Uruguayan Government to make his ship seaworthy. His evaporators had been damaged and his galleys destroyed. To Varela's surprise, he was quite ready to talk about the battle. Impatiently pushing the first-aid man aside, he demonstrated how the British ships had divided his fire, using three fingers of each hand as the two turrets of the *Graf Spee*. He said the battle had been without a definite decision, although he believed he had sunk the *Exeter*. The difficulty had been in having three adversaries. He was able to engage two of the British ships effectively, but three had been too many for him.

Varela was deeply impressed by Langsdorff. It was extraordinary the attraction that the man exercised over everyone who met him. Varela watched with fascination the gestures of the slim hands, he saw the fire and passion in the fine melancholy face, the flashes of elegance and humour. If Dove had been present, he would have also recognised the nervous tension, the desire for human communication, the attempt to explain to himself what had happened by explaining it to others. The man was exhausted but he was like a wound-up spring. And Dove would have seen what Varela did not see: at the back of Langsdorff's eyes a puzzled light, a look of uncertainty, the look of a man to whom the incredible has happened, and who cannot yet believe it.

After a while Langsdorff ceased talking. Fascinated though he was, both as a man and as a professional sailor, Varela realised it was time to withdraw. The blinded German sailor was already on board the corvette. Varela made a little speech to Langsdorff, assuring him on behalf of the Government that everything that could be done to help would be done. Formal calls would be made in the morning, but in the special circumstances if Captain Langsdorff wished to go ashore at once arrangements would be made for a Naval escort and a car to the Germany Embassy. Otherwise, his orders were to request everybody to await the official visit of the Commandant of the Port at 9 a.m.

The interview was over. Langsdorff rose and shook hands, and the two Uruguayans took their leave.

When they came on deck, there were already dozens of small craft, tugs, motor-boats, row-boats, circling the *Graf Spee*. Most of the merchant ships that were lying a few cable-lengths from the *Graf Spee* had switched on all their lights, so that the scene was no longer dark but lit by a ghostly radiance. Already cars were arriving on the Mole and turning their headlights so that they pointed towards the battleship, in a vain attempt to pick her out across half a mile of water. The news was running through the city like a prairie-fire. The cinemas and night-clubs, restaurants and bars, were emptying into the streets. In a cinema where Lotte was sitting entwined with her escort a hastily drawn caption, announcing the arrival of the *Graf Spee* in the Harbour, was thrown across the screen right in the middle of the most exciting part of the action. The director would have been mortified to see his public lose all interest in the film and leap to their feet screaming and shouting in half a dozen different languages. Lotte, who had patriotic reasons for excitement, screamed with the rest. Half-carried, half-dragged by her sturdy escort, she fought her way into the street. So did everybody else and the film was left running to an empty house. (It was 'The Grapes of Wrath'.) In the street, Lotte's escort said, 'Where to now?'

His face was familiar. It was the driver from the British Legation, with whom Lotte was flirting on the beach on the day the *Exeter* sailed.

'Where to? To the Harbour, of course!' screamed Lotte excitedly.

Everybody else seemed to have the same idea. Everybody was streaming down for a glimpse of the *Graf Spee.*

'Come on!' said the young driver, catching Lotte's hand, 'I parked the car down the side-street.' He started to run. As he fumbled with the lock of the door, they saw a macabre. little scene. A man came running up the street, out of breath, and hammered on the door of a shop opposite. A window above crashed open and a man in a nightshirt appeared in a sleepy fury. But at the first words of the messenger his anger evaporated and he started to work himself up into an ecstasy. Lotte's face turned pale as she listened.

'Quick! Quick!' she said, 'We must go to the Harbour! . . . I must see my parents . . . . I must see Julita!'

As the car roared away, the lights of the shop went on and the door opened. It was an undertaker's. . . .

Julita was an orphan and shared a room with Lotte in her parents' house. She was asleep in bed. Lotte was often late these nights and through her sleep she had heard the front-door close and knew that her friend had come in. She wondered sleepily why Lotte was so long in coming to bed. Then she heard the voices of Lotte's parents talking. She was just dozing off again when she felt Lotte's arm around her pillow and Lotte's voice close to her ear, saying, 'Julita. Wake up, Julita,' in a tone which suddenly stopped the blood around her heart. In a second she was wide-awake and sitting up in bed. She switched on the light. The two girls looked at each other. Lotte repeated, 'Julita, you must be brave.'

Her lips opened and she breathed rather than spoke the words, 'What is it? Is it about Billy?'

Lotte nodded. 'There has been a battle off Punta del Este.'

'A battle?' The words were like a moan of pain.

'Yes . . . three British ships against a German Pocket battle-ship . . . the *Exeter* was one of them . . . our ⸺ the German battle-ship is here in the Harbour. She has many killed and wounded. Julita, you must be brave. They say she has sunk the *Exeter*. . . . They say everybody has been killed.'

But the storm of tears had already broken.

'Billy, oh, my Billy . . . Billy, my Billy. You said you would come back to me. . . .'

It was three-thirty in the morning. Yet all the lights were burning in the Cabildo.

In Dr Guani's office there were three men. Dr Guani himself stood at the tall windows and looked out at the lights of his city. He was a very small man with one of the largest and wisest heads that ever sat upon a small man's shoulders. A cosmopolitan, who had made Paris his home for twenty years, he had been prominent in the foundation of the League of Nations after the 1914 War, and had been one of its first Presidents. Streseman's photograph stood on his wide desk, but not Ribbentrop's; Croce's, but not Mussolini's. After a distinguished diplomatic career, he was now the Foreign Minister of his country; and it was fortunate for his country that he was.

The second man in the office was a large German diplomat, who was seated rigidly upon an uncomfortable settee. He looked the successful business man that he was. He was also an extremely shrewd, adroit, power-diplomat. Although it was only an hour or two before dawn, he was shaved and impeccably dressed in frock-coat, top hat, stick, gloves and the rest. He was looking straight in front of him. This was Dr Langmann, the Ambassador.

The third man was Captain Langsdorff. He was seated beside his Ambassador. He had come straight off his ship, although his arm was now in a neat sling underneath his uniform coat with the sleeve pinned across it. The cuts on his face had been covered with plaster but a scratch had started bleeding again, and there was dried blood caked in his neat little beard. He leant back in his corner of the settee making a vivid contrast with the diplo-

125

mat. He was dropping with sleep and his eyes burned in his head, but they were fixed on Dr Guani, in whose hands now lay the life of his ship.

Guani sighed and turned from the window. He walked slowly across to his desk. On the wall above it, behind his chair, hung a full-length portrait of Artigas, the Liberator, the symbol of Uruguay's independence. His hands behind his back, he glanced at the picture for a long moment. That evening there had been a reception for all the diplomatic representatives of the American continent and the little Foreign Minister was in evening dress, with orders and medals. He turned and still standing addressed the two Germans gravely and courteously speaking first to Dr Langmann: 'All I can promise you at this stage, Your Excellency, is to give every consideration to your Government's request within the limits of International Law.' Then to Langsdorff he said: 'In the morning I will send a commission of experts on board your ship, Captain Langsdorff, to assess the damage she has received. You may be assured that the members of the commission will act in the spirit of complete neutrality, and that you will be given all the time necessary for repairs to make you sea-worthy.'

He gave a little bow, and the Germans rose. Guani rang a bell on his desk which sounded in the ante-room. A harassed secretary opened the big double doors. Langsdorff gave a Naval, the Ambassador a Nazi, salute accompanied by the unnecessary words: 'Heil Hitler.'

In the ante-room, the Germans passed a tall, elegant figure in evening dress. It was Mr Eugen Millington-Drake. He and Langmann knew each other well, of course. But since their countries were at war, they ignored each other's existence.

The secretary, who was not used to being in the vortex of world events, announced to Guani, 'His Excellency The British Minister.'

Millington-Drake came in like a man sure of his welcome. He had known Dr Guani since the 1914 War, when Guani was already a Minister and he was a very young Secretary. And their relationship was somewhat in the nature of a diplomatic uncle and nephew. So it was with an affectionate smile, deprecating the formality of his words, that he said, as he advanced across the big room, 'Señor Ministro! The Uruguayan Government with its well-known democratic principles will act in accordance with Intenational Law and intern *Graf Spee* for the duration of the war will it not?'

126

Guani's eyes twinkled and he put his head on one side as he answered blandly, 'Sit down, my dear boy.'

The doors, which had barely closed, opened again and a secretary announced, 'His Excellency The French Minister!'

Monsieur Gentil entered, bearing an impressive, red-sealed Note in his hand. Like Millington-Drake, he was a diplomat de carrière, but he was by no means such a strong personality. He bowed to Guani and said, 'Monsieur le Ministre.' Then he looked across at Millington-Drake and said, 'Ah! Cher collègue!' and bowed again. Millington-Drake bowed gravely in his turn. They had parted only twenty minutes before. Guani, from his desk, looked appreciatively from Millington-Drake back to M. Gentil, who now advanced and offered him the red-sealed envelope with a murmured apology for the lateness of the hour.

Guani took the envelope in his hands and turned it over reflectively. Then he looked enquiringly at the French Minister, 'Another Note, I suppose?'

Gentil spread out his hands, 'By the terms of the Hague Convention – '

Guani interrupted him, throwing up his hands in gentle mockery, 'Ah! That much-quoted Hague Convention! Gentlemen! Please be seated.'

He waited until they had accepted his invitation, seated himself in his big chair, looked from one to the other and then continued, 'The Hague Convention! Article Seventeen says that "Warships of belligerents may not make repairs in the ports and roads of neutrals beyond those necessary for safety at sea; and may not increase in any way the fighting efficiency of the vessel". The Other Side have also quoted the Hague Convention and I assured them, as I do you, that we need no prompting in our duty as neutrals. The Hague Convention will be observed.'

Millington-Drake coughed and said, 'Señor Ministro. May I draw your attention to the fact that since the battle, *Graf Spee* has already sailed three hundred miles?'

'At top speed!' shouted his excitable ally. 'Mon Dieu! Elle a couru comme un lapin!'

Guani yawned politely and said, 'Gentlemen. Since midnight – and it is now ten to four – I have received three diplomatic Notes from the German Ambassador, two from the British Minister and two from the French. We are a small country which has imposed upon itself the heavy burden of Neutrality. Do not, I beg of you, make it any heavier.'

Millington-Drake gazed at the ceiling and went to the limit

127

of diplomatic good manners by murmuring mildly, but with a full consciousness of the seriousness of his question, 'Forgive me for asking, but will you be able to enforce your country's decision?'

Guani started, and turning towards the Englishman, opened his mouth to reply rather sharply. But at the same moment, M. Gentil exploded like a bomb.

'That is it! Where are the guns of the *Graf Spee* trained at this moment? Not at the enemy! No, oh no! All are trained upon the city of Montevideo. *Force majeure*, my dear Guani! *Force majeure*!'

It was blunt speaking. Guani's eyes flashed. He was no longer a patient, cosmopolitan, neutral diplomat, but a fiery Uruguayan patriot. The real issue had been brought into the open and he welcomed it. His nostrils dilated and a strange smile appeared upon his lips as he answered.

'M. Gentil! Mr Millington-Drake! In our short history my small country has survived many threats. We grow fat on threats! Each time we are threatened, my whole country takes a step forward. We are very simple. We are only two million people. We only understand a few things. Law we understand. Justice we understand. Threats we will never understand.'

He rose. He was immensely formidable. The great little man seemed to fill the room, as he finished with passion and dignity, 'See me! I am not big! But I have two million heads!'

There was no more to be said. The Ministers bowed and took their leave. Dawn was in the sky.

CHAPTER X

THURSDAY

MIKE FOWLER HAD seen the sun rise many times in his life, but usually when he was going to bed. On this occasion he was up and about long before the dawn. In the chilly hour before the sun rose, when the calm waters of the River Plate were no longer dark but the colour of lead, when a cold little wind was blowing, when the tall, modern apartment buildings which lined the long beaches of Montevideo were turning a fiery red in the glow from the eastern sky, Mike, driving his station-wagon and followed by three trucks belonging to the Telephone Company, came bumping along the empty beach and outside Manalo's. Manalo was no more an early riser than Mike was, which was just what the American had counted on. The place was shuttered and dark. On the ramshackle terrace, with its superb view over the harbour and city and out over the River Plate, the chairs and tables were stacked. There was nobody about except a small boy with freckles and a jam-jar, going fishing, who stopped and watched with great interest as the telephone engineers started to unload equipment, run out cables, and hook themselves up to the telephone system by land-line, all so that Mike could talk direct to New York. For he had got his commission from the recording-company, it was going to be a nation-wide hook-up, and the sky was the limit! Everything depended now upon getting the best viewpoint in Montevideo, and that was just what Manolo had. Mike knew Manolo and possession was nine points of the law, He had strictly enjoined silence on his helpers and work went ahead with all the orders in pantomime. Mike and Pop moved the chairs off the tables and installed the batteries of microphones at the very best corner table overlooking the beach and Harbour.

Monolo's hangs on the side of the Cerro, the hill which dominates Montevideo, and which is so much the only hill in the lovely and undulating country of Uruguay (for a country no more more than a woman likes to be described as flat) that it is known by no other name than The Hill. On its rocky summit is an old square fort. Long Spanish cannon, upon which children sit astride, point across to the tall buildings of the modern city. The Harbour is a natural one and is an almost perfect circle, two miles in diameter. To the north, on the city side, the tall buildings crowd down to the water's edge, with miles and miles of deep-water quays busy with shipping. On the other side is the Cerro, with long red, dusty cattle tracks winding over the hill and down to the shore, where the white buildings of the canning-factory stand on the water's edge, journey's end for cattle and gauchos after many miles of driving. Mike's station-wagon had been often held up for an hour, during which Pop rolled and smoked a dozen cigarettes, while the long lines of cattle wandered bawling by.

Outside the Harbour, the broad expanse of the River Plate stretched as far as the eye could see, broken only by two rocky lumps, reefs rather than islands, on one of which stood a lighthouse and on the other the old quarantine station. Just before sunrise Mike thought he could make out a plume of smoke and two black dots which could be the two British cruisers, but when the sun rose, a great orange shape, strangely squeezed by mirage into the shape of an hour-glass, they had vanished. Mike may have been right. Harwood was so determined that night not to lose contact with the *Graf Spee* that he closed both cruisers to a few thousand yards from the Harbour entrance during the hours of darkness and withdrew them out of sight as soon as the skies started to lighten.

Up to Montevideo, the river is deep and navigable with the usual shoals and banks clearly charted, but above the city the channel is buoyed and has to be dredged for vessels of deep draught. The Rivers Paraná and Uruguay, which drain four countries, bring every year an immense amount of mud rolling down from the Mato Grosso and the Gran Chaco. These two rivers, and their tributaries, form the immense body of water known as the Rio de la Plata to Latin-Americans, as the River Plata to North Americans, and as the River Plate to the insular and conservative English. A thousand miles is nothing to an American river and river steamers go up that distance and more when the river is high. But, although liners and even the biggest tankers go up to Buenos Aires, very few battleships would risk fouling up their water intake to pay a call on the Argentine capital. For this reason the Argentine Naval base is at Bahia Blanca; and for the same reason the British, from their base at Port Stanley in the Falkland Islands, have always made Montevideo their main port of call in South America; and since they have always been well-received they have come to regard it as practically a British harbour.

130

Some of these thoughts were passing through Jock McCall's mind, a few hours later, as he flew from Buenos Aires to Montevideo in the sea-plane which flies regularly every morning and afternoon between the two cities. Buenos Aires being a full Embassy and Montevideo only a Legation, the Naval Attaché's headquarters were at B.A., although many of his problems arose at Montevideo. This meant a lot of travelling to and fro. McCall found the sea-plane convenient for these trips, especially since the only alternative was an over-night journey in one of the two ferry-boats; majestic, Edwardian creations built by Cammell Laird in 1905, thick with panelling and richly vulgar decoration, including a Chinese dining-saloon and a wonderful, stuffy Bridal Suite which would have made any wedding night a complete fiasco. The ships were built of the best teak and mahogany, had three decks and it need hardly be said that the engines were as good as ever; so that there seemed no reason why they should ever go out of service. If some restless director of the Company should ever want to install two streamlined modern ships, public sentiment will probably forbid it. Except during political storms of short duration, the two cities are as closely connected as Hamburg and Cuxhaven. And the romances, quarrels and tragedies which must have started and finished upon these immense floating hotels must be innumerable. If ever they are retired from service, they should be preserved as monuments, one in either port, for future generations to see where so much was generated.

McCall knew the course of the seaplane by heart and had taken the precaution to seat himself on the starboard side so that he had an excellent view of the *Graf Spee* lying in the Outer Harbour as they approached the city and prepared to come down on the water near the Pocket battleship. There was great excitement as she was identified and all the passengers on the port side stood up and breathed hard down the necks of the lucky ones. But McCall, who owed his position to foresight, yielded not an inch from his own porthole and producing a large pair of Naval binoculars from his brief-case focused them greedily on the battleship.

'Oh, do let me look!' said the lady opposite, 'doesn't she look beautiful.'

'Yes, señora . . . from here,' answered McCall, ignoring the request and answering the question, meanwhile keeping the glasses close to his eyes.

'May I see?' insisted the lady with a winning smile that entirely wasted as McCall was engaged in counting the hits he could see on the superstructure.

He grunted, 'Please excuse me, señora. I have a special interest in the *Graf Spee*.'

The lady said, 'Oh,' and examined him rather doubtfully. He was wearing a light-coloured suit with a United Services Club tie, and in the rack was a Panama-hat with a coloured band of exuberant design. But his brown fingers, hawk-like profile, and keen black eyes, would have picked him out of any crowd.

The lady took another look at him and murmured, 'Isn't she an enormous ship?'

'Yes,' said her neighbour grimly; he added under his breath: 'And in *our* harbour.'

A square-ish lady on the other side of him, obviously an Axis partisan, who had been gazing with ecstasy at the Pocket battleship could contain herself no longer and exploded to the whole cabin, 'What a ship! What splendour! What power! What beauty! My friends! There is no people like the German people. They are invincible!'

This is the kind of positive statement which only embarrasses the English, so McCall gave her a tolerant smile, but his neighbour was at once up in arms and laying about her for the Allied cause, 'What do you mean, Señora? Have not the British chased the Germans into Montevideo?'

'It was a strategic withdrawal!' replied the other lady heatedly, striking her German-language newspaper a blow which would have routed Commodore Harwood himself.

'You talk like Hitler,' retorted McCall's lady-friend with spirit. 'I suppose your invincible Germans shot themselves full of holes in order to impress us neutrals!'

'Neutral, indeed! Ha, ha, ha. Listen to her. Where is her neutrality I wonder.'

'Where is yours?' came the smart retort.

'How dare you? I am a citizen of Uruguay!'

'How dare you? So am I!'

By now the passengers were divided into two camps (curiously enough nobody seemed to be neutral) and McCall, a man of peace while on shore, was preparing to dive under his seat before the two partisans came to grips, when the steward saved the situation by bellowing, 'Please fasten your seat-belts. We are about to land.'

The political discussion was postponed (it was renewed later in the Customs Shed) and the seaplane swept once around the Harbour before coming down on the water. McCall had been concentrating all his attention on the *Graf Spee* from the moment

132

that Montevideo came in sight and it was only now, as they passed over the moles and docks black with people, as he saw the hundreds of boats and small crafts which were thronging the Harbour, and thousands of people on every tall building and vantage point, that he began to realise what a sensation the arrival of the Pocket battleship had caused and what an important international drama, in which he was to be one of the chief actors, was developing before his eyes. The plane banked round. They were only a few hundred feet up and directly beneath him was the terrace of Manolo's bar. It was swarming with people, but he could see that a radio commentator was already installed with his microphone and sound-vans, and he wondered idly how he had managed to establish himself so early in such a unique position.

Much the same thoughts, although expressed more forcibly, were passing through Manolo's mind as he came out, yawning, into the bright sunlight to find microphone cables looping across his terrace like lianas, and Mike installed at his best corner table overlooking the Harbour, testing a direct line to New York while police held back the admiring crowd. Manolo had never had much time for the police – no night-club owner ever has – and the sight of so many of them protecting Mike made him see red. He advanced towards the invader, who was intoning over and over again into his microphone, 'Hello, New York. Hello, New York. Hello, New York. This is Mike Fowler calling you from the waterfront at Montevideo. Testing. Testing. Testing. Testing. One. Two. Three. Four. Are you receiving me? Are you receiving me? . . . Hey, Pop! Do your stuff! Keep checking. What do they say in the van? Are they getting us?'

There were excited voices from the sound-van, forty yards away, then Pop put his head out of the door and shouted, 'Man say no! Keep testing, Mike.'

Mike obeyed and started his 'Hello, New York. Hello, New York,' just as Manolo came out and burst into a flood of furious Spanish, much to the delight of the crowd.

'Hell, Manolo,' said Mike, 'nice to see you. How's the boy? Hey, Pop! Come and tell Manolo what it's all about; I'm busy. Hello, New York. This is Mike Fowler, your special reporter, calling from the waterfront at Montevideo. Testing. Testing. . . .'

He continued while Pop ambled up and went at it hammer-and-tongs with Manolo, who was quite worked up. Pop perched himself on the rail of the terrace and rolled a cigarette. The more furious Manalo became the more Pop seemed to agree with him.

He nodded and nodded again, and finally reported to Mike, 'Manolo say we must clear out from Manolo's bar.'

Mike said, 'Hello, New York . . . Tell him I'm reporting on the *Graf Spee* to the whole of the United States. Tell him that this is the best view in Montevideo. Tell him that we have a permit from the Post Office. Tell him. . . . Well, go on! Tell him! And rub it on about the permit.'

There was another burst of Spanish, then Pop reported again, 'Manolo he say you have no permit from him.'

By now Dolores in a wrapper and painting her finger-nails had come on to the terrace and a waiter in a green shirt had stopped sweeping so that he could listen better. Mike said with angelic patience, 'Testing. Testing. Tell him I'll mention Manolo's bar in my broadcast. Tell him he'll be famous. Tell him his joint will be famous. . . . ' His eye was caught by Dolores' shapely leg and as Manolo followed the look, she yawned and stretched like a cat in the sun. 'Tell him all the Americans will come to Montevideo to photograph the *Graf Spee* and they'll all have drinks in Manolo's bar. Manolo will be not only famous but rich!'

Dolores began to look interested and moved closer to Mike, who went on testing while the two Uruguayans fought it out. Presently Pop reported, 'Manolo he say the British will sink the *Graf Spee* before the American tourists get here, and he can make money now at this table where you sitting. And four people can have drinks at this table, or maybe six.'

He winked at Mike. It was in the bag. From now on it was only a question of negotiation – and of course commission. The crowd breathed and followed the negotiations with flattering interest as Mike replied, 'O.K. Tell him he can bring me six Scotches every half-hour as long as I stay here. Show him the dough.'

A tremendous Spanish palaver gave Mike three minutes' clear testing before Pop announced, 'Señor Mike! Six double-Scotches every quarter of an hour! I think the best we can do.'

Mike looked sourly at Manolo who spread his hands with an ingratiating smile thinking that he had overplayed it; but to his relief the American said, 'O.K. But, Pop, he provides the bottles free to pour the drinks back. I can't drink on the job, but I'm not going to waste good Scotch.'

Manolo, all smiles now, clapped Mike on the back and proclaimed, 'Estamos.'

Pop said, 'It's a deal.'

Mike observed drily, 'He's not knocking himself out any, is he? Get back on the job, Pop . . . Hello, New York. Hello, New York. Testing. Testing. This is Mike Fowler reporting from the waterfront at Montevideo on the *Graf Spee*. Are you receiving me? It is now 11 a.m. local time. This morning at 9 a.m. the official visits started, and a Technical Commission appointed by the Uruguayan Government went on board to assess the damage to the ship. . . . '

If Mike could only have known, one of the biggest sensations of the whole adventure was about to break upon the world, which until now knew nothing of the existence of Captain Dove and his fellow-prisoners on board the *Graf Spee*. The British Consul had been warned that she was carrying English prisoners and a tug had been ordered to take them ashore. But no visitors except the official representatives of the Uruguayan Government and Navy, and the German Ambassador, were allowed on board the Pocket battleship. Compared with the battered condition of the *Exeter* the damage to the *Graf Spee* may have been superficial and her casualty list low, but at a period in history when Germany, with her subject-states, was the greatest Power in Europe, it would have been unthinkable to allow other less-subservient nations to see that she was as vulnerable as the rest of the human race.

This illusion of absolute power and the necessity of preserving it, influenced every move of the Germans in the political battle that was to be waged during the next four days; and since, in a totalitarian State, the politicians call the tune, and compose it as well, they also influenced every decision Langsdorff had to make. It is as well to remember this during the events that led up to the final tragedy.

When well-led, there is no better human material than a German, but what is one to make of a nation which inevitably chooses madmen for its leaders? The crew of the *Graf Spee* was no exception. Most of the seamen were very young and had believed everything that Hitler and Goebbels told them. The sea, with its traditions and its stern realities, is not a good breading-ground for politicians and their slogans, but the canker was there in the *Graf Spee,* and during the next fateful days in harbour, it fed upon doubt and flourished upon dishonour. At sea they had a Captain in Langsdorff whom they would have followed anywhere. They had been shipmates for four months. They had lived together, triumphed, and fought in battle together. They were still a closed community. They were that

135

wonderful thing, a well-worked up ship under a Captain whom they trusted. So they had toiled all night cleaning up, making everything ship-shape, patching the holes with canvas and painting them over, cutting away wreckage and concealing damage, rigging awnings and ladders, until at breakfast-time orders were given for every man to see to his personal appearance before turning in, while the Captain, his Officers, and the watch on deck, still sleepless, shaved and dressed in the formal dress of the day to receive the first official callers. It was a transformed ship, trim with huge, snow-white awnings and gay with flags, with pipe-clayed ropes and with canvas and carpets underfoot, that met the eyes of Dove and his fellow-prisoners when they were finally allowed on deck with their bundles under their arms. They were fit enough, but pale from their long confinement, and they blinked in the bright sunlight. Their old shipmates, Lieutenant Hertzberg and the Master-at-Arms, escorted them for the last time. They looked wonderingly at the tall buildings of Montevideo against the blue sky of early summer, at the crowded shipping around them, and shook their heads in silent amazement. Even Dove was speechless. It was only weeks later that they would find words to describe their experience and its dream-like ending. To the reporters, who later besieged them on shore, they had disappointingly little to say. What could they say? There was either too much or too little to tell: they had been Masters in their own ships, they had lost everything, they had been helpless prisoners for many weeks, they had been in battle and in danger of their lives, and now they were free. So they shook their heads once more and talked together in low tones with Hertzberg and the Master-at-Arms, as they waited for the tug to come alongside. They did not belong in this ship, but they did not belong anywhere else, and it would take days of freedom and the ecstasy of reading loving messages, penned by shaky hands and eyes dim with tears, to wake them from their dream.

A messenger came and spoke to Hertzberg who said: 'Captain Dove! Our Captain wishes to see you.'

Dove had not expected the summons, but he found that he had been waiting for it. He nodded, gave his bundle to Stubbs to hold, and followed Hertzberg to Langsdorff's harbour cabin. Once more Dove and Langsdorff confronted one another and each man thought it was for the last time. The German Captain looked at the burly Englishman with affection and Dove solemnly returned his gaze. Langsdorff looked tired and pale. He wore his formal white uniform with epaulettes; his belt, with the small-sword of the German Navy, lay upon the table ready to be assumed. He had managed to get his wounded left arm into his tunic and only a certain stiffness betrayed it. His scalp wound and the wound on his chin had been cleverly cleaned and dressed, but he had shaved off his dapper little beard and it made him look much younger. His manner, too, had changed: behind his eyes there was a constant question.

Now he looked at Dove's honest face and forgot the troubles pressing on him in the pleasure of their personal relationship. It was with an echo of their previous meetings that he said, 'Well, Captain Dove.'

Dove answered gravely, 'Well, Captain Langsdorff!'

Langsdorff's charming smile played across his sensitive face and he stepped quickly forward, holding out his hand. Dove took it and Langsdorff said with friendly warmth. 'I'm glad you're all right.'

With equal sincerity Dove replied, 'Thanks for everything. You've done your best for us and I can only wish you the best for yourself.'

Langsdorff thanked him and sent his good wishes to the other prisoners. He was insistent that Dove should not forget to wish them well on his behalf. Then with a sudden thought he added. 'Wish them a happy Christmas! Yes. A happy Christmas.'

For a moment his thoughts were far away. Then he returned to the present with a jerk and said, 'Is there anything else I can do for you?'

Dove nodded slowly, 'If you wouldn't mind, sir, could you tell me the names of our ships that engaged you?'

Langsdorff's eyes flickered and he answered, 'There were three of them: the *Exeter*, the *Ajax* and another of the same class. I think it must have been *Achilles*.'

Dove said anxiously, 'What happened? Were any of them sunk?'

Lanksdorff shook his head, ' . . . We badly damaged the *Exeter* but she was still afloat the last time I sighted her . . . we could have fought two of your ships, but three was too much for us.'

Dove said gently, 'Would you mind telling me what happened?'

Langsdorff nodded and said, 'Yes.' But he did not speak at once. He walked over to his big chart-table and bent over the chart of the River Plate. Dove waited. After a little Langsdorff started to speak, living the battle over again in his mind, 'It was a classic action. Both sides fought well. My men – my young boys and men – fought magnificently. Their courage was beyond praise. Both sides could claim a victory – I suppose both sides will – and they would both be right. The British Commander was a brilliant strategist. He divided my fire from the start. I concentrated my guns on the biggest cruiser. I could have sunk her but the others pressed me so hard that they made me divide my fire again. I had three ships to fight and I couldn't take my eyes off one of them.'

His voice changed, and it was with open admiration that he continued. 'The *Exeter* was magnificent. I put her forward turrets out of action. I smashed her bridge. She was on fire, out of control and veering round in figures of eight. But the Captain regained control and went on fighting. They only had one gun left and they fought me with that! They kept on attacking me.'

Dove was spellbound.

Langsdorff paused, then made a gesture and said, 'When you fight brave men like that, there is no enmity. You want only to shake hands. The *Ajax* and her sister-ship came at me like destroyers. They couldn't do much harm with their six-inch guns and they tried to torpedo me. They fired ten torpedoes. Some were very close. I said to myself, "They would never dare to do this unless they were supported by big ships". . . . '

He paused again then continued ' . . . Yes . . . I thought they were trying to drive me out into the guns of bigger ships. . . . '

He ceased speaking though he continued to look down at the chart. Dove waited but he had obviously said all he had to say. Finally Dove asked, 'What shall you do now, Captain?'

For the first time in their relationship Langsdorff spoke unnaturally. He straightened up and answered, as if he were making a statement for publication, 'I have asked the Uruguayan Government to let me carry out necessary repairs. These things are governed by International Law. There is a Technical Commission on board now. My galleys have been wiped out, my store-rooms shot away. I cannot feed my men.'

He hesitated, then added in the same tone, 'I am not going to take my men out to sea to commit suicide.'

Suddenly he recollected to whom he was talking, drew himself up and said rather formally, 'Well, I suppose you have to go?'

Dove nodded. Langsdorff picked up two black cap-ribbons printed with *Admiral Graff Spee* in letters of gold, which had been lying on his chart-table, fingered them for a moment, then suddenly handed them to Dove, saying, 'Take them . . . from the caps of two of my men who fell in battle . . . souvenirs!'

Dove took them and held them in his big hands, and said slowly, 'Thank you – very much.'

The door opened and Captain Kay came in. He nodded to Dove and said to Langsdorff in English, 'The Uruguayan Technical Commission have finished their inspection and are about to leave.'

Langsdorff nodded and called his servant, who appeared and helped him to buckle on his belt and sword. Dove stood waiting to say good-bye, but Langsdorff seemed almost to have forgotten his presence. Then, as he picked up his cap, he saw him and said, 'Good-bye, Captain. We are not likely to meet again.'

But he was wrong.

The Technical Commission consisted of the two officers who had visited the ship the night before: Captains Varela and Fontana. Although their report and their recommendations were vitally necessary to Langsdorff, a good deal of the damage had been concealed from them. For this the Gestapo and Dr Goebbels' propaganda-machine were responsible. German pride and prestige were at odds with the hard facts. The Commission was hurried by much of the damage; much else was already camouflaged. They had seen little the night before and their main impression had been of the human casualties, the sight of the dead and wounded. Great play was made now for their benefit of the damage to the galleys and store-rooms, and nothing was said about the far more serious damage to the evaporators. The few hits that could not be concealed, particularly those near the water-line, were dismissed as superficial by the Germans themselves. By the time the Commission took their leave, they believed in all good faith that the damage was far less than in fact it was.

Both on their arrival and at their departure, they were treated with respect and formality that one Power owes to another on such occasions. However much the German Ambassador ashore might try to bully Dr Guani, Captain Langsdorff, as a sailor who had been reared in the traditions of the Imperial German Navy, knew how to conduct himself. He and his Officers formed up on the quarter-deck beside the gangway and there was a Guard of Honour. After saluting the Commission, Langsdorff chatted a moment with Varela. He said that his ship would need a fortnight in port for repairs. He wanted to know how long they would allow him and said that the life of the ship depended upon it.

It has already been described in what way Varela had formed different conclusions. He respected Langsdorff, but not knowing all the facts he saw no reason to change his opinion. He was a man of high principle and, like the rest of his Government, he acted throughout in a spirit of complete neutrality. He was always emphatic that no pressure was brought to bear upon him by any Foreign Power. He answered Langsdorff that it was not in his power to say how long a time would be granted. He could only report to his Government who would then make their decision. Langsdorff nodded and stepped back to his Officers. The two parties saluted each other again, the Uruguayans went over the side and returned to the *Lavalleja,* where they stood to attention once more and saluted as the corvette drew away. Like the Germans, the officers of the Commission were wearing full dress and swords.

After the seaplane from Buenos Aires had landed, there was an irritating delay before the passengers got ashore. The motor boat which should have been in attendance was away taking sightseers to look at the *Graf Spee.* As soon as he landed, McCall took a taxi to the British Legation, which was situated in a pleasant house, with its own garden, on the edge of a park outside the city. He found Millington-Drake with all the books on International Law spread out on the desk in front of him and, at the moment when the Uruguayan Technical Commission was going ashore, the British Minister was expounding his tactics.

'It all comes down to this: according to International Law, no beligerent warship can stay in any neutral harbour longer than twenty-four hours without being interned. After that everything turns upon the Emergency Clause. If the Germans want to apply it and ask for time to carry out repairs to make the ship sea-worthy, I shall resist it with every pressure I can bring to bear.'

McCall asked, 'I suppose the French will help?'

'Certainly. You can be sure of that. We consult together on every move we make – but we make the moves separately.' He smiled. 'You know Monsieur Gentil, don't you? The prestige of France is quite safe in his hands. Of course the ideal thing would be for Uruguay to stick her toes in and threaten to intern *Graf Spee* after twenty-four hours, which would drive her out to where Harwood is waiting for her. But I'm afraid there's no hope of that. They're bound to grant an extension. How long depends upon the Commission's report.'

McCall said thoughtfully. 'I wish I could be sure what Harwood wants.'

'Admiralty are talking to him every hour by code through the Falklands. You could do the same.'

'That wouldn't do. I must see him.'

Millington-Drake raised his eyebrows. 'At sea? Won't that be a bit difficult?'

McCall murmured, 'Ray Martin will find a way.'

The Minister looked alarmed and said, 'Now don't bring me into your cloak-and-dagger manoeuvres! I'll look after the political side. . . . I suppose you're keeping a watch on the *Graf Spee*?'

McCall answered in the same tone, 'Ray Martin is.'

There was a knock at the door and Miss Esther Shaw, the Grey Eminence of British politics in Uruguay, put her head in.

'Minister! Have you seen the crowd outside? I think we shall have to ask for police protection.'

The two men went to the window and Millington-Drake stepped outside. He was greeted with the sort of screams which are usually reserved for film stars. He blenched, for although enormously popular, he was a modest man and, after giving a half-hearted Royal-from-balcony wave, he stepped hastily back into the safety of his office. The telephone on his desk buzzed and Miss Shaw answered it.

'Yes. But who is it? . . . He won't give his name? . . . Yes, Captain McCall is here. . . . Very well. Put him on.'

Meanwhile the Minister was wandering back, shaking his head, 'Who are they all? I never saw such a thing in Montevideo. And at this hour in the morning, too.'

'It is a great tribute to the splendid work you have been doing here, Minister,' said Miss Shaw with decision. One felt that she included herself in the compliment, and rightly. 'I've had enquiries made, and they're all people of British sympathies who have come here in person to tell you so, and to offer their services to the Allied cause.'

There was no more to be said. Like a competent executive, she had wrapped the situation up into pithy sentences and disposed of it.

Millington-Drake said, 'Ah,' rather weakly, but in a gratified manner, McCall said breezily, 'Take their names, Miss Shaw. We'll screen them later. We've got to keep a twenty-four hour watch on the *Graf Spee* and we shall need plenty of volunteers.'

Miss Shaw nodded and said on the telephone, 'Yes. This is the Minister's office. Yes, Captain McCall is here. Who is speaking? . . . Yes, but who is speaking? . . . Very well.'

She put her hand over the receiver and said, in the indulgent tone of a mother whose children are playing cops-and-robbers,

'Mr Martin is calling, Captain McCall. He won't give his name, but I know his voice.'

'One up to you, Miss Shaw,' said McCall. 'Will you have a cigar or a bag of nuts?' Miss Shaw always brought out the schoolboy in him. Fortunately she had a weak spot for Naval officers. She answered, 'Nuts, please. Brazils,' handed him the telephone and left the room as efficiently as she had entered it.

Ray Martin was down by the docks. Like Mike, he had a good eye for a commanding position. However, it was not so much of the *Graf Spee* that he was interested in but the people who visited her. He had installed himself in a shack with a wide window which overlooked the Harbour and commanded every movement between the Pocket battleship and the shore. It might have been a ship-chandler's office, or a time keeper's office, or a Customs office, or all three, for Martin was a secretive man and is not likely to write his memoirs. But for four days and three nights it was known as Martin's Look-Out, and we know that from it he, McCall, and any others who were involved in their nefarious plans, had their quarry always before their eyes, night and day.

Insignificant as ever, Ray Martin was sitting in a sea of newspapers, chain-smoking and throwing the half-smoked butts into an old can which he invariably missed. He was a man who smoked in his bath and in his bed. He was not considered a good insurance risk either by his friends or by his invisible employers, but somehow nothing ever seemed to happen to him. In those days anyone who wanted a telephone installed in Montevideo had to wait six months, yet by some unknown means Ray Martin had one hooked up two hours after he had moved in. A marine telescope stood on a stand beside him, trained upon the starboard gangway of the *Graf Spee,* the one where all distinguished visitors were received, and one of his wide-open pale eyes was glued to it while he waited for McCall to speak on the other end of the wire.

Presently he said, without taking his eye from the telescope, 'That you, McCall? Our friends have already delivered a Note to the proper quarter. It is being studied now . . . two weeks my informant says . . . yes – well you'd better get down here as soon as you can. . . . Our old friend, Langsdorff? Yes. I'm looking at him now. He seems to be a high-class person.'

McCall said, 'I'll be down before lunch. Yes, I'll bring some sandwiches,' and rang off. Thoughtfully he remarked, 'Martin says they have asked officially for two weeks to make repairs. Do you think they'll get it?'

'Not if I can help it,' was the reply. 'What's their strategy?'

McCall considered. 'It can only be to lull everybody off their guard and then to make a dash for it,' he decided. 'Our two cruisers are no match for the *Graf Spee*'s guns, but they've got the legs of her. They've re-fuelled by now and they've got their oiler with them. *Graf Spee* will sail with full tanks, too, but this time she won't have the *Altmark* standing by. Harwood will never let her out of sight, if he knows when she is sailing. So Langsdorff's only chance is to have several nights to choose from and to make a dash out to sea on one of them under cover of darkness. He might get away with it. The human element comes into it. The strain on the watchers is terrific but the quarry can choose his own time. Yes, I'm sure that's his plan. Our job is to get him out – or interned – within twenty-four hours, if possible. . . . Any news of the *Cumberland*? That would make things a bit more even.'

H.M.S. *Cumberland*, a three-funnel cruiser, had been heard of last on the eve of the battle cleaning boilers in the Falkland Islands, and was not expected to be in service again for at least ten days. She was the nearest capital-ship to the River Plate and, with her eight-inch turrets, would certainly make a formidable addition to Harwood's small force.

'Nothing further,' replied Millington-Drake. 'She must be keeping wireless silence. As you know, the Admiralty ordered her up from the Falklands yesterday afternoon. But I suppose, at the most optimistic guess, she couldn't be here before the week-end, could she?'

'Afraid not,' grunted McCall. 'But you haven't answered my question. Will H.M. Government put enough pressure on Guani to throw the *Graf Spee* out?'

'You're asking a good deal,' said Millington-Drake drily, 'but you can count on us to do our best. There are Notes going every hour, of course – from both sides. Meanwhile the report of the Technical Commission is being considered. The crucial interview between Guani and Langmann is at seven o'clock.' He permitted himself a smile, 'He is seeing our French Ally at five o'clock and myself at six, so he should be well-primed for his interview.'

Millington-Drake's remark was a bit cynical although, of course, it was true that the utmost pressure was being brought to bear by the Allies upon Uruguay to turn the hunted ship out.

Equal pressure was being brought to bear by Germany to let her stay. The alternative was internment. Uruguay's wish, on the other hand, was to get rid of her unwelcome visitor as quickly and as politely as possible. But although a strict interpretation of International Law meant that the *Graf Spee* must sail at the end of twenty-four hours (after sunset on that very evening), there were also the decencies of international relationships to be observed. Millington-Drake might brag a little to McCall that relentless pressure was being brought to bear upon Dr Guani, and it was true, but he was the most tactful of men and nobody knew better than he that, although Guani's sympathies were well-known, and although German influence was very strong in South America, particularly in Uruguay's nearest neighbour across the River Plate, the Foreign Minister was a man of great personal and moral courage, and could be relied upon to implement his country's decision with strict impartiality and as firmly as if he had been the Foreign Minister of a great Power. Since Uruguay was a well-governed country, his colleagues knew this and, having reached a decision, left him to handle it alone.

At a few minutes before seven that evening when Millington-Drake, with many polite courtesies and small chat, took his leave, Dr Langmann and Captain Langsdorff were already waiting in the ante-room. Although affecting to ignore his two enemies, the British Minister glanced covertly at the German Captain as he passed by. A student of human nature, he simply could not resist it. He decided that the fellow looked a first-class serving-officer and every inch a sailor. Langsdorff was dressed for a formal call. The white uniform with its gold trimmings suited him. The German Minister was seated, but the German sailor stood erect, staring straight in front of him, his only movement a light tapping of his hand on his sword-hilt. Millington-Drake passed directly across his line of vision yet he gave no sign of having seen him. Perhaps he had not. His eyes were far away. Millington-Drake was impressed and, he admitted aferwards, moved. That was long afterwards for, in diplomacy, emotion is only a counter in the game: something to be exploited in your opponent and concealed in yourself. Still this man's reputation for humanity and good seamanship had already impressed the world and now here he was, slim, ardent, pale and younger than Millington-Drake had expected. What was passing through his mind, the Englishman wondered?

It was still a minute or two to the hour. Guani's buzzer sounded and the secretary went in. There was a murmur of

144

voices. The two Germans waited patiently. Neither looked at the other; there was nothing to discuss. Precisely at seven o'clock the secretary reappeared, opened the doors wide and announced them. After some rather stiff courtesies at the door they entered, Langmann leading the way.

Dr Guani had already risen to receive his visitors. Langmann gave a flip of his hand, à la Ribbentrop, which passed for a Nazi salute to a small nation, and said, 'Señor Ministro. You have already met Kapitan Hans Langsdorff, Commandant of the *Admiral Graf Spee*.'

Langsdorff saluted. Guani bowed and said, 'Please sit down, gentlemen. Let's forget formalities.'

Langsdorff flashed him a quick smile but continued to walk quickly up and down as if he were on a quarter-deck, at some distance from the two politicians. Langmann sat down carefully on the same uncomfortable sofa and said, 'Your Excellency is well aware of the facts.'

Guani took him up smoothly, 'Let me see if I have got them right.' He put on his glasses, searched on his desk, and, finding a particular paper, read it aloud, 'Early yesterday morning, off Punta del Este, a Naval battle took place. The German Pocket battleship, *Admiral Graf Spee,* was engaged by three British cruisers, the *Exeter,* the *Ajax* and the *Achilles.* In the course of this engagement, the German battleship gained a victory. The British cruiser *Exeter* was seen to be shot to pieces and the other British cruisers fled. The *Graf Spee* herself received a few minor hits – '

Langsdorff abruptly stopped his quarter-deck walk and looked meaningly at his Ambassador, who hastily interrupted: 'That is not correct.'

'No?' said Guani.

'No,' was the firm reply, 'the *Graf Spee* has suffered serious damage. She is not seaworthy.'

With an air of astonishment, Guani exclaimed, 'But I am quoting the official communiqué of your own Government, quoted by your own official agency, the Deutsches Nachtrichten-bureau, issued today at 13.15, Greenwich Mean Time.'

Langmann forced a smile at the Minister's little joke and explained laboriously, 'Your Excellency knows that official news in wartime has to take into consideration the psychology of the people, the maintenance of morale, the – but, of course, Your Excellency is joking.'

Guani smiled politely and waited to see if the German Ambassador was going on, but he said no more. So the Foreign Minister turned in his chair and addressed Langsdorff, who had remained silent and motionless during the fencing-match between the two diplomats. It was a direct question that Guani put to him: 'Captain Langsdorff, how would you assess the damage to your ship?'

Langsdorff thought carefully before he answered, 'My galleys have been destroyed. I cannot feed my men. As for other damage . . . you have sent a Technical Commission on board and I have shown them everything.'

Guani nodded and, still addressing himself directly to Langsdorff, replied, 'I have their report. How much time would you say was necessary to make you seaworthy?'

It was a straight question calling for a straight answer. Langsdorff knitted his brows and made some quick calculations. Before he could answer Langmann cut in quickly, saying firmly, 'My own assessment is two or three weeks.' He paused and then repeated with meaning emphasis, 'At least two weeks,' and fixed his protruding eyes upon the Foreign Minister.

Guani said, 'My Commission suggests forty-eight hours.'

The blow was a direct one. Langmann nearly had a seizure. Langsdorff said sharply, 'Your Excellency! There are sixty-four hits on the superstructure alone!'

Guani looked calmly down at the report in front of him and answered, 'Sixty-five.'

The two Germans exchanged a look of utter amazement. The little Foreign Minister rose and, in the most formal tones, said: 'In view of this report and of your Government's request to extend the twenty-four hour period under the Emergency Clause of International Agreement, my Government has decided to grant an extension of seventy-two hours in order to render your ship, the *Admiral Graf Spee,* seaworthy, the time-limit to expire at 8 p.m. on Sunday the 17th December – ' He paused. Langmann had made a sudden violent movement forward. The veins stood out on his head as he glared across the wide desk at this calm little man, who was treating the express wishes of the great German people as if they were a routine request to be dealt with on its face-value. He would have spoken, but Guani held him with his eye, and without raising his voice or altering his tone, continued, ' – but prohibiting, in accordance with the Articles of the Thirteenth Hague Convention any repairs for the purpose of increasing the fighting strength of the vessel.'

Langsdorff listened with bowed head. He said nothing. For him it was a death sentence.

Langmann and Guani stared at one another. The German's eyes dropped first. He looked at Langsdorff and back at Guani. He tried to speak and could find no words. He was in a situation which had not been envisaged by his superiors, and he could see no way out of it. Himself a bully, he was completely unprepared for the knock-out blow which his small adversary had just given him. Guani's eyes were fixed steadily upon him, gentle but inflexible; behind him on the wall hung the portrait of Artigas; and behind the picture the whole force of law and of democracy. It was in a strange, heavy voice that the German Ambassador said at last: 'I most strongly protest!'

Guani answered coldly, 'I note your protest,' and rang the bell for his secretary to show the two visitors out.

After they had gone, he walked to the window and stood there thinking, his hands behind his back. The sun was setting and the lights were coming on in the city. It could have been a symbol of the event in history which had just taken place. For a long time Guani stood there, his mind full of many things, as the room faded into darkness, while out on the broad bosom of the River Plate the shadowy forms of the two hunters closed silently in.

The final event of that eventful Thursday came at 2200 hours, when the lynx-eyed Swanston, who could apparently see as well in the dark as he could in the daytime, reported, 'Bearing Red Three-Eight. A dark object. Bearing Red Three-Eight.'

The two cruisers had closed Montevideo Harbour in company to a distance of about four miles, so that they could be sure to detect the *Graf Spee* if she sailed. They were steaming at cruising stations about eight cables apart. The night was dark but clear, and visibility with glasses was about two miles – for normal eyesight. Swanston's dark object seemed to be about three or four miles away. It was quite impossible for *Graf Spee* to have slipped out, but this ship, if ship it were, approaching from the south-east and showing no lights, could only be a warship. Sound carries a long distance across water at night, so Swanston's report was given in quiet tones, which made the words sound even more ominous than they were.

Although at cruising stations, Captain Woodhouse was on the bridge. During most of the nights off Montevideo he slept there. So did Parry, whose legs were so stiff that he couldn't sleep much anyway. He had a deck-chair brought up on

Achilles's bridge and took cat-naps. His wounds were painful but were healing well. He wasn't very mobile but he was able to get around.

At Swanston's words, every glass on the bridge of the *Ajax* was levelled to starboard and the gun control-tower started to swing round. The report was confirmed. It was a large ship approaching from the south of English Bank. Meanwhile Harwood, having been informed of the presence of a strange ship came on deck. Woodhouse gave a quiet order, 'Alarm starboard. Prepare to challenge.'

To the Yeoman of Signals he said, 'Make to *Achilles*: "Alarm Starboard, Bearing Red Three-Eight. A dark object".'

Shaded lights started to wink between the two ships and their gun turrets swung round. All this was done very quietly and orders were given in whispers while the two ships continued to slip along through the water at twelve knots. The tension was almost unbearable as everyone strained their eyes through the darkness to identify the approaching vessel. In the control-tower the Gunnery Officer reported, 'Target!' over the voice-pipe to the bridge, and gave the order to the turrets to load and come to the Ready. Harwood stood close to Woodhouse, with his eyes to his glasses like everybody else. All this had taken not much more than a minute. 'Guns' reported in a low but clear voice, 'Captain, sir! Ready to open fire!'

Woodhouse glanced at Harwood, who nodded, and replied, 'All right, Guns.' Then to his Yeoman, who was standing like a terrier at his elbow, he ordered, 'Challenge!'

It was a breath-taking moment. The Yeoman had in his hand the same shaded directional signal lamp with which he had been signalling *Achilles*. He raised it and, sighting the strange vessel, he made a short signal. The clicking of the lamp sounded unnaturally loud in the breathless hush which had fallen. He stopped. The reply might easily be a full broadside. 'Guns' put his thumb on the firing bell. Then through the darkness a lamp started to wink in reply.

The message was in English and was as follows:

'*CUMBERLAND* TO *AJAX* SORRY BUT I'M A STRANGER HERE.'

At the same time the G.C.T. reported that the strange object was identified as a three-funnel cruiser.

After the first roar of relief and amusement, Harwood said, 'It's a miracle!'

Woodhouse nodded. 'Miracle or not, sir, we can certainly do with her.'

The same thought was being expressed, in a slightly different way, in *Achilles,* where that romantic realist, Washbourn, was saying to Parry: 'Good old *Cumberland*! She'll be the first target if and when *Spee* comes out. While she's throwing bricks at *Cumberland,* we can get in and torpedo her.'

'Ask her how the blazes she managed to steam a thousand miles in thirty-five hours,' exclaimed Harwood, who still couldn't believe that he had another eight-inch cruiser here in the River Plate under his command. The signal was made and acknowledged.

'*Cumberland* answering, sir,' reported the Chief Yeoman.

The Captain of the *Cumberland* was a master of the laconic style, as was proved by his answer:

'ANTICIPATION.'

CHAPTER XI

FRIDAY

'IT'S MIDNIGHT, BILL,' said Mrs Thompson to her husband, 'time to call General Bowes.'

Bill Thompson, who was a brewing-engineer, took the binoculars from his eyes, rubbed them, nodded, yawned, then opened the door of the car and climbed out of the driving seat. He looked critically at the headlights, which were full on, and said, 'Battery needs charging. Start the engine up, darling.'

Mrs Thompson pressed the starter and the Dodge began ticking over. Bill walked down the long row of private cars which were lined up on the quay, with all their headlights pointing towards the *Graf Spee*. Late on Thursday, she had moved from the Outer to the Inner Harbour to facilitate repairs which were going on day and night, and she was only a few hundred yards from the quay. Her own lights had been repaired and she was surrounded by tugs and lighters which were burning flares. Welding was going on. The headlights of the cars illuminated her from stem to stern. She looked like the star of a show lit up by spotlights. The owners of the cars were all in them taking watch and watch, some sitting with binoculars in the front seat, others taking their turn to sleep in the back. They were all British volunteers. Bill Thompson came to an old-fashioned Rolls Royce at the end of the line. He looked into the lush interior where General Bowes, a portly, retired soldier, was slumbering on red leather upholstery and framed by silver-mounted speaking-tubes, cigar-cutters, vanity cases, mirrors and flower-vases. He contemplated this splendid spectacle for a moment, but duty was duty. He leant across to the driving seat, where the chauffeur was snoring profoundly, and put his lips to the vulcanite mouthpiece of the old-fashioned speaking-tube, through which he blew a creditable imitation of a rousing bugle-call. The General stirred and the chauffeur started and hit his head. Bill said, 'Wake up, General! Your turn as sentry.' But the General was already climbing out, keen as mustard. Bill handed over the binoculars and said, 'You're on till two o'clock, then you wake Mrs Attwater and hand over to her.'

'By gad! Never thought I'd be rousting Mamie Attwater out of bed at two in the morning,' chuckled the General. 'Shows what war does for you. Anything happened?'

'Work still going on,' reported Thompson. 'The German Ambassador went on board just now.'

'Hah!' said the General thoughtfully. 'Did you tell the Secret Service boys?'

Thompson said, 'Yes,' with a jerk of his head towards Ray Martin's Look-Out. 'But they don't miss much.'

Martin and McCall were eating bacon sandwiches and drinking strong tea which they had made for themselves on a primus. The big telescope was trained on the illuminated *Graf Spee* and this time McCall was on the watch. Ray Martin, who was lying on a battered cane chair staring at the ceiling, was recounting a recent experience between bites of his sandwich.

'I found him in his office looking damned unco-operative. I said, "Chemineau! I want to hire your shipyard until Sunday night." He said it wasn't for hire. I said, "I'll double any other offer you get." He looked at me as if he were going to hit me and said, "That is not necessary, Señor Martin. I have refused the Germans already." '

McCall grunted, 'Stout fellow. Did you ask him why?'

Martin said, 'No. Why should I care so long as he refuses.' He munched his sandwich and added: 'He told me anyway. He had two reasons.'

'What were they?'

'One was that his grandfather was a Frenchman. I said just to tease him, "But you're not French. You're Uruguayan." He looked at me very sourly and said, "That's my other reason".'

McCall nodded. 'Yes. The Uruguayans are all right. They don't like the Nazis any more than we do. What's the news from B.A.?'

'A tug is coming. . . . Hamburg-Amerika line . . . bringing welding equipment and sheet metal . . . should be here by the morning.'

McCall remarked wishfully: 'If I were the Uruguayans, I'd put an embargo on the stuff as soon as it entered port.'

Martin murmured, 'You've given me an idea.'

After a ruminative pause, he said, 'I'm worried about the *Tacoma.*'

McCall repeated, 'The *Tacoma?* That's the big German merchantman that's been lying up here for some time, isn't it?' Martin nodded.

'What about her?'

'They could use her in several ways,' was the answer. 'As a decoy duck; or for passing messages; or even for smuggling somebody on board. She could be very useful to them. Her Captain is a bit of a swashbuckler and he's bound to do anything he's asked. I'll keep an eye on them. If we can trump up some excuse we might get them interned for actively aiding a belligerent warship,' he added with relish. Intrigue of this sort was meat and drink to Martin.

McCall reported, 'Langmann's just leaving.'

'He's probably been to discuss the arrangements for the funeral. They're going to make a big splash of it. Don't blame them. Nothing like a funeral to get popular sympathy,' said the cynical Martin.

'When is it? Tomorrow?'

'Today,' replied Martin, looking at his watch, '16.00 hours.'

There was a long silence while McCall watched Longmann go ashore and drive away, and Martin stared at the ceiling. He broke it by remarking, 'We ought to be doing more.'

McCall said briskly, 'Quite agree. Harwood would want us to attack. He won his battle by the use of the offensive spirit. He expects us to do the same.'

Martin murmured with an exquisite accent, ' "De l'audace, en encore de l'audace et toujours de l'audace!" '

McCall repeated it meditatively, with a Dartmouth accent, and asked, 'Who said that?'

'Danton.'

McCall observed, 'I never hear a foreign quotation without thinking that an Englishman would have said it better.' He thought a moment, then added, 'And shorter.'

Martin grinned, 'Example? In this case?'

But the British Navy was, to mix a metaphor, on firm ground. 'Harwood has said it better,' replied McCall: ' "My object: destruction." '

'You win!'

Towards 7 a.m. the tug from B.A. arrived and tied up alongside the Customs Shed for inspection. An hour later thirty-six coffins arrived in the undertaker's vans and were ferried out to the battleship. It was again McCall's turn to be on watch. 'I'll have to be going soon,' he said.

'Go ahead,' replied his companion, 'I'll take over. Get back as soon as you can. You'd better have a shave and smarten up or the Commodore will put you in the Log.'

McCall remarked, putting on his coat and hat, 'Langsdorff

hasn't been to bed all night either.'

The man who was doing more than anyone to ruin the German Captain nodded and said with sincerity, 'Poor devil. . . . '

McCall was staying with Millington-Drake and he had to fight his way in and out of the Legation. It was still being besieged by volunteers. The queue was orderly enough, but it blocked the entrance and stretched far down the street. His car was waiting under the trees on the other side of the road, and the driver, Lotte's boy-friend, was walking up and down on the path with a worried expression. He turned to see if McCall was coming, then glanced at his watch again. Then he looked up the street. Suddenly his face cleared. Glancing back at the Legation to see if anybody was watching him, he waved briefly.

Lotte, swinging along the pavement in a light summer frock, waved back. As she came up, he said, 'I thought I'd miss you.'

'Why?' she asked, 'Have you got an early job?'

He nodded. 'Can I see you tonight?'

'What about lunch-time? We had a date on the beach.'

The young man looked unhappy. 'Sorry. I can't today.'

His quick eye caught sight of McCall coming out of the Legation and he added, 'Look out. Here he comes.'

'Who?'

'The English Captain. I'm taking him on a special job.'

Lotte's eyes narrowed and she said, 'You're always wanting me to go down to the beach, and I always go when you ask me. Now, the one time that I ask you. . . . '

She got the information she wanted. The driver said, 'We're going to Punta del Este.'

She could afford to be nice now. She said, 'Oh, well. That's different. What does he want to go to Punta del Este for?'

'D'you think he'd tell me? He wants to get some sea-air, he said.'

McCall was coming up, so he added hurriedly, 'What about tonight?'

Lotte gave him a ravishing smile and said, 'Of course,' then went off down the street with a side-glance at Captain McCall which he thoroughly appreciated. As he climbed in beside the driver, he asked, 'Who was that?'

The driver answered proudly, 'My girl friend, sir.'

He let in the clutch with a bang and they shot off. McCall refrained from saying, 'Well, I hope you have a lighter hand with the girls than you have with a car,' and settled himself comfortably for the two hours' drive.

As they turned the corner into the main road, the driver kept his eye open for Lotte, but she was nowhere in sight. There was a drug-store on the corner and she was in there telephoning. As the coin dropped, she said, 'Hello. Is that the German Club? I want to speak to Herr von Ritter. It's a lady who knows him. . . . '

Every night during the long watch off Montevideo, Harwood closed his ships into the Harbour and then drew off at dawn to a distance of about forty miles. On this Friday morning, with three ships again under his command, he felt for the first time at his ease. He had drawn off to the mouth of the river and *Cumberland* was patrolling south of the English Bank. *Achilles* guarded the north channel and *Ajax* was lying only a few miles off Punta del Este, on the south side of Lobos Island. He was there by arrangement, for it was time to take stock and he wanted to talk to McCall as much as the Naval Attaché wanted to talk to him.

The arrival of the Commodore's barge from *Ajax* in the little port of Punta del Este caused a considerable flutter. Captain Rodriguez, Uruguayan Navy, the Captain of the Port, who spoke excellent English, received two separate and completely contradictory accounts of the battle from the Coxswain and the seaman with him before McCall's car arrived. McCall went to Rodriguez' office to pay his respects before going on board the barge. The Captain of the port knew, of course, that he was going to see Harwood and, although bursting with curiosity and excitement, was too polite to ask any questions, much to McCall's relief. After giving him the latest news from Montevideo, he walked down to the barge which had been freshly painted and lay alongside the quay with its brass gleaming in the sun. War or no war, battle or no battle, Captain Woodhouse liked a smart ship. The crew, too, were extremely smart and, having spotted McCall a few minutes ago, were standing easy waiting for him and ignoring the questions in various languages which were hurled at them by fishermen and visitors. McCall was in civilian clothes, but as soon as he approached the barge, with his easy air of authority, the Coxswain sprang to attention and said, 'Captain McCall, sir?'

McCall nodded and stepped on board.

'Carry on, sir?' asked the coxswain.

McCall said, 'Yes, please,' and sat down on the snow-white cushions.

With McCall's eye on them and with half the waterfront population of Punta del Este breathing hard, plus the knowledge that they were bleeding heroes fresh from battle, the crew reached

154

a standard of efficiency seldom achieved outside the Royal Tournament. Hardly had the orders, 'Let go for'ard! Let go aft! Shove off!' left the coxswain's mouth than they were carried out. Mercifully the clutch didn't slip (it had been giving trouble the last few days), and McCall, outwardly impassive, left the harbour in the style befiting a British Naval Attaché on an important mission.

As he rounded the lighthouse at Lobos, H.M.S. *Ajax* came into view and McCall's heart leapt at the sight. Harwood had not anchored, and the cruiser was lying motionless head on to the light breeze that was blowing. As the barge altered course and rapidly approached the flagship, McCall could see that there were working-parties all over her: some were cleaning the guns, scraping off the blistered paint and leaving the long barrels bare; shipwrights were working on the deck where the force of the blast had lifted the planking; the shot-off main-mast had been sheered off and the aerials between the fore and main-mast were being fixed neatly to the stump, so that they looked quite normal. Everything was being made as ship-shape as possible. Only the forward turret, which had been put out of action by the salvo from the *Graf Spee*, remained at an angle to the others, its guns cocked at different elevations.

The ladder was down on the port side, and the Officer of the Watch had obviously notified the Commodore that the barge was approaching for McCall saw white figures arriving on the quarter-deck. It is not every day that a Naval Attaché with the rank of Post Captain visits a victorious Commodore after an important Naval engagement, and McCall keenly appreciated Harwood's sense of the fitness of things as his barge came smartly alongside the ladder and, stepping on to it, he climbed deliberately up to the quater-deck to be greeted by Commodore Harwood, Captain Woodhouse, Commander Everett, Lieutenant-Commander Medley, the Officer of the Watch, a midshipman, a Petty Officer and two boy seamen, all at the salute. McCall took off his Panama-hat, rather conscious of the gaudy hatband, and put it on again. It would be nice to report that his first words were something for the Oxford Book of Quotations, and if he had been a Frenchman, a nation which has the gift for these things, he would no doubt have hauled off and spoken half a page for the books, but his actual words to Harwood were, 'Hello, sir!'

Harwood seemed to find them adequate. He said, 'Hello, McCall! Very glad to see you. You know Woodhouse, don't you?'

Here was another opportunity for McCall to say something memorable. He said, 'Hello, Woodhouse,' and they shook hands.

Harwood added, 'And Medley, my Staff Officer.'

McCall did the hat trick by saying, 'Hello, Medley.'

He said good morning to the others and then turned and looked at Harwood. That was a moment they both remembered. Harwood's eyes sparkled and emotion rose in McCall. Words came jostling into his mouth, but he was saved by Harwood grasping him by the arm, shaking him roughly and growling, 'Come on! Come on! Over here!' He led him across the quarter-deck away from the others, who remained within call, but just out of ear-shot, in the background.

'Now McCall,' he said, 'you've got to stop her sailing!'

McCall's jaw dropped and he stared at the Commodore. 'Stop her!' he exclaimed, 'but we've been moving Heaven and earth to get the Uruguayans to throw her out!'

Harwood brushed that on one side. 'Yes, yes. I dare say. Quite natural under the circumstances but quite wrong.'

McCall said as heatedly as a Post Captain can to a Commodore, 'In fact we have persuaded them!'

'Well, now you can unpersuade them,' said Harwood. 'You've got to keep her here.'

McCall's head was whirling. 'But how can I now, sir?' was all he could find to say.

Harwood was quite ruthless. 'That's up to you and Martin. Use every possible means. Invoke the Twenty-Four Hour Rule. Anything!'

He saw McCall's amazed and aggrieved face and altered his tone. He became charmingly confidential. He said, 'The point is this. My three ships aren't enough to make the issue certain. You know how long it took us to corner her, eh?'

Mc Call nodded and Harwood went on urgently, 'The mouth of this river is a hundred miles wide . . . if she gets away again —' he gestured towards the open sea, then said with extraordinary vehemence, 'And she might! She might! . . . I was very lucky on the thirteenth, I'm not so sure that I'll be as lucky a second time.'

McCall said glumly, 'I see.'

Harwood saw that he had rammed home his point and altered his tone again. He raised his voice, 'Admiralty have ordered a concentration on Montevideo. All Hunting Groups have been directed this way. But look at the chart!' He had beckoned Medley and Woodhouse to approach and, at a sign from him, Medley

156

unrolled the chart. Harwood stabbed a blunt finger at the north of South America and said, 'Force K. . . .'

Medley murmured: '*Renown* and *Ark Royal*. . . .'

' . . . Six hundred miles east of Pernambuco,' completed Harwood. 'Twenty-five hundred miles away.'

Woodhouse added, 'And they'll have to re-fuel at Rio.'

Harwood nodded, 'Yes. That's Sunday . . . Monday . . . Tuesday, eh?'

Woodhouse agreed.

Harwood went on, 'Tuesday's the earliest they can be here. *Neptune* and the French Force X are even further. The *Dorsetshire* left Cape Town on Wednesday . . . four thousand miles to steam. . . . You see?'

McCall saw.

Harwood finished up emphatically, 'You've got to keep her here until Tuesday at least.'

McCall said philosophically, 'Well, I'd better get a move on.'

'That's the spirit,' exclaimed Harwood. Turning to Medley he said, 'Warn the boat's crew. Oh, and – ' he murmured something to Medley who nodded, smiled and hurried off.

The three senior officers stood chatting for a few moments, then strolled across the quarter-deck to the ladder. McCall had quickly got over his chagrin and was already chafing to get back to Montevideo.

'Poor old Millington-Drake!' he said. 'I can just see his face when I put him into reverse.'

'He must be enjoying himself,' remarked Harwood.

'He is. He's doing a wonderful job. He takes it all in his stride: Ministry of Marine, Defence, Foreign Office. . . . He's at 'em all, day and night, waving the Hague Convention.'

'By George, yes,' said Harwood thoughtfully, 'Guani, Luisi, Campos – why, I was playing golf with them only a few days ago. And now they have to decide a matter of life and death for us all.'

The midshipman panted up with a strange-looking blackened object, and Medley took it from him as Harwood added, 'And talking of golf. Look at my clubs!'

Medley showed the tattered bag, the forlorn, decapitated sticks. McCall looked at them sympathetically, 'Are those golf-clubs?'

'Toothpicks!' roared Harwood, 'that's all they are now. Toothpicks! One shell took all their heads off! Good shooting, eh? On a fair-ground it would have won a teddy bear!'

By now they were at the ladder. The boat was standing by, and Harwood and the other ship's officers prepared to see McCall off as ceremoniously as they had greeted him. The sun shone, the blue sea lapped the slowly-moving cruiser, the white uniforms were bright in the sunshine, nobody would have guessed that death was so near.

Behind Harwood's back, the Officer of the Watch handed a signal to Medley and, in a strange tone which made Medley glance sharply at him, said, 'Signal for the Commodore, sir.'

Medley took it and read it. He exchanged a look with the Officer of the Watch, who was now grinning broadly. Then seeing that Harwood was chatting to McCall, he silently showed the signal to Woodhouse, who in his turn showed it to the Commander. On all their faces, wonder, amazement and glee, at the expense of their Chief, were variously expressed. Quite oblivious, Harwood was saying to McCall, 'Now don't get arrested for smuggling! Tell Rodriguez I'll bring him some gin in a few weeks' time.'

McCall looked squarely at Harwood and there was a gleam in his eye as he said in a peculiar tone, 'You know, sir, that the South American states claim all the River Plate as territorial waters – all of it, between Punta del Norte and Punta del Este?'

Harwood looked just as squarely back and replied, 'Yes. I do.'

McCall went on, 'Suppose *Graf Spee* breaks away up-river for Buenos Aires. Will you try and stop her?'

He had hit the nail on the head and Harwood appreciated it, but he was giving nothing away. Perhaps he didn't yet know the answer, but he was a good diplomat. He said, 'McCall, I never was much good on a horse, but I know the drill: don't take your fences until you have to.'

McCall smiled and said, 'Good-bye, sir.' They shook hands. Harwood saluted and the others followed suit. McCall raised his hat and went down the ladder.

Woodhouse still held the mysterious signal for the Commodore in his hand and was waiting for the proper moment to give it to him. Harwood stood at the rail for a moment watching the barge carry McCall swiftly back to Punta del Este and the job he had to do. The Naval Attaché's last words had brought into the open the problem which had been at the back of his mind for the past forty-eight hours. This was his second period of service on the South American Station, and he was throughly familiar with local sensibilities and local problems. In the running fight up-river, they had already violated territorial waters and he had no

158

doubt that the Chancelleries of the various American countries, including the United States, were already humming with the news. His fingers beat a tattoo on the rail, as he watched the barge disappear round the point of Lobos, then he turned and said, 'Medley, make a signal to Admiralty from Commodore, South Atlantic – '

Woodhouse seized his opportunity and cut in, 'I beg your pardon, sir, but that signal is incorrect.'

Harwood was so taken aback that he just stared, 'But I haven't said anything yet.'

'You have, sir!' said Woodhouse with irritating blandness.

The veins on Harwood's neck started to swell. He glared at his Captain as if he had gone mad: 'I've just said "Signal to Admiralty". What's wrong with that?'

Woodhouse was thoroughly enjoying himself. 'And then you went on "From Commodore, South Atlantic".'

Harwood looked from Woodhouse to Medley and back again and growled, 'Well, I am Commodore Harwood, am I not?'

'No, sir,' said Woodhouse magnificently, 'You are Rear-Admiral Sir Henry Harwood, Knight Commander of the Bath.'

He held the signal out to Harwood who, staring, took it in one hand. Woodhouse seized the other and shook it with warmth and emotion, saying, 'My congratulations, sir!'

The new Admiral was suddenly surrounded by smiling faces, warm words of praise. As for Henry Harwood-Harwood, for the first and only time in his life, he was completely at a loss and speechless. But the joke was not only on him. A second signal was handed to Woodhouse, who glanced at it and exclaimed, 'Oh, I say!' He looked up and found Harwood's eyes fixed upon him as if he already knew the contents.

'Well? What is it? Bad news?'

Woodhouse said weakly: 'I've been made a Companion of the Bath. . . . So have Parry and Bell.'

Then Harwood started to laugh. The laugh grew to a roar and the roar to a gale, while Woodhouse stared in amazement at his Chief. Still roaring, Harwood grabbed him in a bear-like grip and half-pushed him, half-led him to their wrecked quarters, where a blaspheming group of artificers and plumbers were working, disentangling broken cables from wrecked plumbing. Harwood pointed to what was left of the two bathrooms and roared, 'Look at us! One Commander and one Companion of the Bath. And not a blooming bath-tub between us!'

In case it may be thought that these Officers were treating

too frivolously the great honour which had been bestowed upon them on the field of battle, an event rare in history since the days of chivalry, it would be as well to quote the text of the Signal which Rear-Admiral Harwood made to the ships under his command on that memorable day:

> 'I hope that every one of you will take to yourselves the credit for the honour which has been bestowed upon me and your Captains by His Majesty The King. No Commander could receive better service from his Captains, nor I, nor they, as displayed by the Officers and Men concerned in the battle of the River Plate.'

The Royal Navy has a prose style of its own. It is everything that the purists demand and seldom achieve. It is direct, vigorous, colloquial, terse, masculine and Anglo-Saxon. It is an excellent prose and it would perhaps be of interest to place beside Admiral Harwood's signal the text of the signal by another Master of prose, not unfamiliar with Naval affairs, who was, at that time, in charge of the Admiralty: the signal which Admiral Harwood received:

> 'From Admiralty.
> In recognition of a gallant and successful action fought by His Majesty's ships *Ajax*, *Achilles* and *Exeter* against the German armoured ship *Admiral Graf Spee*, the First Lord desires me to inform you His Majesty has been pleased to appoint Commodore Henry Harwood to be a Knight Commander of the Most Honourable Order of the Bath, and Captain Parry, H.M.N.Z.S. *Achilles*, Captain Woodhouse, H.M.S. *Ajax* and Captain Bell, H.M.S. *Exeter* to be Companions of the same Order. Commodore Harwood has also been promoted to be a Rear-Admiral in His Majesty's Fleet to date from 13th December, the date of the action.'

At the risk of being boring, it should be repeated that there is something about the Royal Naval style. They know what they are saying and they know how to say it. It is a style that repays study by politicians, leader-writers – and writers of books.

It may be remembered that during McCall's interview with the Admiral the latter suggested that the Twenty-Four Hour Rule could be used to delay the *Graf Spee*. Since we hear a good deal of this during the next day or so the reference had better be explained. It is already clear that a belligerent warship can only stay twenty-four hours in a neutral port unless granted an extension of time for adequate reasons. But if during that time a merchant vessel belonging to the Power with which her Government is at war sails from the harbour, then the warship herself is not permitted to sail until twenty-four hours later, and the Neutral Power, as the authority on the spot, has the obligation to detain her. Behind this Rule there is partly the old, old idea of giving the fugitive a fair start; the other intention is to avoid unpleasant incidents on the doorstep of neutral nations. McCall put this suggestion of Harwood's into immediate action. After a word with Rodriguez, he set off for Montevideo. His driver was only too delighted to see him back so soon – he might meet Lotte on the beach after all – and they beat the record back to the city. The British Legation was on the way, so McCall stopped there first to report to Millington-Drake. To the relief of the driver he was only with the Minister for about ten minutes. Then, hurrying out, he asked to be dropped at the Dockyard gates.

It was very hot in Martin's Look-Out, although Martin himself didn't seem to notice it. He was a hot-house plant. He listened calmly to McCall and then said, 'So we go into reverse?'

'Yes. We've got to keep her here until Tuesday.'

Martin nodded, 'Twenty-Four Hour Rule, eh? Good idea. There's a French meat-boat with steam up. You'll have to get the French Consul and see the Captain. . . . Have you told Millington-Drake?'

McCall said admiringly, 'He didn't turn a hair. I suppose the Foreign Office is used to looping the loop. I'm just a simple sailor.'

Martin said slowly, 'I brought off a little something since you went away. It was just a little pin-prick but it may fall in line with Harwood's strategy.' He was smiling like a Siamese cat.

McCall grinned too and asked, 'What have you been up to? You look very pleased with yourself.'

Martin looked more and more Siamese as he told his story.

'You gave me the idea yourself. You know, about getting an embargo put on the stuff from B.A. After you had gone, I telephoned Grimley, told him to stop playing with railway-trains (Grimley was the British Manager of the Uruguayan railway, amongst other activities), and to come down here and take over from me for a few hours. Then I got to work. The Germans had sent an Engineer-Commander ashore to clear the stuff, but the Customs don't come on till nine, and it was easy enough to delay the inspection – and then the clearance. Where there's good will already. . . . '

He grinned devilishly.

'I was satisfied they wouldn't get any sheet metal aboard *Graf Spee* before lunch-time. So leaving the Jerry brass-hat pacing up and down, and looking at his watch, I went up-town. Do you know the Chief Customs Officer?' he asked unexpectedly.

'Isn't he a big fellow with a fine pair of moustaches?' said McCall hazily.

'That's him. He's quite a one for the girls; hot Spanish blood and all that sort of thing. He's always in the Café Rincon every day at twelve. I was there, too, with a lady whom we will call Madame X: she's one of our volunteers – was vouched for by Grimley. She's a translator . . . works for a radio company. She doesn't speak English very well, but she claims to be British on both sides. Her sides are all right with me. She has the kind of curves that catch the eye – and particularly the Latin-American eye. She didn't arrive with me, of course; she was there already, carrying three or four brand-new German cameras and sitting at a table by herself, waiting for someone.'

'Someone like you,' said McCall admiringly.

'Correct. When I came in I saw Señor Moustaches was already throwing passionate glances in her direction. So far so good. I went over, bowed in my best manner and sat down at her table. I must say she was very good. She'd been told to play a femme fatale. She's a model wife and mother really, but good women have as much talent as the other kind for that sort of thing. I felt my own temperature rising. Presently I caught our victim's eye, smiled and nodded and he came over; the rest was easy. I pleaded another engagement, left them alone together, and in half an hour the lady was in gaol there was a Customs embargo on all goods going in or out of the *Graf Spee*. It's still on.'

McCall mopped his brow and said apologetically, 'Excuse me for being dense, but why is your lady-friend in gaol?'

'For buying smuggled German cameras from the sailors of the *Graf Spee* and trying to re-sell them to Moustaches for two hundred pesos a piece,' said Ray Martin coolly. 'He was caught between love and duty, but duty won, I am glad to report. Of course, Langmann will go to Guani and protest, and an enquiry will be held, the embargo raised and Madame X will be bailed out by me, but that will all take time. And by then we'll have come up with something new. You'd better buzz off and see the French Consul. That meat-boat ought to sail at 18.00 hours.'

162

While these guerilla skirmishes were being fought, a more serious note was introduced by the burial ashore of the *Graf Spee*'s dead. All the severely-wounded men, some fifty of them, had been brought ashore early on the previous morning and were being cared for in Montevideo's excellent hospitals. The German colony in the city had rallied round to a man, and the young sailors were looked after as if they had been their own children. When the *Graf Spee* sailed, they would be interned, of course, but it would be a benevolent internment. The youth of the *Graf Spee*'s crew had inspired surprise and pity in Uruguay. Though wars may be fought by young men, they are not made by them and when hostilities ended, many of these boys were to stay in Uruguay and become valuable citizens. On this afternoon, their thirty-six dead comrades were to be buried in ground made available for the duration of the war in the British Cemetery. Already the long rows of coffins, covered with the Nazi Naval flag, and laid upon the deck of a lighter, were being brought ashore under a Guard of Honour. Crowds of people had been assembling for some time and the great, black, Spanish-style hearse, órnamented with crowns and crosses, and shining like ebony in the sun, stood out, sombre islands in the sea of faces. Excitement and sympathy became intense as tugs brought off hundreds of the young seamen who were to attend the funeral, loo!.ing very smart in their white caps, short white blouses with black scarves and blue bell-bottom trousers with black shoes. Then Captain Langsdorff and all his officers, in their white uniforms and carrying their swords, came ashore. Permission had been given to march through the city to the cemetery, and the procession started to form up. Six young seamen were assigned to each flowered-covered coffin, and a Leading Seaman or Petty Officer, picked for their fine appearance, marched between. Hundreds of Uruguayans of German stock or sympathies joined the procession or assembled at the cemetery, while many thousands of men and women, who were neither pro-German nor pro-British, lined the route of the procession, some out of curiosity, but most of them out of respect – for youth and courage and idealism.

It was perfectly true, as Roy Martin observed, that the arrangements for the German funeral were made with an eye to propaganda and were calculated to extract the utmost popular sympathy. The press photographers and news-reel cameras were busy. But under Langsdorff the ceremony was conducted with dignity and good taste from first to last. It was only afterwards, when the Nazi propagandists got their hands upon the photographs and the reports, that vilifications set in, truth was distorted, and noble sentiments were labelled base. On this day in Montevideo there were no lies, no hatred. Men thought only of dead shipmates. Many of the crowd were curiously moved to see, walking in the procession, a group of the senior British merchant-marine officers who had been prisoners in the *Graf Spee*. Captain Dove, Captain Stubbs and the others had come because they wanted to; because, seamen themselves, they wished to pay their last respects to the young seamen with whom they had been shipmates, and who had died as they themselves might well have died in the terrible experiences which they had shared together. There had not been much discussion. It was not a concerted movement. Nobody had organised it. But one had said to the other at the English Club, 'Are you going? . . . So am I. . . . Might as well. . . . ' And now there they were, standing in the British Cemetery, a solemn little group. Some had been lucky enough to preserve their best uniforms and wore them. Others like Dove, wore plain, blue, decent serge. Dr Goebbels, who had already told the world that the British had used mustard-gas shells in the battle of the River Plate, was to put out a story that these British merchant-seamen spat on the graves of the fallen German sailors. But on this day, as they stood near Langsdorff beside the graves, there was no thought of the brilliant inventions of a diseased, club-footed paranoiac. There was only a fitting meloncholy and a feeling of kinship which covered the whole human race.

Langsdorff's appearance and personality had made its usual impression. He had walked with his officers at the rear of the procession, letting his dead seamen have their rightful place of honour. After the ceremony he got into a car with the German Ambassador and went to the Embassy where he remained in conference for several hours.

As Ray Martin foretold, Langmann had had a stormy scene with the patient Dr Guani, reproaching him for having subordinates with pro-Allied and anti-German sympathies, and requesting him to raise the embargo at once on the equipment and material which had been sent for, in an honest attempt to comply with the time limit he had himself imposed. Guani, who was anxious to get rid of the *Graf Spee* as soon as possible, promised to speak to the Chief of Customs himself. The sheet-metal was released towards sundown. But hardly had he settled back in relief from solving this problem, when a solemn French Minister

164

requested an immediate interview and informed him that since the French Frigorifico, *Cote d' Azur*, had sailed at 18.00 hours for Rio de Janeiro, the French Government requested the Uruguayan Foreign Minister to prevent the *Graf Spee* from sailing, by force if necessary, until twenty-four hours after the departure of the merchant vessel; which as His Excellency, of course, knew was according to the Hague Convention, etc., etc., etc. . . .

The harassed Guani replied rather reasonably that, to the best of his knowledge, the *Graf Spee* had no intention of sailing during the next twenty-four hours and that even if she did, he hadn't the force to stop her, although it was true that there was a Uruguayan Naval Guard boat alongside the battleship to see that no technical violations of the Agreement were committed. To the Foreign Minister's bewilderment, however, Monsieur Gentil was most insistent that Captain Langsdorff should be informed of the new situation which had arisen, and that Uruguay would be held responsible for any violation of the Twenty-Four Hour Rule. Guani could only shrug his shoulders politely and send the requested Note to the German Embassy for forwarding to the Captain of the *Graf Spee*.

'Nice work,' said Martin to McCall when he came back to the Look-Out at sunset. 'So they can't make a dash tonight without breaking the Law. Tomorrow we'll sail that Houlder Line boat at the same time, and on Sunday at 13.00 hours we'll sail that grain-ship. If Guani does his stuff, that'll keep Langsdorff here until Monday . . . by then we'll fix something else. The only trouble is that we'll run out of ships. You'd better put Johnston on to see who's in B.A.'

McCall nodded and said, 'If the earliest that Force K can get here is Tuesday, we'd better start putting out propaganda that they're here already.'

He little knew what he was letting himself in for when Ray Martin looked meditatively at him and murmured, 'You've given me an idea.'

It was now nearly dark and the warship was brightly lit-up, so that there was hardly any need for the motor-car headlights. Work was going on day and night, and the big ship was surrounded by tugs, floating cranes and lighters.

'But in spite of that, we're going to lay great stress on the Twenty-Four Hour Rule,' McCall told Martin. 'Millington-Drake and I have been granted an emergency audience at Government House by Dr Guani at 11.30 tonight. We are going to urge that a Uruguayan picket should be placed on board the *Graf Spee,* as we feel it would be difficult for her to sail with them on board; and if they were pushed off, there would be a definite act of violence. Of course it's only a forlorn hope but it shows we're in earnest.'

When they faced Guani across his wide desk that night, the Foreign Minister, although not committing himself, said patiently, 'Gentlemen! I will give you this last satisfaction to-night by consulting the Minister of Defence on the telephone if I can get him.'

This he proceeded to do and, whilst not directly supporting the request, said he considered it reasonable. But General Campos prudently refused it, stating that the Naval Guard boat which was already alongside, was the most that he was prepared to do.

There was a pause after Dr Guani conveyed this refusal to the Englishmen. The little Foreign Minister seemed to be puzzling something out, and his eyes rested upon them with an expression of gentle enquiry. It was five minutes to midnight. There was nothing more that they could do. They glanced at each other and rose to say good night. Guani rose also, still with the same quizzical expression on his face. Before they could speak he said, in the tone of an uncle to a favourite nephew, 'My dear Millington-Drake!'

Millington-Drake replied politely, 'Señor Ministro?'

Guani continued, his eyes on his old friend, 'Why are you and your agents now trying to delay the sailing of the *Graf Spee*? Explain this change of attitude.'

'Oh, but Your Excellency,' replied Millington-Drake promptly, 'it is not a change of attitude.'

Dr Guani considered this reply for a moment, as a connoisseur savours a mouthful of vintage port, before saying, 'No?' There was a smile appearing in his eyes and on his lips and the same smile hovered over the impassive, well-bred features of the British Minister as he answered, 'No, Señor Ministro. It is a change of strategy.'

CHAPTER XII

SATURDAY

In the morning the civilian offensive continued unceasing and, as usual in battle, the innocent suffered with the guilty.

It will be remembered that there was a leakage on the telephone line between the British Ministry at Montevideo and the Embassy at Buenos Aires. The devious Martin had decided that now was the time to take advantage of this: with the result that the unfortunate Captain McCall found himself seated in the British Legation early the following morning, next to a sign saying, 'Take care! The enemy has his ears everywhere!' and feeling like an amateur actor about to go on as Hamlet, while Miss Shaw tried to get Buenos Aires on the telephone. They were in Millington-Drake's own office. The Minister sat at his desk, rather disapproving but resigned. Miss Shaw stood beside it with her ear to the telephone. Ray Martin lounged on a sofa watching McCall. The two cloak-and-dagger exponents had not slept for two nights, apart from occasional naps. They looked a bit brown around the edges but were otherwise full of fight.

McCall saw Martin's malicious eye fixed upon him, stirred restively and said, 'After this I shall never be any good again as an ordinary Naval Attaché.'

Martin crossed his legs, twiddled his thumbs and said, 'Who cares?'

Exasperated by his callousness, McCall said impressively, 'You realise that, for your own evil ends, you are asking me to violate one of the – '

He was interrupted by Miss Shaw saying, 'Good morning, Your Excellency. The Minister wishes to speak to you.' She handed the receiver to Millington-Drake, who thanked her and then, seeing that she was inclined to linger, said, 'Leave us please.'

On the telephone he said, 'Is that you, Ovey? McCall wants a word with you. . . . What's that? . . . Oh, we're in the thick of it all right,' he laughed then said, 'Very nice of you to say so. Well, I'll give you McCall.'

He held the receiver towards the reluctant Post Captain. McCall exclaimed to the world at large, 'Well, here goes my professional reputation!' He took the telephone and said, 'McCall

167

here, sir. An emergency has arisen over the *Graf Spee.*'

Millington-Drake writhed in his chair and murmured, 'Oh God! Oh Montreal!'

The Ambassador warned, 'Careful, McCall! Security!'

McCall blushed and said, 'I know, sir, but this is most urgent.'

There was an extension on the telephone. Ray Martin grabbed it and listened in as McCall went on.

'I have just heard by Admiralty Code that two of our capital ships are – '

The Ambassador's voice blasted the telephone: 'Are you mad, McCall? I'm going to hang up!'

Martin grinned cruelly at the unfortunate Naval Attaché, who said desperately, 'Sir! I must insist! In this case urgency over-rides security.'

He got an approving nod from Martin and a stupefied gasp from Sir Esmond Ovey. But he didn't hang up, and McCall was able to finish his message:

' . . . Both these capital ships will be calling in the next few hours at Bahia Blanca to re-fuel. They will be down to their last drop when they arrive. They have steamed at full speed to the vicinity of the Plate – for obvious reasons. They request that we arrange for two thousand tons of fuel oil to be available in tankers as from midday today.'

He paused. He was sweating in streams. There was no immediate reply but he could hear a murmur of voices at the other end of the wire. He looked at Martin then said into the telephone, 'Did you understand my message, sir? Shall I repeat it?'

At once Sir Esmond's voice answered him. 'No. That's all right, McCall. We got your message. There's no need to repeat it.'

He was about to hang up thankfully when the Ambassador's voice added, drily, 'McCall!'

McCall said, 'Yes, sir.'

'The next time you do a thing like that you might give me some notice.' And Sir Esmond Ovey hung up.

'I think he twigged it,' said McCall to the others, mopping his forehead.

Millington-Drake looked at the ceiling, silently dissociating himself from the whole deplorable incident.

Ray Martin said, 'Don't worry, old boy. Liars are born not made.'

'What result do you expect to obtain from this manoeuvre?' enquired Millington-Drake courteously.

'I expect to hear the afternoon paper-boy screaming that half the British Fleet are off Punta del Este,' replied Ray Martin. 'But I'm going to give them some corroborative detail. McCall! Do you remember that girl who came in yesterday for news of the *Exeter* and said she knew the lighthouse keeper?'

McCall nodded, 'What about her?'

'I've got her waiting in the next room. Come on! I think we can use her.'

He was already on his way out with a nod to the Minister, who looked at McCall expressively. The Naval Attaché avoided his eye and said hurriedly, 'Well, I must get on with it! Thank you, Minister! You won't forget about the Houlder Line boat sailing at 18.00 hours today?'

Millington-Drake slowly shook his head and McCall made his escape thankfully.

In the other room Ray Martin was listening to Julita who was saying, 'But I know that the *Exeter* has been sunk!'

'How do you know?' said Marin.

'My cousin works at Punta del Este in the Lighthouse Service. He is stationed on Lobos Island. He has seen only two ships when the battle was over, and the *Exeter* was not one of them. . . . '

Julita was dressed in black. She looked thin and pale, but had herself well under control. Ray Martin said to McCall as he closed the door, 'She had a boy friend in *Exeter*. Boy called Roper.'

McCall said gently, 'And you liked each other very much?'

Julita nodded, 'Yes. Very much. I wish to know – I wish to know the truth. When he went away before, he promised he would come back . . . and he did come back. And this time he promised . . . and now his ship has been sunk and . . . I am sorry . . . I have no words. . . . '

McCall said, 'Señorita, you know that in war many things must be kept secret.'

She nodded. And he went on, 'But I will tell you that the *Exeter* has not been sunk. There were many men killed and wounded, but she has not been sunk. This very morning she arrived safely at the Falkland Islands!'

This was news to Martin. McCall went on steadily: 'At the Falklands the wounded can be properly attended to. So you must hope, and if you give me a letter to your boy I will try and see that he gets it.'

Julita's face was radiant and full of hope once more. Martin said, 'And will you do something to help us in return?'

Julita nodded and listened to what he told her.

The midday papers, as Martin had foretold, were full of rumours of a vast Naval Force assembling outside the River Plate to bottle up the *Graf Spee*. The names of *Renown* and *Ark Royal* were freely mentioned as well as half a dozen other capital ships. But the item which gave Martin and McCall the greatest pleasure was a highly-authentic report from the lighthouse keeper on the Island of Lobos: he had sighted and identified the battleship *Barham* and other powerful units of the British Fleet operating with Admiral Harwood's Squadron. Ray Martin said with satisfaction, 'That's what I mean by corroborative detail.'

McCall said, 'That cousin of Julita's must have very good eyesight. The *Barham*'s in dry dock in Gibraltar. . . . '

The news which Captain McCall had compassionately revealed to Julita was quite true. That very morning, Captain Bell in H.M.S. *Exeter,* had sighted the rocky, barren coast of the Falkland Islands. And an hour or so later, they entered Port Stanley to a wonderful reception from the Governor and the local inhabitants. During the three days of the voyage, the engineers had never ceased working on the electrical compasses, telephones and communications between the bridge, the helmsman and the engine room. At last on the night before they arrived at their destination repairs were sufficiently advanced for Bell to reoccupy his proper position on the forebridge, with compasses working correctly and normal communications re-established. It was fitting that their Captain should be back on the bridge for their first landfall, and the men worked day and night to bring it about.

At Port Stanley, Bell received his orders from the First Sea Lord to make the ship seaworthy and to return with all expedition to the United Kingdom. So there he remained for the following six weeks; while for the next thirty-six hours both he and the Governor, and every living person on the Falkland Islands, as well as in the rest of the world, were glued to their radios listening hour after hour to the descriptions of the mounting drama in Montevideo, event which tended to be dominated more and more by one voice – the voice of Mike Fowler.

'It is now nearly a quarter after nine, folks, here in the great city of Montivideo on this Saturday, the 16th of December. We hear that there's a blizzard blowing in New York, but on this side of the world it's a lovely summer evening and half the population are out *on paseo* – that means out on the town. There

170

must be half a million people milling around in sight of me at this very moment. They are thronging the quays and jetties of the Harbour, they are crowding the beaches, and the roofs of all the tall buildings in the city – and while I watch still more are coming to see the next act in this unique drama of the *Graf Spee*. I have been talking to these citizens of Montevideo, and I have several of them standing here right beside me to give you listeners exclusive news of what is happening behind the scenes. Here, for example, is Señor Casuelo who is a gardener at the German Embassy. Step forward! Señor Casuelo! Say a few words to the millions of listeners in the United States. . . . '

But after a long pause all that the eager listeners heard was a sepulchral 'Hello', followed by a torrent of apologetic Spanish off-mike. Mike hastily cut in again. 'Señor Casuelo assures us that when Captain Langsdorff, the Captain of the *Graf Spee*, visited the German Embassy last night both he and the Ambassador were talking to Berlin and, probably, to Herr Hitler himself. These high-level political discussions are still going on for, with the recent news that the British and their Allies are concentrating vast forces at the mouth of the River Plate, the fate of the German Pocket battleship, the Pride of the German Navy, hangs in the balance. I also have here beside me a radio amateur. . . . Your name, señor? . . . '

There was no shyness about the next speaker who had evidently grasped the microphone as firmly as the nettle, Danger, and announced in ringing tones, 'Señor Torres! Hello! Short-wave hams of the United States of America! I am broadcasting every night on my – '

Mike sounded rather put out as he cut in again, 'Thank you. Thank you. That was Señor Torres, folks. This young man has picked up on his home-made short-wave set powerful signals on the secret wave-length used by the German Embassy for communicating with Berlin. But although his wife, Minna, is of German stock . . . say a word, Minna! . . . '

Minna was not backward either: 'Hello listeners! I am second generation Uruguayan and good democrat, and my grandfather was from Linz, Austria. Hello! Cousin Thea in Minneapolis! Are you listening?'

Mike again: 'Thank you Minna! Now, as I was saying, although both these young people understand German, the signals to Berlin were scrambled or in code and so couldn't be understood. And now we have Dolores del Monte, the inter-

171

national singing star . . , Hiya, kid! . . . who has agreed to appear – '

There was a pause, and a sound of a slight scuffle and an argument in Spanish, then Mike came on again, 'Apparently she's agreed to disappear. Even in Montevideo you can't keep the customers waiting. Ha ha! Now it's more than an hour since the sun sank beneath the waves of the River Plate, but it's still quite light and the lightest spot of all is round the vast bulk of the Pocket battleship, *Graf Spee,* where work is going on by night as well as by day. I have had my glasses on her all the afternoon and evening. There has been a great deal of activity. At one point I could see hundreds of officers and men assembled on the after-deck. . . . Some sort of meeting was taking place and it didn't look too disciplined a meeting to me. Nobody knows what was decided at it. Nobody knows what was said to Herr Hitler today or what will be said tonight. But there is a constant traffic of launches and lighters between the Pocket battleship and the S.S. *Tacoma,* the German merchant-vessel which was in Montevideo when the *Graf Spee* arrived, and is now lying a few hundred yards away from the battleship . . . I can't make out whether the launches are bringing stores on board the *Graf Spee* or whether they are taking them off. . . . What's that, señor? What can you see? Oh, yes . . . I've just been told that the *Graf Spee* is transferring heavy equipment into the two tugs which lie alongside. Of course! That's the welding equipment from Buenos Aires with which she has been repairing her scars of battle. Folks! The *Graf Spee* is transferring her welding equipment. That means she has finished repairs! That means she is ready to sail! But when? Her only chance is to make a dash for the open sea under cover of darkness. And she can only do that by breaking International Law. Today, at six o'clock in the evening, a British cargo boat left Montevideo Harbour and, according to the Twenty-Four Hour Rule which is applied by neutral nations, she must be given twenty-four hours' grace to get clear before a belligerent warship can sail after her. So the *Graf Spee* cannot legally sail until six o'clock on Sunday evening, that is to say only two hours before her time-limit, set by the Uruguayan Government, expires. These are the legal aspects of the matter. But I am standing right here in Montevideo, in the middle of this great drama of the sea, and I can tell you, folks, that International Law is one thing and Captain Langsdorff's personal position is another. The facts are that the *Graf Spee*'s engines and armament are virtually undamaged. She is still one of the fastest and most powerful battleships afloat. She is still in a position to make a dash out to sea at any time that suites her and the British Admiral, Admiral Harwood, is well aware of this. Night and day, every hour, every minute, the question upon everybody's lips and in everybody's minds is – will the *Graf Spee* dare to come out?'

CHAPTER XIII

SUNDAY

THERE WAS VERY little sleep for anyone that night. With the fall of darkness, the three British cruisers closed the Harbour until they could be sure to detect the *Graf Spee* if she were to sail. But there was no sign of it. She still rode at her moorings. On shore, thousands of eyes watched her all night. At three a.m., Langsdorff came ashore, went to the German Embassy and spoke once more and for the last time to Berlin. It was then that he received his final orders and, as soon as he returned to his ship, the watchers saw a great intensification of activity. Another mass meeting was held and, by the sounds that came across the water, it was more like a political meeting than an address by a Captain to his ship's company. Very strange things were happening that night to the soul of the great ship and to the heart of her Captain.

At dawn of the day upon which his quarry must sail or be interned, Harwood withdrew his small force forty miles down-river, out of sight. It might be for the last time. The decision was not in his hands. He could hope for no further reinforcements before Tuesday but that did not worry him. His only concern was to see that the *Graf Spee* did not slip through his fingers. To avoid this meant constant vigilance, day and night. There was a slender hope that Millington-Drake's application of the Twenty-Four Hour Rule might keep the battleship bottled up in harbour but he put no faith in it. And he was wise, for early that morning Dr Guani urgently requested the British Minister to attend at his office. He had learned of the intention to sail a third merchantman at 1 p.m. that day, and he requested Millington-Drake on no account to do so as his great anxiety was, naturally, to get rid of the *Graf Spee* as soon as possible, and within the time-limit. Faced with this direct exposure of his tactics, Millington-Drake could only agree. Since the *Graf Spee* was still there, moored in the Inner Harbour, and the time-limit expired at sundown, the issue was plain: she must either be out of territorial waters by 8 p.m. or be interned: a simple dramatic situation whose significance the whole world could easily grasp, particularly through the agency of Mike:

'Ladies and gentlemen, it is Sunday morning, 10.15 the 17th

of December, the day upon which the time-limit given to the *Graf Spee* will expire. To be exact, at 8 p.m. local time, she will have to be out of territorial waters or the Uruguayan Government will intern her. It is rumoured that outside the mouth of the Rio de la Plata there are five, possibly seven British warships waiting for her. Another rumour says that the Germans, too, are sending reinforcements, so that a Naval battle even greater than Wednesday's is imminent. We figured that the *Graf Spee* would make a run for it last night during darkness but she is still here this morning. Throughout the night her Captain, Captain Hans Langsdorff, worked with the Nazi diplomatic authorities towards one of Germany's most important decisions since the war began. Will he take the battered vessel out of the haven of the River Plate? Will they make a dash for Buenos Aires, four hours steaming up the channel? Will it be a fight to the death? Nobody knows. An hour ago Captain Langsdorff returned to his ship. He had spent many hours ashore. The German Minister, Dr Langmann, accompanied him to the quay and, as they shook hands, was heard to say, 'Until tomorrow.' Naturally he said it in German. I am giving you a translation of his words. . . . '

The tireless voice went on and on, vivid, resourceful and penetrating until it seemed as if the whole world were listening to Mike's words. Admiral Harwood certainly was. An elaborate system of espionage, and the transmission of news via the Falkland Islands and the Admiralty had been worked out many months before, but by an irony of science it was Mike, broadcasting to America, re-transmitted to the B.B.C. and thrown out again to the rest of the world all in a matter of seconds, who kept the British Admiralty informed, not only minute by minute, but also second by second, of his enemy's action and intentions. In a mater of seven seconds, Mike's voice bounced round the world and came back to every man in the three British ships over a rough hook-up to their loudspeaker systems. The voice was hypnotic. It was impossible not to listen to it. Men went about their jobs half-automatically, their ears cocked for the latest bulletin. When Mike went off the air everybody waited for him to come on again. Sometimes the circuit was left open, so that the noise of the crowd came through, mixed with faint sounds of music from Manolo's orchestra and, once or twice, the distant blast of a ship's siren. It was weirdly and intolerably dramatic. Montevideo and the enemy were out of sight and yet it seemed as if an invisible eye were watching them. It would not have surprised the British if Mike had started to describe their own movements and feelings as well.

The three ships were far apart patrolling the mouth of the Plate, off the English Bank, and maintaining contact by sight. The Flagship was patrolling within sight of Lobos Island. It was a glorious day and very hot. Harwood and Woodhouse were both on the bridge, listening like everyone else to the voice of Mike. Medley brought a signal to Harwood who read it, touched Woodhouse's arm and jerked his head towards the starboard range-finder. It stood in a little wing on the side of the bridge and was a good place for a private talk. Swanston, having nothing else to do and being incapable of idleness, was polishing the brass with pitiless zeal. Harwood said, 'Buzz off, Swanston,' and stepped up on to the platform where Woodhouse joined him. He passed him the signal with the words, 'From our Ambassador in Buenos Aires.' It read 'Strong rumour current here that *Graf Spee* will sail tonight.'

Woodhouse nodded, handed back the signal and said, 'So she is coming out.'

Harwood grunted, 'Is she? What would you do if you had the *Graf Spee* under your command?'

Woodhouse always liked a plain question. He turned the answer in his mind and then said slowly, 'Well – I'd come out as soon as it was dark and try to dodge the ships that were waiting for me outside, and get to the open sea again. And if I failed to dodge them, I'd fight to the finish. Isn't that what you would do, sir?'

Harwood nodded slowly. 'Sounds simple. I wonder if it sounds that simple to Longsdorff?'

'Why not?' asked Woodhouse and he sounded genuinely surprised.

After a moment Harwood replied like a man thinking aloud. 'He's got plenty of headaches . . . Headache number one: he doesn't know what force we've got out here. Headache number two: he can let himself be interned in Montevideo, but Uruguay might come into the war later on, on our side, and then the *Graf Spee* would fall into our hands. . . . Of course, he might make a dash for B.A., but the channel's narrow – '

Woodhouse ventured – 'and shallow – '

Harwood nodded – 'and muddy – if he fouls up his water-intake he'd be a sitting duck. . . . '

Suddenly he made up his mind and struck his fist on the edge of the steel bridge, 'Yes! He'll come out!'

Woodhouse said quietly, 'When do you think he'll move?'

'Now! . . . at noon! . . . at sunset! . . . any time! He can choose his own time. But he's lost the value of surprise because that fellow will tell us every move he makes,'

He jerked his head towards the loudspeaker on the bridge which was now playing a samba. Woodhouse said temptingly, 'Let's go and trail our coat on his doorstep.'

For a moment Harwood looked tempted and he gave a boyish grin of delight, then he groaned and said, 'Captains of warships, my dear Woodie, are not only Naval Officers: what we do or don't do is being constantly interpreted one way or another by our friends and enemies – or by neutrals.'

But this was no problem to Woodhouse: 'If we sink her it can only be interpreted one way!'

Harwood shook his head. 'I'm not so sure. Think a bit, Heart of Oak! If we open fire within the River Plate, we shall be accused of violating neutral territory. Think what little Goebbels will make of that!'

But Woodhouse was not to be drawn. He had his ship to fight and that was enough for him. 'Well, that's up to you, sir,' he announced, putting the problem squarely back into his superior officer's lap.

Harwood shook himself like a bear and growled, 'Yes. Thank you very much.'

Woodhouse caught his eye, burst out laughing and went for'ard.

Harwood glanced again at the Ambassador's message. Suddenly the music stooped and Mike's voice came again over the air. 'Flash! Mike Fowler reporting from Montevideo. General opinion here is that it is quite possible that the Pocket battleship will make a dash to another neutral port . . . to Buenos Aires . . . or Bahia Blanca . . . keeping in territorial waters all the way. . . . Activity is intense around the *Graf Spee*. She has now rigged a canvas awning over her starboard gangway, presumably to hide whatever it is she's loading into the tugs which are sailing continuously between the warship and the S.S. *Tacoma* . . . a gentleman has just been telling me that the *Graf Spee* is transferring dozens of men – I beg your pardon, señor? Oh, thank you! Si. Comprendo. Correction! The *Graf Spee* is transferring hundreds of men to the *Tacoma*. They are carrying their kit and as soon as they go on board the *Tacoma*, they are being sent below out of sight. . . . I can assure you, folks, although we can follow every move, none of us can tell what is going to happen. The suspense here is unbelievable. The best guess is that the

177

Graf Spee will sail with a skeleton crew, I might call it a suicide crew, to do as much damage as possible against hopeless odds and to go down fighting in a – !'

Mike's voice was suddenly interrupted by a loud crash, followed by screams and yells. Several hundred million people listened in suspense. There were some strange buckling noises, then Mike came on again, a bit breathless: ' . . . Sorry, folks. I was standing on a table in this café, where I am broadcasting, and it collapsed right under me . . . No harm done, sorry if I scared anyone. Guess you thought the *Graf Spee* had sailed.'

A couple of hundred symathetic citizens helped to pick Mike up and re-set his battery of microphones. Pop picked up and re-counted the bottles of whisky which had been under the table. There were now thirty-seven of them, all carefully filled up and re-corked by Pop himself. As Mike turned from reassuring his public he saw that his host and landlord, Manolo, was on his knees talking earnestly to Pop, who was turning a more or less deaf ear to his argument.

Mike said, 'What is it, Manolo?'

Manolo smiled ingratiatingly, spread out his hands and said, 'Whisky terminado.'

'Manolo he say no more whisky,' said Pop cutting in swiftly. 'No more whisky because no more delivery. Too many people.'

Manolo nodded, beamed at Mike and said, 'Si, claro,' then favoured Pop with a burst of Spanish and pointed to Mike's store of whisky.

Pop said drily, 'Manolo he say he like to buy whisky from you.' He winked at Mike, who looked solemnly back. This was his great moment. Pop's too.

Mike said carelessly, 'Well, I guess we can let him have half a dozen bottles – at a price.'

Pop translated, 'Seis botellas.'

Manolo still didn't see where he was going. He said impatiently, with a sweeping gesture, 'Seis? Tu tonto? Para todas!'

But Mike just shook his head and held up six fingers, 'No! Seis! Ask him how much he'll pay?'

About six hundred heads turned to Pop who translated the question. Then the heads turned again like a tennis match back to Manolo who said, with a look of astonishment which was almost convincing: 'Lo mismo!'

Pop beamed. This was really too easy. He looked at Mike and said pityingly, 'The same you pay him.'

Manolo nodded anxiously and said, 'Veinte-cino pesos.'

Mike smiled angelically and shook his head. Manolo looked him in the eye. Mike said, 'I'll double you. Cincuenta pesos.'

It was too much for Manolo. His business instincts deserted him. He screamed, 'Cincuenta!' and his voice cracked. Then he said, 'No!'

Mike smiled.

'No, no, no.'

Mike's smile broadened.

'No, no, no, *no!*'

Mike laughed out loud, then he suddenly grew quite solemn, fixed Manolo with his eye and said, 'Well, Is it a deal?'

The crowd waited breathlessly.

Without answering, Manolo dropped on one knee and gathered up the six bottles, then he rose and said, 'Is a deal!' and pushed his way through the crowd.

It was now midday and Sunday dinner-time, which is as serious in Montevideo as anywhere else and considerably more lengthy. Sunday dinner in Latin-American countries is followed by the sacred hour of the siesta, and not even the *Graf Spee* could cut into that. Gradually the quays and beaches, the jetties and roof-tops, and even Manolo's bar, emptied and Mike was left alone except for Pop who, having seen six bottles bring back a hundred per cent profit, was working out the probable profit on the remaining thirty-one. Mike yawned and stretched himself and looked around. Except for a few children and loafers there was no one in sight.

Only on the *Graf Spee* busy figures moved to and fro, tugs and launches continued to pass between the battleship, the shore and the *Tacoma* and — yes! a working party was starting to strike the awnings. Suicide crew or not, she was getting ready to sail.

But out of sight of Mike a great deal of activity was taking place and, in particular, one meeting which was to have important effects upon the history of the Western Hemisphere. This was the meeting on Sunday afternoon at the Ministry of Foreign Affairs to which Dr Guani summoned all the diplomatic representatives of the American continent. (South Americans use the word 'Americano' to include North and South America). It was about 3.30 p.m. when the day was at its hottest and Millington-Drake was sitting in his shirt-sleeves at his desk, when Miss Shaw came in to say the Consulate had telephoned to say that their Observer had just seen all the American Heads of Missions and also the Ambassadors of the U.S.A., Argentine and

Brazil drive one after the other up to the Cabildo and go in by the private entrance. As a matter of fact, Millington-Drake had had advance information about the meeting. It is interesting to recall the frame of mind of North and South America at that time. From his Geneva experience, Guani knew the value of collective action, and he knew also how to strike when the iron was hot. This moment, when the Western Hemisphere was still reeling under the effect of finding itself in the battle area, was the moment to chrystallise opinion and to concert action. He concealed nothing from the assembly. Lucidly and frankly, he set forth to them the attitude of the Uruguayan Government and their reasons for it. Dr Guani would have been listened to with respect at any time, but the fact that while he was making these revelations no one present really knew what was going to happen at eight o'clock that evening, gave added importance to every word he said and held his listeners tense from first to last. It must have been an extraordinary meeting. There was food for thought for many of those present when the Foreign Minister mentioned the pressure brought to bear upon him by both Governments, by His Majesty's Government as much as by Herr Hitler's, and said that, at certain moments, it had been quite intolerable. Then, with a smile, he admitted that the pressure from the British had been slightly more tolerable because exerted through the tactful personality of his friend Millington-Drake. . . . The admission brought a smile from the uneasy assembly, for they all knew Dr Langmann and his methods. But the polite little joke brought no easing in the tension and the realisation that something must be done. It will be remembered that a few weeks later all the American countries, including the United States, published an Agreement stating that any Naval combat within a very wide belt of the American coasts (some two hundred miles and clearly defined) woud be an open breach of neutrality. Of course this was only an extension of the Monroe Doctrine which, although not in the written Constitution of the United States, binds that country to act in concert with other American states against an act of aggression. But the fact that the Agreement tried to extend the traditional three-mile limit to one of several hundred miles shows the extent of the impression made upon America at that time and the length that all the Western countries would go to to keep out of the war, whatever their sympathies. Looking back from a period of history when the United States is not only the acknowledged leader in political influence but in striking power as well, the thoughtful citizen should be comforted. What Kipling happily referred to as 'The Ties of Common Funk', once only bound the British Empire together; now they bind the whole world.

By the time the meeting was over, it was six o'clock and the siesta was over too. Once again crowds were starting to pour on to the beaches and the quays, and the loudspeakers that were turned on in every room and by every window, and were even patrolling the streets, were beginning to blare the latest news and rumours of news. Mike's voice could be heard clearly by Millington-Drake on the eighteenth floor of the Palacio Salvo, where he had gone with his family and personal staff to see what could be seen. From there, high up on the balcony, the three small dots of the British cruisers were clearly visible on the horizon but not to Mike several hundred feet below and going at it hammer and tongs.

'Here I am, folks, reporting from my water-front ring-side seat at Montevideo. I had to go off the air just now because the crowd was so immense they broke my microphone cable. However, thanks to the gallant police of Uruguay order has been restored and the line has now been repaired. As you know, the time-limit for the *Graf Spee* to be out of territorial waters was 8 p.m. local time, and it is now 6.50, just over an hour to go! And she hasn't moved yet. It is hard to describe the scene here as tension mounts by the minute. The sun is sinking fast but it is still bright sunshine here in Montevideo, and visibility is about twenty miles. But the waiting British warships are out of sight. The latest rumour says that thirteen Allied warships, including the *Renown* and the *Ark Royal* are waiting outside. . . . '

'Good old McCall!' said Woodhouse, 'He did his stuff.'

The three cruisers were moving at twelve knots up the river, in line abreast with the Flagship. As sunset approached, Harwood was concentrating his forces. Everybody was at Action Stations. The next hour was the decisive one they all realised. As seamen, they knew from the continuous reports of activity throughout the day that something would happen that evening. The general opinion was that the *Graf Spee* would come out with a reduced crew of volunteers for a death-ride!

When Woodhouse spoke, Harwood glanced at him but made no reply. It was a moment of decision for him too. Mike's voice went on over the loudspeakers.

'The tugs and lighters have cast off. One of the tugs is nosing up alongside the *Graf Spee*. There are men working now down on the buoy. I believe they are casting loose her moorings. Yes!

181

I believe she has started her engines. I can see the slight churn of her propeller in the water!'

Harwood said suddenly, aloud, 'All right, Woodie. Here we go! Chief Yeoman! Make to *Achilles* and *Cumberland*: "Form Single Line Ahead".'

The Chief Yeoman said, 'Aye, aye, sir,' and ran to the voice-pipe aft.

Woodhouse gave a contented smile, but made no reply, as the Yeoman's voice was heard: 'Flag-deck! Bend on and hoist order one!'

Medley was already at Harwood's elbow with his binoculars, and passing the strap over his head as Harwood eased them on his broad chest. And, as the answering pennant flew from *Cumberland* and the white cruisers swung round into their station, he remarked to Woodhouse, 'And it's an outsize in bowler hats if this goes wrong.'

But although he had taken his decision, he still listened to Mike. He couldn't help it. Nobody could help it. For these short glorious hours, Mike had become one of the most important people in the world. His persistence, his vitality had ended by mesmerising everybody. He stopped everything. He started everything. He dictated policy and reversed it; it seemed that it was he who sent the British cruisers on to eighteen knots and started the *Graf Spee*'s diesels turning over. And still the tireless, hypnotic voice went on.

'The sun is sinking. . . . The evening is fine and clear. . . . The crowds gathered here on the beaches, on the quays and on the roof-tops would put the Army and Navy football crowd to shame. . . . All afternoon we have watched men being transferred to S.S. *Tacoma* . . . there can only be a suicide crew left on board. . . . A moment ago we heard, for the first time since Thursday, the sound of the *Graf Spee*'s engines. . . . Now her diesels have started again . . . her mooring is cast off . . . her anchor is being raised . . . there is black smoke coming out of her funnel. . . . Excuse me while I gulp some water, my throat is dry with excitement. . . .'

Medley swallowed, 'So's mine!' he said feelingly.

' . . . The vast crowd which has been so noisy all the afternoon seems to have lost its voice as well . . . everybody is watching in silence. Now! . . . No! . . . Yes! . . . No! . . . Yes! Ladies and gentlemen, the Pocket battleship *Graf Spee* is moving!'

Woodhouse looked at Harwood who ordered, 'Go on to twenty-five knots. Close the Harbour!'

The Navigator gave the order. Woodhouse said, 'Steer two-seven-oh. Due west.'

'Port ten,' said the Navigator with one ear on what Mike was saying.

' . . . Yes, she's moving! . . . the great battleship is moving, moving out from the Harbour under her own power. The steamship *Tacoma* is following her. Oh, brother! Anything can happen now!'

Woodhouse ordered, 'Catapult aircraft!'

The order was repeated in each case almost before it had left the mouths of the Officers. Woodhouse gave a little laugh. By now all three ships were getting up to speed and a foaming wave was springing up at their bows. The boiler fans were whining. The wind was twanging in the stays. With a roar and a crash the aircraft was catapulted off, and Drunkie Lewin and his Observer headed joyfully westward to see for themselves. In a few seconds the sky-line of Montevideo became visible and the tall tower of the Palacio Salvo, black against the setting sun.

At the moment that the *Graf Spee* got under way and started to move from the Inner Harbour, Millington-Drake turned his glasses quickly on the British cruisers and saw that they had altered position. He saw the aircraft mount into the sky and, a moment later, *Ajax* started to make smoke which blotted all three of the ships out for some considerable time. He turned back to the *Graf Spee*. It was extraordinary how impressive the great ship looked moving slowly and majestically out of the harbour. Now she was nearing the Outer Breakwater, and the *Tacoma* was following her at a few cables distance The vast crowd watched breathlessly, most of them in silence. Some men waved to her, some cursed her, many women were on their knees praying. Now she had passed the mouth of the Harbour and was in the deep channel leading to Buenos Aires. Mike's voice cracked with excitement as he reported the fact. It looked as if she were going to make the dash into another neutral harbour which he had prophesied. Then, when she was some miles out she turned eastward and headed towards the British cruisers whose smoke was now visible on the horizon. The sun was rapidly sinking and the time was about 7.30. The *Graf Spee* appeared to be barely outside the three-mile limit when Mike reported to the world that she had stopped! A moment later Lewin, from his aircraft high up above the battleship, was reporting the same startling news to the *Ajax*. The *Graf Spee* had stopped! She lay there without movement on the calm waters of the Plate as the

183

minutes ticked by. For a while the whole world was in suspense, then Mike reported that first one and then two other launches had left the side of the *Graf Spee* and were heading towards the *Tacoma*. Through his glasses, he could see that the launches were full of men.

It was 7.55. The edge of the sun touched the sea. On the vast calm expanse of the River Plate the Battleship lay motionless.

The sun had nearly gone.

At the very moment when it disappeared beneath the waves, a tremendous explosion was heard and an inferno of fire shot up out of the *Graf Spee*. Great columns of smoke rose into the air while again and again new explosions occurred. On the shore people screamed with horror and excitement, with fright and with exultation. A great inarticulate roar of sound filled the whole city. More and more explosions burst from the doomed vessel. The whole of her armament seemed to be blowing up. In the space of a few minutes she was blazing from stem to stern. Mike clung to his microphone, shrieking and stammering, trying to describe the indescribable, to convey the unconveyable. 'Another explosion! . . . and another! Smoke is pouring out of her. Flames! Red and yellow flames. . . . Listen! You can hear the thunder of the explosions from here. It's fantastic! . . . A gigantic witch's cauldron of fire . . . !'

On the bridge of the *Ajax,* everybody, even Harwood, was silent. Harwood's face became red then white. Suddenly he walked to the front of the bridge and rested his head on his hands. Nobody said a word. Far, far away, dead ahead of them a great pyre of black smoke was mounting into the sky. Over the loudspeakers on the ship Mike's voice was still stammering and shrieking, while behind him could be heard again and again the screaming of the crowd and the thundering of the explosions from the dying ship. At last Harwood turned and looked at Woodhouse, his eyes red, his voice hoarse as he said, 'Well, Woodie, That's that.'

Woodhouse said quietly, 'Yes, sir.'

Harwood collected himself. All eyes were upon him now. He stepped forward and said, 'Chief Yeoman! Make to *Achilles* and *Cumberland* – '

He thought for a moment, composing the words in his mind, and then said, 'Make to *Achilles* and *Cumberland*: "Many a life has been saved this day".'

The Yeoman saluted in silence and went to make the signal. Harwood added briefly, 'Recover aircraft.' And turning away, he fixed his eyes on the distant pyre of smoke.

Woodhouse looked affectionately at the Admiral's back then said matter-of-factly, 'All right, Pilot. Make a slick to starboard.'

Medley stepped to the voice-pipe and said, 'Guns! Tell the aircraft to return and land on the starboard side.'

Picking up an aircraft on a hook out of a 'slick', is a tricky operation and many an aircraft has been lost at it. But Drunkie Lewin's judgement was faultless and he was hooked on and hoisted up at the first try. By the time the manoeuvre was completed, the *Ajax* was practically stationary and the *Achilles* was coming up on her port beam. For a few seconds, in the failing light, the sister ships were alongside at only a couple of cables distance. In both ships the word had been passed that everyone not actually required on watch could come on deck. In both ships almost the whole ship's company had taken advantage of the position. Gun-house crews filled the tops of the turrets. Every point of vantage was black with figures. Then the two ships started cheering each other, and cheered again and again until they were all hoarse. *Ajax* started to sing 'Roll out the Barrel'. In *Achilles*, Maoris were dancing a war dance on one of the turrets. The new Zealanders started singing 'Aroho pumai' and other Maori songs, and the whole ship's company took it up and accompanied it with guitars. *Ajax* replied singing, cheering and shouting in mad triumph. Suddenly the whole tremendous relief from the tension of the last four days was shown; in fact it was the only emotion that anyone showed during the whole of the four days.

The most demonstrative of all was the Canteen Manager in *Achilles* who opened his doors and made his stock free for all.

Gradually the excitement died down and hands started to go below. Harwood roared, 'Chief Yeoman!'

'Sir!'

'Make to *Achilles* and *Cumberland*: "Follow Father!" Pilot! d'you see that bonfire over there to westward?'

'Yes, sir!'

'Well, steer straight for it!'

On the balcony of the Palacio Salvo, Millington-Drake drew a deep breath and looked at his watch. It was exactly eight o'clock. The sun had quite disappeared and a lurid light filled the sky.

'Timed to the second,' he said. 'Exactly at sunset.' Then after a moment, 'The Twilight of the Gods. . . .'

185

As darkness fell the sight of the great ship burning became more and more terrible. She was still being rent and torn apart by vast explosions while her whole length was a roaring mass of flame. The water all around the ship was boiling and bubbling. As the ammunition caught fire in different parts of the vessel, whole chains of explosions would go off one after the other. Masses of metal hurtled into the air and fell into the boiling sea. Pieces of the steel superstructure broke off and came crashing down. The battleship had been lying in shallow water and was already settling down on the mud with her back broken. Her decks were awash. And still the explosions tore at her and dis-membered her, and she seemed to shudder where she lay. She was to burn for three days.

The *Tacoma* lay about half a mile away, surrounded by the launches of the *Graf Spee*, a tug from the Argentine and several open lighters into which the crew of the *Graf Spee* were being transferred. The dark shapes of the ships were lit up by the lurid glare from the burning *Graf Spee*. The sound of the explosions drowned the shouted orders in Spanish and German. It was a strange, wild, uneasy scene. A Uruguayan gun-boat came racing up to the vessels, her searchlights trained upon the *Tacoma*. Beside the Commander on the little bridge stood Captain Dove. The Commander called over the loud-hailer, 'Capitan! Capitan *Tacoma!*'

A heavy German voice answered, 'Hier!'

'I am ordered to detain you in the name of the Republic of Uruguay! You have been actively helping a belligerent warship in Uruguayan territorial waters – '

'I protest! This is a merchant vessel! It it not on my country's War Reserve.'

'You have left Harbour without clearance papers and without a Pilot. You are under arrest. Send over your launch!'

There was a moment of consultation on the bridge of the merchant-ship. Finally, the Captain answered, 'Very well. What do I do with all these officers and men?'

'You can bring them back to be interned,' was the answer, 'Or you can send them to Argentina to be interned there, which is, I believe, your intention. Is Captain Langsdorff on board?'

A tall figure which had been standing on the lower deck of the bridge of the *Tacoma* now came forward and called out, 'Yes!'

'I am coming on board you!'

The Commander and Dove transferred to the launch and went

on board the German ship. They climbed to the lower bridge. The tall figure of Langsdorff stood there, his back half-turned to them, his eyes on the burning ship in the distance. Meanwhile, the business of putting a guard on board the *Tacoma* and getting the *Graf Spee* sailors transferred into the lighters proceeded. The Commander saluted and said, 'I have orders not to detain you, Capitan Langsdorff. Nor any of your men.'

Langsdorff saluted and nodded at the words but made no reply. Dove stepped forward and said, 'Captain Langsdorff.'

Langsdorff turned with a start. Their eyes met. There was a long pause. At last he said, 'Well – Captain Dove!'

Dove said, 'They let me come out to see you. I was glad to come. Things have changed a bit for you since we said good-bye four days ago. . . . ' He paused.

Langsdorff said abruptly, 'Yes,' and continued to look at him.

Dove stumbled on, 'I had sort of unofficial orders to come and see you – because there is a rumour in Montevideo that you perished with your ship.'

Langsdorff looked at him for a long moment, then turned and moved across to the rail before answering, 'The safety of my crew comes first.'

But Dove had not finished what he had come to say. He moved a little closer to the Captain and said in his deep, gentle voice, 'I want you to know, Captain, that everyone on shore who has come in contact with you respects you very much . . . and – I can only say this as a private person, of course – even your enemies.'

Langsdorff nodded slowly. Dove persisted, 'I am sorry to see you in this situation . . . and alone.'

Langsdorff had turned once more to look at his blazing ship. 'Every commander is alone, Captain,' he answered. Suddenly he turned and, holding out his hand, took Dove's and shook it warmly. 'Good-bye,' he said, 'This time it is good-bye . . . and thank you.'

Then he turned abruptly away and put his cigar, his inevitable cigar, back in his mouth, and his hands on his glasses. He stood there like a statue looking at the burning *Graf Spee*. And that was how Dove left him.

About midnight, the three British cruisers came up with the wreck of their enemy, and circled around it. There was no cheering now. They looked at the burning hulk in silence. There were many small craft out, even at this late hour, so Harwood turned away and ordered the Squadron back on patrol again until the relief should arrive. One enemy was destroyed, but there were still others. They were still seaworthy and battleworthy. They went back on the job.

CHAPTER XIV

MEN AND SHIPS

IN THE EARLY hours of December the 20th, in his room at the Naval Arsenal in Buenos Aires, Captain Hans Langsdorff wrapped the flag of the Imperial German Navy around him and shot himself. He had seen his men safely to the capital of Argentina where they had been received with all honours due to men who had fought bravely, and who were now fugitives seeking shelter. Quarters were found for them for the first few days in the Naval barracks. Later on they were moved to an internment camp up-country, but it was a light and honourable internment. Many of the crew remained in Argentina after the war; most of the officers escaped under the light surveillance during the next eighteen months and, by devious routes, found their way home to fight again.

But their Captain whom they had followed through triumph and battle into exile and disgrace lay buried in foreign soil, while his ship which he had destroyed with his own hand settled deeper and deeper into the mud of the River Plate. Nobody had the wit or the imagination to seek permission that he should be buried at sea beside the smouldering broken corpse of his ship, to plunge there into the rolling yellow flood of the river and lie there beside her. It would have been fitting.

The initial mistake of seeking shelter within the River Plate had been his; but when once he had deserted the tradition of the Navy and had allowed a politician's dirty hand to guide the destiny of his ship, when he had allowed the simple issue of 'Come out and fight – win or lose' to be in debate, when he had accepted and obeyed Hitler's shameful orders to scuttle his ship and intern his men, then, being the man he was, he had ended his career and had nothing more to live for. Being the man he was he had first seen his men to safety. A lesser man, guided by the same traditions and principles and making the same decision, would have feared to meet the eyes of his men during the next forty-eight hours and, at Buenos Aires, the inevitable questioning by reporters, the endless interviews with Ambassadors and Consuls, the glances of scorn from enemies and, even worse to bear, of pity from friends, and would have gone down with his ship. Not so Langsdorff. He had told Dove that a Commander is always alone and no man was ever more alone than he was during those final hours. In the battle and in the chase that followed he made some fatal errors, but they were human errors caused by lack of fighting experience and the lack of a long sea tradition at his back. It is no disrespect to the qualities of Harwood, Woodhouse, Parry and Bell to state that when in battle they made a decision, Nelson, Anson and Francis Drake made it for them. The Offensive Spirit cannot be taught, it is sucked in with our mother's milk. The Royal Navy, thanks to politicians, has had its ups and downs but its Captains have at their back three hundred years of sea experience and of fighting ships.

With all his heroic, simple and noble qualities Langsdorff did not have this. But he had other qualities, and they stood him in good stead during the dreadful hours of that Sunday which followed the return to his ship before dawn after his final telephone conversation with Hitler. He assembled his principal officers, gave them their orders and, with characteristic thoroughness, saw that they were carried out in every gruesome detail. His orders had been to destroy his ship utterly and beyond possibilities of salvage: an almost impossible task with a heavily-armoured ship like the *Graf Spee* which was virtually unsinkable. All day long while the rest of the crew was being evacuated to the *Tacoma*, men were toiling below decks to prepare her for her end. Magazines were emptied of their deadly cargo which was distributed all over the ship. On every deck high explosive shells were stacked in beds of cordite. Charges were laid to every fuel tank. Hosepipes were connected to tanks of petrol and diesel-oil so that, at the turning of a cock, the decks would be flooded with inflammable liquid. At first men worked half-heartedly, then they became like men possessed. The ship that they had cherished and cared for became an object to be destroyed. Human ingenuity worked wonders. Man is a limited being; only his capacity for destruction is limitless. In addition it was an Order. It is well-known that an Order absolves well-trained subordinates from any responsibility, moral or aesthetic. So, while Langsdorff sat in his cabin writing his report all through that long, hot Sunday, while Mike kept the world in suspense at their radios, while Admiral Harwood with his small force patrolled the River Plate, and politicians invoking the 'Ties of Common Funk', altered the laws to fit the facts, while the eyes and ears of the world were concentrated upon the enigmatic shape of the *Graf Spee*, as she lay quietly at her moorings in Montevideo Harbour, within

190

her splendid body the men who loved her and had served her scurried to and fro like feverish, malevolent ants intent to maim her, dismember and destroy her.

The huge crowd of half a million people who watched her sail an hour before sunset little suspected that the magnificent ship which left the Harbour so calmly and majestically and made her way out into the waters of the River Plate, was a vast floating bomb timed to explode at 7.55, five minutes before the time-limit allowed by the Uruguayan Government expired. Over each ammunition hoist on the port and starboard sides, the war-head of a torpedo was suspended, operated by a time fuse which, at the appointed second, would send the ton and a half of metal and explosive plunging down five decks to explode in the magazines and send a column of flame and blast half a mile into the still air. It took brave men to set such an infernal instrument and equally brave men to make it harmless: for one of the time-clocks failed to work and, days later, engineers penetrated the smouldering hulk, found it still hanging and (since what men have done men will do), neutralised it. So it was no longer a ship but a vast funeral pyre, a sacrifice to colossal egotism which Captain Langsdorff left behind him, floating in the River Plate, as he boarded the last launch to leave the *Graf Spee*.

Such was Hitler's solution for saving German face in the first Naval battle of the war. A drawn battle which could have been turned by luck and daring into a German victory was converted to an ignominious defeat. Propaganda fed and flourished on the theatrical gesture, and the issues and decisions which caused it, the responsibility and the blame, the truth of the matter remained and has remained obscure to most of the world until this day. But by the political stroke he condemned a loyal and faithful servant to death and a fine ship to an ignominious end. He dealt a mortal blow to the traditions of the German Navy which its Admirals had been at such pains to build up, and he destroyed their confidence in him. Warships may be regarded by politicians as instruments of policy, but they are not political instruments to the men who man them and command them. They would not remain long afloat if they were. So when the *Graf Spee* did not come out to fight, but scuttled herself instead; when Langsdorff paraded his men in the Naval barracks at Buenos Aires and addressed them briefly, reassuring them of the arrangements for their welfare, thanking them for their loyalty and comradeship and bidding them farewell; when he gave a dinner that night to his officers, laughing and toasting the ultimate victory and bidding them sleep well until the morning; and when he tossed the Nazi flag on one side and wrapped himself in the German flag before putting a bullet through his brain, the German Navy needed no further explanation. It understood only too well Hitler's solution and it did not like it. It was the first of a number of such solutions which were to occur to the German Fuhrer, the last of which was acted out in the Berlin Bunker in 1945, when he perished amid the ruins of all that he had created, cursed by the people who had idolised him and haunted by the ghosts of ten million men and women whom he had personally caused to be slain. *Quem deus vult perdere prius dementat.*

On that evening in December, 1939, when the German shadow lay over the whole of Europe and half the rest of the world, and no champion had arisen, nor seemed likely to arise, to fight for freedom, Millington-Drake's intuition was right: it was the Twilight of the Gods.

THE END